£9·99

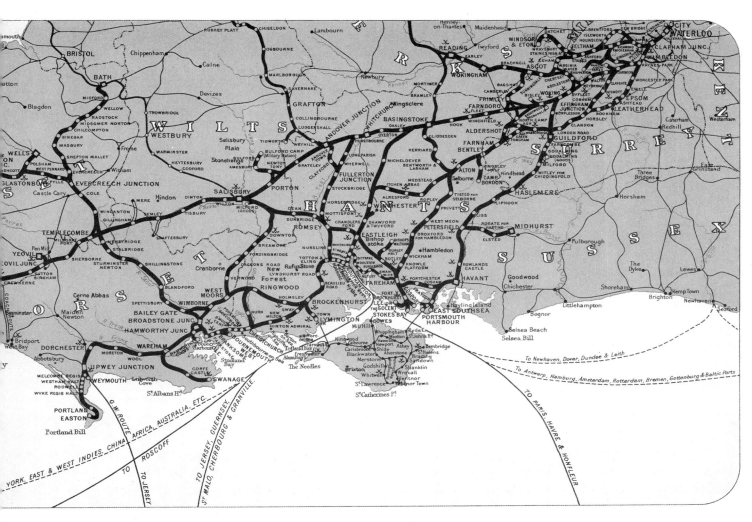

...ESTERN RAILWAY SYSTEM.

LSWR
WEST COUNTRY LINES
THEN AND NOW

LSWR
WEST COUNTRY LINES
THEN AND NOW

MAC HAWKINS

David & Charles

Frontispiece: **Halwill Junction** (190 SS 454001) This view looking northwards from Halwill's down platform towards the junction of the branches shows N class 2–6–0 No 31835 passing by with an afternoon freight to Exeter. No 31835, from Exmouth Junction (83D) shed, was withdrawn a month later and was finally scrapped by Bird's, Swansea, in December 1964. *Photo: P. J. Lynch.*
Date: 26 August 1964.

There is not much to indicate that there was ever a station here – let alone a junction – for the same location is now taken over by the 'Stationfields' housing development, which is nearing completion, as can be judged from the bungalow in the process of being built.
Date: 28 February 1993.

Location map scale

Scale $\frac{1}{2500}$ being 25·344 Inches to a Statute Mile or 208·33 Feet to One Inch.

Links 100	0		5		10		15		20		25		30		35		40 Cha
Feet 100	0			500		1000			1500			2000				2500	2600 Feet

N.B. – The representation on this map of a Road, Track, or Footpath, is no evidence of the existence of a right of way.

The author and publishers have made every effort to ensure that the 'then and now' photographs are exact equivalents. Due to normal production and printing practices, certain details may have been 'bled off' by the binding or trimming of this book.
The differences will be minor and therefore it is hoped that they do not detract from the accuracy that this publication endeavours to achieve.

A DAVID & CHARLES BOOK
Copyright © Mac Hawkins 1993
First published 1993

A catalogue record for this book is available from the British Library.

ISBN 0 7153 0122 5

Designed by Michael Head
Typeset by Ace Filmsetting Ltd, Frome
and printed in England by Butler & Tanner Ltd, Frome
for David & Charles
Brunel House   Newton Abbot   Devon

CONTENTS

FOREWORD

Mac Hawkins is to be congratulated on producing his series of *Then and Now* railway books, which are a valuable and interesting record of how what we all thought was an essential part of the British landscape has changed – sometimes to the point of obliteration – over the last thirty or forty years. Those of us old enough to remember some of the railways portrayed in this book as they were will be glad to see them once again, alongside such a remarkably accurate set of photographs taken in the same locations now, showing either the reduced, more efficient, railway of today, or an area of waste land reminiscent of an abandoned battlefield, or something totally new and different, such as a school, factory, or housing estate.

I think, however, that perhaps more might have been said in the text in one respect. We are told about the station master's widow, still living in the old station house, now named 'Beeching's Folly'; and several times Mr Hawkins writes that the decline of the rural railways shown was part of an inevitable process. Yes and No. As you came out of Callington station, for instance, you could look left and right along the road, and see hardly a house as far as the horizon. Quite a hopeless case. But Tavistock, nearby, is surely a town which should never have lost its trains – and as Mr Hawkins says, the short-sighted sale and development of the railway land now means that the proposal to bring trains back faces an unnecessary problem. Again, he describes the rationalised, reduced, cheaper and more efficient modern rural railway, as well as the old, stick-in-the-mud, labour-intensive and expensive one, without asking how many lines that were closed still in the full lavish panoply of Victorian operation, could have been saved if the will was there to reform them instead of closing them down. The lines covered in this book never carried a great amount of freight, for instance, but there was the once well-known seven-day-a-week and potentially very profitable trainload of milk brought to London via Salisbury until the 1960s, cast carelessly to the roads and now almost forgotten. The real hidden message of this book is one of lost opportunity.

THE HON SIR WILLIAM MCALPINE, BT

PREFACE

As a small boy in the 1950s living near the village of Chagford on the edge of Dartmoor, periodic trips were made to Exeter – and civilisation. These afforded me the opportunity to become fairly familiar with the former LSWR routes in the area, although I never travelled on them. Exeter St David's was a place of both sheer misery and joy for me, for it marked the point of embarkation at the start of a school term, which involved a journey to Sussex via Paddington and Victoria. I always went that route and not by the Southern's, for an 'honorary' aunt in London awaited her real nephew and me to show us some of the capital's delights – and anyway, my grandparents always intercepted the train at Taunton to lavish both food and comics upon us for our hateful trip; but the return for holidays was one of delirium!

I was not totally oblivious to the presence of Southern trains at Exeter St David's, but must confess I was a Great Western fan through and through and they never really interested me. My experiences of Exeter Central were limited to waving goodbye to an adored girlfriend, who was off to distant parts never to be seen again – and I never quite forgave the Southern for that! On the other hand, a canoe which I had built at school was safely delivered from Sussex and I can remember with gratitude collecting it from Central station, for it provided hours of fun during that summer holiday in 1958.

So much for boyhood. I did travel on the SR route during my time in the army and usually caught a train from Chard Junction. A change was necessary at Yeovil to catch a London-bound express to Woking, from where I returned on a local train to Farnborough. As the training camp was adjacent to the main Southern line, one got used to seeing endless expresses flash past at great speed heading either to Salisbury, Weymouth or further west to Exeter and beyond. Other memories are of the twilight days of steam in 1964 and I recall seeing what must have been some of the last express workings, also probably of the 'ACE', on the Waterloo–Exeter route by Bulleid Pacifics as they thundered through Sherborne where I had gone to see my mother, who was a house matron at the well-known boys' public school.

Following the publication of two previous titles, *The Somerset & Dorset Then and Now* in 1986, and *The Great Central Then and Now* in 1991, I was sufficiently encouraged by their general acceptance to look for a suitable subject as a follow-up. The former LSWR routes in the West Country were the obvious choice, for they are highly popular in terms of interest and diversity.

Initially, I decided to limit the area of study from Templecombe westwards, linking in nicely with the Somerset & Dorset book. However, as time progressed it became apparent that the exclusion of the section between Salisbury and the former interchange station was a mistake, since great changes had taken place over the years and it was relevant to highlight them.

After obtaining from a wide source innumerable original photographs of good quality upon which my study could be based, I started in earnest the daunting task of recording what remained of the system in the West Country. Several exhausting months of hard graft ensued and many sorties were made between the summer of 1992 and the spring of 1993, often returning to individual locations several times before certain shots could be satisfactorily obtained, particularly those taken in the winter months in bad lighting conditions. This process resulted in over 3,500 photographs being taken, some of which then had to be matched with the originals and printed – a long and tedious job in itself. By the end of that period my task was all but complete – apart from the writing and compilation of the book itself!

I have endeavoured to select photographs both for their quality and content and have tried to include as many as possible that have not been published before, but make no apology for a few others that have: for being the best or only ones available of a particular location, they have served my purpose well. My one regret is that many superb examples of the original photographs gathered have not been included, either because they duplicated areas already covered, or it was impossible to take an accurate equivalent and at best the end result would have been disappointing.

Virtually all stations and important locations along the route have been included, and only a very few could not be represented, either because they were impossible to retake, or no suitable photographs could be found; I trust this will not spoil readers' enjoyment. However, I hope the comparison photographs selected and the accompanying text give some flavour of how the former LSWR West Country lines and branches, including those of the 'withered arm', have changed over the years.

Mac Hawkins COSSINGTON, SOMERSET, *1993*

INTRODUCTION

If one stands on the concrete bridge at Seaton Junction today overlooking the scene of dereliction and decay, it is hard to imagine what it was like just 30 years earlier when the 'Atlantic Coast Express' used to thunder through here. This once-busy junction on the London & South Western Railway's former main line to the West Country is reduced to a single track as in 1860, when it was first opened to Exeter. This was a far cry from when the line was eventually doubled and extended to Plymouth to become a major trunk route, enabling it to compete adequately with its arch rival, the Great Western.

During the 1860s the system expanded rapidly, and smaller companies which had built or promoted lines to seaside towns in Dorset or East Devon were soon absorbed, adding to the prosperity of the LSWR. With the granting of leases and eventual absorption of other local companies, by 1862 the LSWR was spreading its tentacles further west and soon Plymouth was reached, with other branches fingering their way across the high ground of Devon and into Cornwall. Although the LSWR's network was largely completed within a few years, it was not until 1899 that its furthest outpost in Cornwall was reached at Padstow. The coming of the railway soon brought prosperity to the towns along its routes and encouraged the transportation of freight from the region's fishing and agricultural industries, together with other locally manufactured products, which could be sent to distant markets.

The steady rise of tourism was encouraged by, and soon provided increasing custom for, the railway and brought seasonal prosperity to the region. Over the years efforts were made to increase the popularity of coastal resorts served by the system by offering prestigious services to the public, hence the 'Atlantic Coast Express', inaugurated in 1926 and promoted by the Southern Railway. In 1947 the 'Devon Belle' Pullman service was introduced, but it was withdrawn in 1954. Perhaps one is best reminded of those years when Britain was emerging from its period of post-war austerity, and those wishing to travel by train from Waterloo often caught these trains to embark upon a holiday to the sunny Atlantic coast of north Cornwall or glorious Devon. The expresses were often hauled for part of the journey – certainly beyond Exeter – by Bulleid West Country class Pacifics named after towns or villages on the routes. These locomotives, a lighter derivative of the successful

Merchant Navy class, were primarily designed to cope with the difficult grades and limited axle loads encountered on the SR lines west of Exeter, where their heavier counterparts were prohibited from working.

Going down in history as one of the most multi-portioned trains in existence, the 'ACE's' fame is now legendary. The trains were split at strategic junctions along the way and then the divided portions were hauled separately to their respective seaside destinations. The Exmouth and Sidmouth portions were detached at Sidmouth Junction, before splitting at Tipton St John's. At Exeter Central, the Plymouth and North Cornwall portions were detached from those for Torrington and Ilfracombe – the latter would proceed separately before dividing at Barnstaple Junction. After detachment from the Plymouth coaches at Okehampton, the Bude and Padstow portions would be split at Halwill Junction, on part of the old LSWR lines west of Exeter which became affectionately known as the 'withered arm'. In reality, the name was more applicable just to the 31¼-mile Bude and 49½-mile Padstow branches, for the LSWR operated as a main line to Plymouth, terminating at Friary station near the city centre. On a typical summer weekday in the early 1960s, the 'ACE' ran in two parts: the 11.00 for Ilfracombe, Torrington, Exmouth and Sidmouth; the 11.05 for Bude, Padstow and Plymouth. On a summer Saturday it was run in no fewer than four parts, leaving Waterloo at 10.35, 10.45, 11.00 and 11.15.

Forced to compete with the ever-increasing popularity of the motor car, the railways lost much of their trade, and therefore had to be modernised and the infrastructure rationalised. The Beeching report of 28 March 1963, *The Reshaping of Britain's Railways*, was to sound the death knell for many former LSWR/SR lines beyond Exeter, then operated by the Southern Region. The routes to the Atlantic coast, when compared with the former GWR rival, served only relatively small population centres and had also missed out on the lucrative holiday traffic to the more popular south coast resorts of the West of England. From September 1964 the 'Atlantic Coast Express' was withdrawn, and henceforth all its Waterloo–Exeter services were put under the control of its old rival, the Western Region – still dominated by GWR loyalties. The line was downgraded to a secondary route and from west of Sherborne it was controlled by the WR, who diverted much of the traffic, particularly freight, to their main line. Steam trains no longer ran, being supplanted in August 1964 with Class 42 'Warship' diesel-hydraulic locomotives, which took over the Waterloo–Exeter services. However, the progressive rationalisation of local services reduced passenger loadings rapidly.

It was inevitable that the Southern's route could no longer compete with its former rival and in 1967 the Waterloo–Exeter main line was singled west of Wilton, with provision only for passing loops located at various points along its length. The branch lines to Lyme Regis, Seaton and Sidmouth were closed, leaving only the one to Exmouth. West of Exeter, both the Bude branch and North Cornwall line to Wadebridge closed on 3 October 1966, but Padstow remained open via the old GWR line from Bodmin Road until January 1967; however, the celebrated Wenford Bridge section – opened in 1834 – was to live on until 1983 for china clay traffic. The through route to Plymouth closed between Okehampton and Bere Alston in 1968, leaving the GWR's tortuously graded and winding coastal line as the only option. A further contraction of services took place in 1970 and the line from Barnstaple to Ilfracombe, with its notoriously steep gradients of up to 1:36, then reduced to a single track, finally closed. Although passenger services on the line between Barnstaple and Halwill Junction were an early casualty, being withdrawn entirely on 27 March 1965, Torrington remained open until 1980 to handle fertilisers – milk traffic having ceased two years earlier. However, clay continued to be transported using the remaining portion of the line between Meeth and Barnstaple Junction until 1982, when it too closed.

There was little or no investment in the offing and the Waterloo–Exeter route soldiered on until 3 October 1971, when the Class 42s were supplanted *en bloc* by lower-powered and inferior Class 33 diesel-electrics. Times were slightly extended, and as a result services went into further decline. This was to continue until the late 1970s, when a more forward-thinking management of the Southern and Western Regions realised that with investment there was a potential source of revenue to be gleaned from the route in terms of commuter and leisure traffic, due in part to the increase in population of the towns along its route. However, this could not be satisfactorily achieved with ageing locomotives and the existing rolling stock, largely comprised of MkI coaches. Little happened until May 1980, when the Class 33s were replaced by the much more powerful Class 50s and MkII coaching stock, which had been superseded by IC125s on the Western InterCity routes. As a result, timings were improved by reducing the average journey between

Waterloo and Exeter to around 205 minutes.

As time went on, revenues began to rise and further development took place: in October 1983 Pinhoe reopened along with Templecombe, once the busy interchange station with the Somerset & Dorset Joint Railway and closed in 1966, along with other intermediate stations, although Sidmouth Junction had reopened as Feniton in 1971. At a cost of £435,000, a passing loop was installed at Tisbury in 1986 in an effort to improve timings. From September that year the Exeter line became part of Network SouthEast and some of the locomotives and coaches began to appear in the sector livery of white, blue and red. By 1990, the reliability of the Class 50s was poor and, as a result of mechanical breakdowns, the schedules also suffered. Despite an intensive maintenance programme introduced at Laira, it became painfully evident that they would have to be replaced, which was duly done with the gradual introduction of Class 47/7s previously used in Scotland on the 100mph Glasgow–Edinburgh push-pull route, so they were not in the best of condition and Class 33s still deputised for them on occasions!

It was agreed that total route modernisation and upgrading should be carried out and a major investment programme embarked upon. After much deliberation on the choice of traction and rolling stock, it was decided to go for 22 new-build Class 159 units at a cost of £33½ million. In addition, a major rebuilding programme of the stations was undertaken to cope with the new NSE South Western Turbo units. By the spring of 1993 this work, as part of a £46½ million package, was largely completed and the Class 47s were being gradually replaced by the Class 159 units throughout the year, this being finally achieved on 12 July 1993.

The Waterloo–Exeter route is set for a much brighter future, and a determined management is aiming to maximise its potential to the full, although it will never compete with the faster service offered on the InterCity route to Paddington. With the announcement of privatisation of some railway services, the route may well be the target for a private operator, but only time will tell, *if* legislation is passed by Parliament.

Today, all that is left of the former LSWR routes in Devon and Cornwall west of Exeter are the lines to Barnstaple, operated as the 'Tarka Line'; some stone traffic from Meldon Quarry, just beyond Okehampton – although this is much reduced; and the Gunnislake–Plymouth branch, now called the 'Tamar Valley Line', still used by commuters and providing an easy and quick link to Plymouth, which is difficult by road.

GRADIENT PROFILES

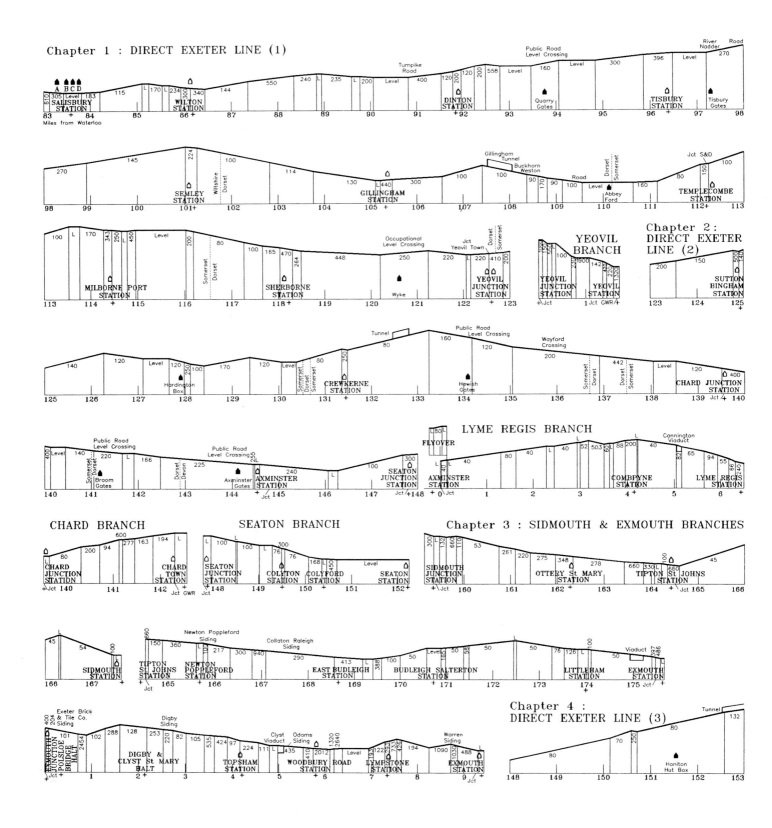

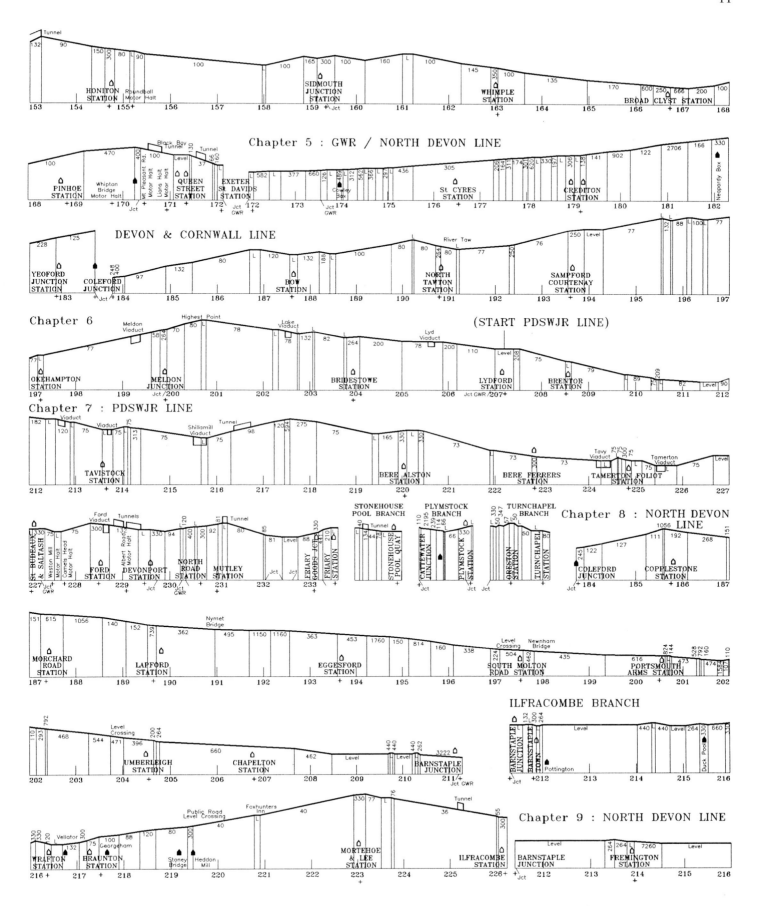

Chapter 5 : GWR / NORTH DEVON LINE

DEVON & CORNWALL LINE

Chapter 6   (START PDSWJR LINE)

Chapter 7 : PDSWJR LINE

Chapter 8 : NORTH DEVON LINE

ILFRACOMBE BRANCH

Chapter 9 : NORTH DEVON LINE

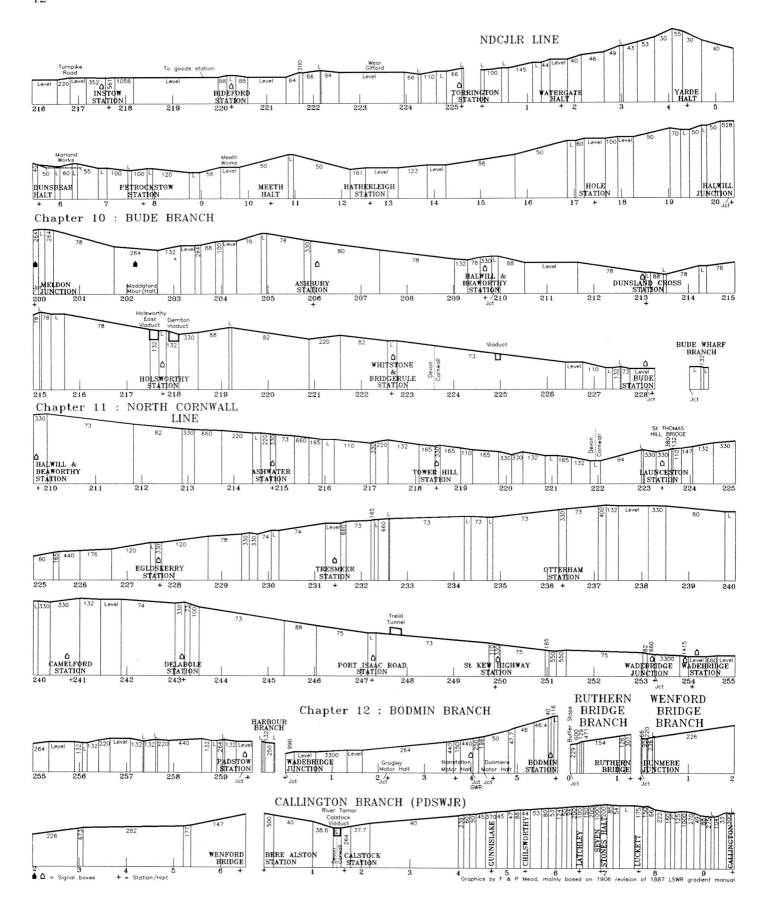

SALISBURY–YEOVIL

14

LSWR's Salisbury–Exeter route

Operated by the LSWR, the Salisbury & Yeovil Railway Co's line from Salisbury to Gillingham opened on 2 May 1859; from Gillingham to Sherborne a year later on 7 May 1860; the section from Sherborne to Yeovil on 1 June 1860, meeting the Bristol and Exeter's (later GWR) branch from Taunton at Hendford. Hendford, superseded by Yeovil Town station exactly a year later on 1 June 1861, was to remain the main line terminus only for a few weeks, when the LSWR's Exeter to Yeovil Junction line opened on 19 July 1860. However, Yeovil Town was to remain the LSWR's (SR's) terminus throughout its existence: the only through workings were GW trains between Taunton and Pen Mill.

1 (Previous page)
Salisbury station (east end)
184 SU 138301

This is how many will remember the Southern's main line to the West Country: its premier express train seen at Salisbury station, a railway crossroads, in the capital of Wessex. Merchant Navy class No 35022 *Holland America Line* leaves Salisbury for Waterloo with the up 'Atlantic Coast Express' ('ACE'), whilst a westbound train waits to depart from a down platform. The banner signal on the up centre road was installed for the benefit of the 'Devon Belle', which was scheduled to pass Salisbury non-stop.

The roof of the building on the extreme right is that of the ex-GWR terminus which closed on 12 September 1932. From that date GWR trains ran into one of the four platforms of its rival's station, the curving layout of which is clearly depicted here.
Photo: George Heiron. Date: c1955.

A vanishing sight: Class 47/7 No 47708 *Templecombe* makes a spirited start from platform 3 with the 08.10 Exeter St David's–Waterloo service. The Class 47s gradually replaced the much-lamented Class 50s, the last of which, No 50033 *Glorious*, was withdrawn from service on the Waterloo–Exeter route during 1992. Soon there will no longer be locomotive-hauled passenger services on the line and during 1993 the Class 47s will gradually be replaced by Class 159 turbo-diesel units. On the left a nine-car Class 159 set stands at platform 4, having arrived from Waterloo with the 08.35 service. The front three cars will be detached and continue to Exeter St David's, scheduled to arrive at 12.17; then the unit will return from there forming the 14.22 service to Waterloo, but once again form part of a nine-car train from Salisbury. This is a pattern set to continue into the foreseeable future.

In this aspect of the station, apart from minor track and signalling changes, there have not been significant alterations to the main fabric – save the removal of the footbridge and part of the canopy over the bay platform in the foreground, which has lost its connection with the main line near the buffers. A new purpose-built depot for the 159 units has been erected on the site of the former GWR terminus, its roof can just be seen over the building on the extreme right, which has been re-roofed over the years.

Today No 35022 survives in rebuilt form and is preserved on the Swanage Railway, but has not been restored. Date: 5 May 1993.

COMMENT: *The curvature of the line here always represented a challenge for locomotives starting out from the station with heavy eastbound trains, particularly for the unrebuilt Bullied Pacifics, which had a propensity to slip. George Heiron relates one occasion when he was some yards from the station sitting in a nearby café having a cup of tea, when a Merchant Navy was heard slipping violently, and obviously having great trouble in restarting its train. The ground was shaking so much that the ceiling of the café fell down, with the result that the once dark-haired waitress serving was instantly blessed with a head of pure white locks from the cascading plaster dust!*

Map 1: Salisbury (1925)
Note proximity of the GWR terminus to the north side of the LSWR station.

2
Salisbury station (west end)
184 SU 136301

The photographer captures for posterity one of the workings which was to endure to the end of through services in 1967 on the Southern main line to and from Plymouth. West Country class No 34106 *Lydford* enters Salisbury with the 11.10 Plymouth Friary–Brighton train. The 'Brighton', which ran between Plymouth and the south coast resort with a Portsmouth portion joined or detached at Fareham, was much used by naval personnel travelling between the two ports. No 34106 would be detached here to wait for a return working, whilst this train was hauled to its destination by Type 3 (Class 33) diesel-electric No D6535. Until 1950, when through engine working was introduced, Salisbury was the frontier post where engines were changed and could be inspected before tackling the severe gradients further west.

The signal in the foreground was a hybrid, the main post being of SR construction but with LSWR dolls and upper quadrant SR arms, operated by pneumatic cylinders. Visible over the locomotive is the 93-lever GWR Salisbury 'C' signal box. Beyond the SR's 64-lever 'B' signal box in the middle distance, with its attendant tank for the pneumatic signals, Salisbury MPD (70E) can just be made out.
Photo: Ronald A. Lumber. Date: 28 August 1964.

The outgoing passes one of its usurpers: Class 47 No 47708 *Templecombe* enters Salisbury with the 08.10 Exeter St David's–Waterloo train, whilst in the background a Class 159 turbo-diesel unit enters the new depot constructed on the site of the former GWR station. Apart from the obvious signalling changes, the trackwork has been rationalised slightly in the immediate foreground, but has radically reduced in complexity beyond the west end of the station and has been removed altogether on the left of the platform with the exception of the down bay line.
Date: 5 May 1993.

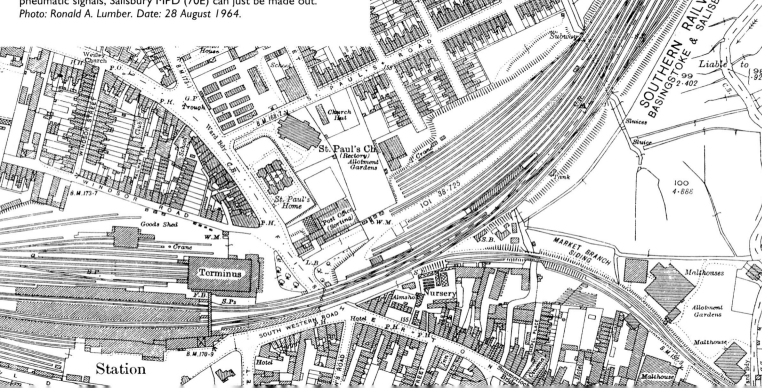

3
Wilton (South) station
184 SU 099317

Although the station is obscured in this view, the camera captures a unique occurrence: the much-vaunted 'Devon Belle' Pullman to Ilfracombe and Plymouth was ostensibly a non-stop service between Waterloo and Sidmouth Junction. To avoid stopping at Salisbury for water, as there were no troughs on the Southern, it was decided that an engine change should be carried out at Wilton – which was not counted as a scheduled stop for passengers. Seen here is Merchant Navy Pacific No 35009 *Shaw Savill* starting out from Wilton with the down 'Belle', whilst No 35011 *General Steam Navigation*, having been detached from the train, waits in the loop to return to Salisbury.

Introduced for summer weekends from 16 June 1947, and from 1949 to five days a week, the service ran to Ilfracombe and Plymouth. Six cars plus an observation saloon went to Ilfracombe, whilst the Plymouth portion of four coaches was detached at Exeter; but by mid-summer the train could be composed of 14 Pullmans, weighing some 575 tons loaded. The 'Belle' was not a commercial success and the Plymouth portion ceased to run in 1950. After a gradual reduction in the frequency of service and length of train, it was withdrawn altogether at the end of the 1954 season. *Photo: Les Elsey. Date: 26 July 1952.*

It is still possible to take a photograph from the same position today, although one is not likely to witness the same spectacle! With the driver keeping an anxious eye on the photographer, who had his arms outstretched over the fence, here Class 47 No 47716 *Duke of Edinburgh's Award* passes the disused station at Wilton with the 11.15 Waterloo–Exeter service.

Along with others between Salisbury and Exeter, Wilton closed for passengers on 7 March 1966, but had closed for goods traffic on 6 July 1964. Further rationalisation occurred on 2 April 1967 when the line was singled westwards just a few yards from the station. The former station master's house is a private dwelling and has been fenced off from the up platform, a portion of which is seen here. The down platform was demolished some years ago and a stout fence erected in its place.

Happily, both No 35011 and No 35009 are preserved by the Brighton Railway Museum, Preston Park, Brighton, but are as yet not restored; and the LSWR-style signal box now resides on the Mid-Hants Railway at Medstead & Four Marks. *Date: 5 May 1993.*

Wilton (South) as it is today. The old up platform remains in good condition. *Date: 5 May 1993.*

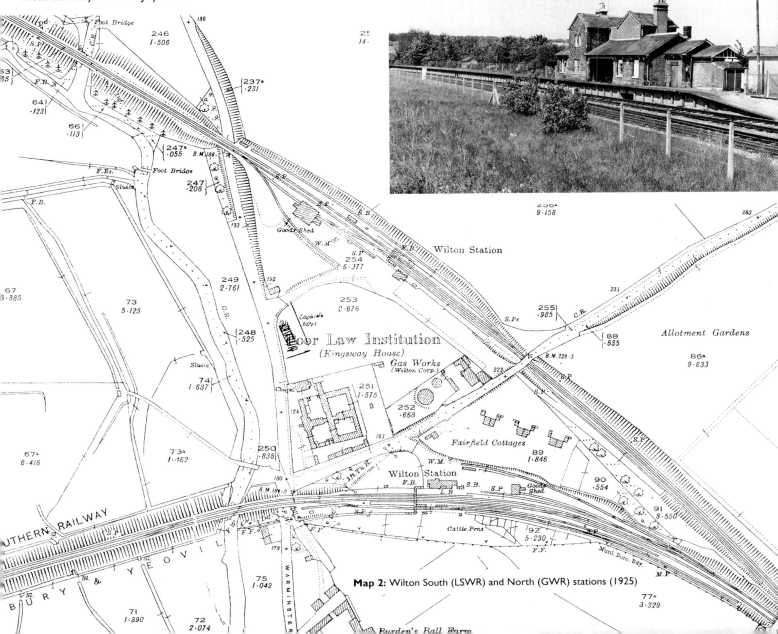

Map 2: Wilton South (LSWR) and North (GWR) stations (1925)

4
Dinton station
184 SU 010309

The small village of Dinton was served by this station located about a half-mile to the south. Both platforms extended beyond the minor road bridge. What would appear to be the original signal box still remains on the up platform, but another was built just off the west end of the down side. This was eventually replaced with a 32-lever box, which opened on 8 November 1942, controlling access to the sidings leading to the stores and ammunition depots of Baverstock (Admiralty) to the east, and Dinton Depot, which abuts the south side of the station. Another controlled the depot sidings at Chilmark (Royal Air Force) to the west, until singling of the line.
Photo: C. L. Caddy. Date: 5 September 1964.

A direct facsimile was not possible, but the changes are evident in this comparison study taken from the road bridge, seen in the 1964 view. The main station building survives in private ownership and still retains the old signal box on the platform. The down platform has long since been demolished.

When the line was singled in 1967, access was maintained to the MOD sidings via a ground frame on the down line into Dinton Depot, whilst the former up line came into use as a long siding, which connected both the Chilmark and Baverstock depots. Access is gained from the running line by means of a crossover obscured by the train, which is the 09.45 Exeter St David's–Waterloo service, with Class 47 No 47702 *St Cuthbert* in charge. The ground frame and points for Dinton Depot are immediately to the rear of the train. The MOD still occasionally uses its two Rolls Royce-engined Sentinel shunters in the depots, which have comprehensive standard gauge networks. In addition, the MOD currently uses seven locomotives operating on the internal 2ft gauge systems, but in the 1990s movements are infrequent. *Date: 5 May 1993.*

COMMENT: *Whilst standing on the bridge, I was approached by the MOD police, who wanted to know what I was doing in the vicinity of the depot with a camera, which goes to prove that if I had been lurking in the bushes near the site of the former down platform, besides trespassing on BR property, I might have not been so lucky with my answer, 'only photographing trains, officer'!*

5
Tisbury station
184 ST 946290

Set on the side of a hill on the south side of the village near the confluence of the rivers Nadder and Sem, the station was reasonably equipped with passenger facilities and sported a lengthy waiting shelter on both platforms. To handle goods traffic, sidings were provided on both sides, with the goods shed located on the up side, which can be seen in the background beyond the signal box. This opened on 12 October 1958 and closed nine years later on 5 February 1967, the same year as the sidings down line were lifted. Goods facilities had been withdrawn on 18 April 1966.
Photo: Lens of Sutton. Date: c1960.

Access to the site of the former down platform can still be gained by crossing the line on Chantry Path, immediately off the east end of the station. The site is now owned by Parmiter's, agricultural engineers and manufacturers of farm machinery and implements, examples of which are seen here. All trains stop at Tisbury, which provides good custom for the line.

Almost as an admission that a grave error of judgment had been made in singling the line, a passing loop was constructed immediately to the east of the station in order to improve time keeping; this opened on 24 March 1986 and remains the only section of double track until the passing loop at Gillingham is reached. Over the past few years, there has been much talk that further sections of the line are to be doubled, but with funding restrictions and privatisation in the offing, all such suggestions have tended to be quashed.
Date: 5 May 1993.

6
Semley station
183 ST 875267

The station was located just off the Shaftesbury to Warminster road (A350) and about a mile west of the village it served. Standing on the minor road bridge east of the station looking west, one had a good view of the extensive layout of the sidings afforded here. The station footbridge at one time had a covered, fully glazed roof, but had been demolished by the time this photograph was taken. The signal box just off the end of the up platform was replaced and the new one opened on 29 January 1961. The large chimney on the right belongs to a milk factory, which provided much traffic and revenue for the railway up until 1980. General goods services were withdrawn on 5 April 1965. *Photo: D. Cullum. Date: 1955.*

This is another sign of the demise of the railways – particularly as far as freight traffic is concerned: today only the single-track line runs past the remains of Semley station, whose platforms are all but demolished or overgrown, although the main building survives as a private house. The goods yard and much of the foreground, as well as a plot of land to the east of the bridge, is used by a salvage company specialising in agricultural equipment. *Date: 5 May 1993.*

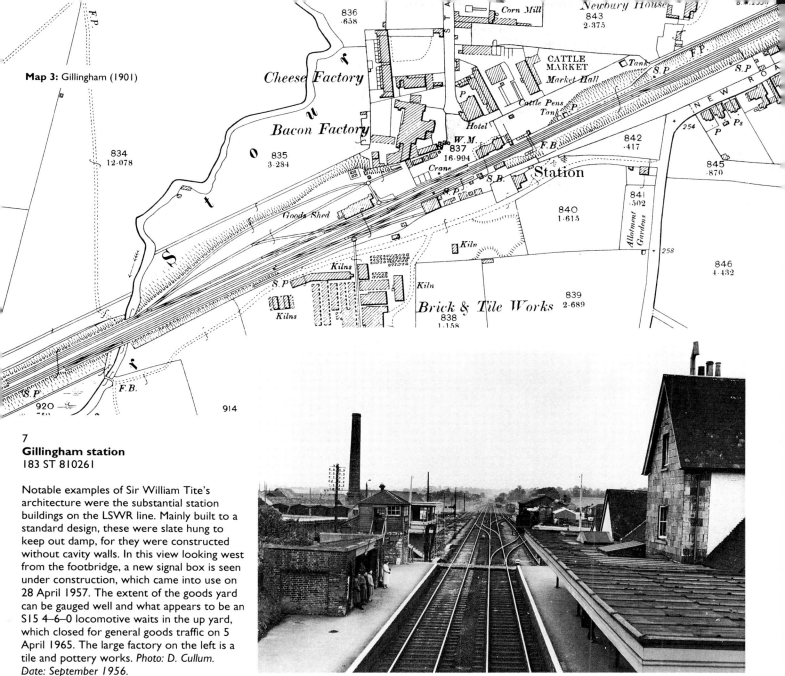

Map 3: Gillingham (1901)

7
Gillingham station
183 ST 810261

Notable examples of Sir William Tite's architecture were the substantial station buildings on the LSWR line. Mainly built to a standard design, these were slate hung to keep out damp, for they were constructed without cavity walls. In this view looking west from the footbridge, a new signal box is seen under construction, which came into use on 28 April 1957. The extent of the goods yard can be gauged well and what appears to be an S15 4–6–0 locomotive waits in the up yard, which closed for general goods traffic on 5 April 1965. The large factory on the left is a tile and pottery works. *Photo: D. Cullum. Date: September 1956.*

Only a similar viewpoint could be gained, for the original footbridge was demolished and replaced in 1967 with the one from Dinton and positioned slightly further back from the main building, the face of which has been shorn of its slate tiles. Today the signal box is the only operational one between Salisbury and Templecombe. The remaining sidings on the up side serviced a large UKF fertiliser depot for a weekly delivery by pallet vans from Ince, Cheshire; this ceased on 15 April 1993 when the price for rail transportation doubled to £15 per ton. Gillingham is a passing point and both platforms are still used, but the up line is reversible when this facility is not required. *Date: 5 May 1993.*

8
Templecombe station
183 ST 708225

The station was totally rebuilt by the Southern Railway in 1938 when a new signal box and enclosed concrete footbridge were also constructed, both of which are seen to good advantage in this view taken after closure. Although still *in situ*, the down line had already been taken out of use, as can be judged by the new electric signal erected on the track. Warship diesel-hydraulic No D821 *Greyhound* speeds past the disused platform on the 09.10 Waterloo–Exeter St David's service. Just visible between the locomotive and signal box is platform 3, which was exclusively used by trains for the Somerset & Dorset line. *Photo: Ronald A. Lumber. Date: 28 August 1968.*

Running to time, Railfreight Distribution-liveried Class 47/0 No 47231 *The Silcock Express* brings the 13.15 Waterloo–Exeter St David's service to a stop at Templecombe. The new waiting room is seen adjacent to the locomotive, and in the background the ex-LBSCR footbridge, complete with decorative lanterns tastefully adorning it and, with the signal box appearing to be in better condition than in the 1968 photograph, the station has a well cared for air about it.

When the line is further upgraded in a few years' time, not only will the signalling be replaced, the section of double track from Sherborne is planned to be extended from a few chains west of the station to run past the former down platform, which will then be brought back into use, enabling a passing loop to be provided here.

Today, Class 42 No D821 is preserved on the North Yorkshire Moors Railway, Grosmont. *Date: 5 May 1993.*

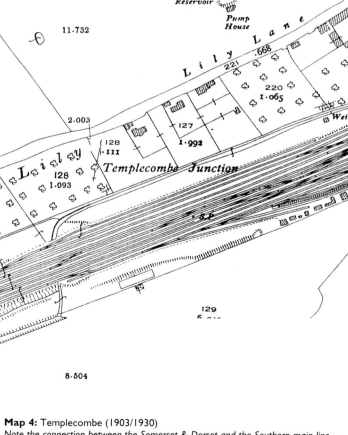

Map 4: Templecombe (1903/1930)
Note the connection between the Somerset & Dorset and the Southern main line. The eastern spur to the LSWR from the S&D was taken out of use in 1870 and then utilised as a siding.

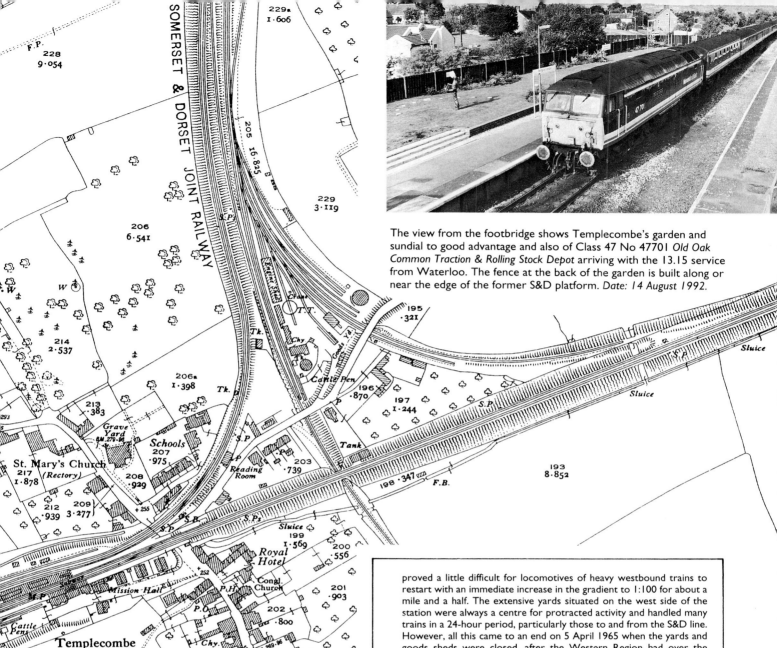

The view from the footbridge shows Templecombe's garden and sundial to good advantage and also of Class 47 No 47701 *Old Oak Common Traction & Rolling Stock Depot* arriving with the 13.15 service from Waterloo. The fence at the back of the garden is built along or near the edge of the former S&D platform. *Date: 14 August 1992.*

Templecombe station

Although situated in a small village, Templecombe was a busy interchange station with the Somerset & Dorset Railway, which arrived here as the Dorset Central in 1862, just two years after the LSWR, and the majority of the local population was connected with the railway to some degree. Although an improvement over the previous method used to gain access to the LSWR, from 1870 trains from the S&D arrived at the 'upper' station by a still rather complicated method via Templecombe No 2 Junction. A down train from Bath would enter the station via a spur, then be hauled out by another locomotive attached to the rear to a point just beyond No 2 Junction, where it was uncoupled. The train then continued its journey south to pass the shed, Templecombe lower platform and then under the LSWR main line. With up trains the procedure was reversed: the second engine was coupled to the rear just beyond No 2 Junction and having hauled it up the spur to the SR station, it would then be detached and left standing alongside Templecombe's No 3 platform, whilst the train continued its journey northwards.

The LSWR line from the east of the station inclined for some distance at 1:80, which eased to 1:150 past the platforms; but even this sometimes proved a little difficult for locomotives of heavy westbound trains to restart with an immediate increase in the gradient to 1:100 for about a mile and a half. The extensive yards situated on the west side of the station were always a centre for protracted activity and handled many trains in a 24-hour period, particularly those to and from the S&D line. However, all this came to an end on 5 April 1965 when the yards and goods sheds were closed, after the Western Region had over the previous few years diverted much of the freight traffic away from this and the S&D line.

When the Somerset & Dorset line closed on 7 March 1966, so did the station here along with others on the Waterloo–Exeter route, but like a phoenix rising from the ashes, Templecombe was reopened on 3 October 1983 for a three-year trial period. This came about due to the good offices of Somerset County Council and the Templecombe Station Working Committee, a pressure group formed from local residents and enthusiasts. The scheme proved successful and today the station has a promising future. When reopened, half the upper floor of the signal box doubled as a ticket office and waiting room, but from 1988 a small platform shelter was built; this was added to in 1990 by the construction of a new building with lavatory and other facilities provided. At the same time, a footbridge which had been in use on the former LBSCR at Buxted in East Sussex was re-erected here, thus removing the need for passengers to cross the line at the west end of the station.

Through the hard work of dedicated volunteers of the Station Promotion Group, Templecombe has won awards for the best kept small station. It now sports well-tended flower beds and a lawn, upon which an attractive sundial sculpture, commissioned by British Rail and titled 'Tempus Fugit', is placed. The inscription on the pages of the 'book' held by the bronze figure is well worth reading for its humour and apposite observations on train timetables!

9

Milborne Port station

183 ST 675208

Situated 1¼ miles north of the village it served, the station was of typical LSWR design. Freight handling facilities were also provided with short sidings and goods shed, as well as a cattle loading dock. This view looking west taken in the early years of this century shows the staff standing on the down platform; they include the station master, three porters, booking clerk and a signalman. The goods yard closed on 6 November 1961, when the station also became an unstaffed halt. The signal box closed on 21 June 1965 and trains ceased to stop here from 7 March 1966. *Photo: Lens of Sutton. Date: c1910.*

The station house now forms two private dwellings. The down platform has been scalloped away and a stout boundary fence constructed along its remaining portion. Although overgrown, the up platform survives reasonably intact, but the edging stones have been removed along its length and it is inaccessible to the public. *Date: 28 January 1993.*

COMMENT: *By means of a stout aluminium pole upon which a camera was mounted, this shot was taken in safety from private property behind the railway boundary fence to simulate the position once taken by the original photographer, which is not legally possible today!*

Sherborne station
183 ST 640162

The station was built on the southern outskirts of the town, noted for glove manufacturing and its two castles, once the homes of Sir Walter Raleigh. Sherborne is also famous for its lovely fifteenth-century abbey church and its two public schools, which provided peaks in railway traffic at the beginning and end of term. A milk factory nestling on the bank of the River Yeo to the north-east of the station, and adjacent gasworks on the south side, also provided revenue for the railway.

The station lost its building on the down platform, which was replaced in 1962 by a canopied shelter using the original columns as support; the signal box was replaced with a modern structure, which became operational on 18 December 1960, but only remained in use for nine years before Yeovil Junction took control of the area on 4 January 1970, when full lifting barriers were also installed for the level crossing situated at the east end of the station. The line was operated as a single track from here to Chard Junction on 7 May 1967, but due to the excessive delays caused, the double-tracked section was reinstated on 1 October the same year.

In this photograph a DMU stands at Sherborne with a down stopping train. These units were used for such purposes between 1964 and 1966. *Photo: C. L. Caddy. Date: 16 October 1965.*

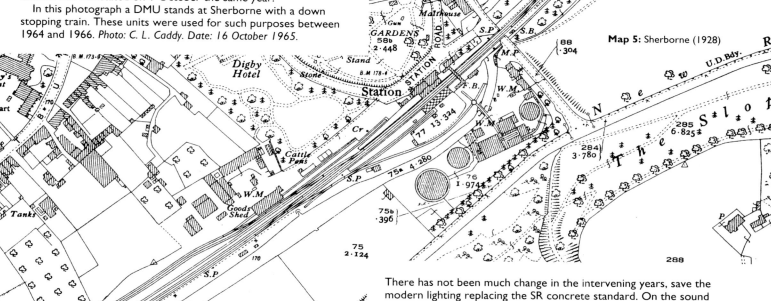

Map 5: Sherborne (1928)

There has not been much change in the intervening years, save the modern lighting replacing the SR concrete standard. On the sound of a warning bell heralding the approach of a train, the duty station staff have to walk to the end of the platform to operate the crossing barriers, which are controlled from a box on the end of the up platform. Entering the station with the 15.15 ex-Waterloo is Class 47 No 47702 *Saint Cuthbert*. Earlier the locomotive had worked the 09.45 up service from Exeter St David's. *Date: 5 May 1993.*

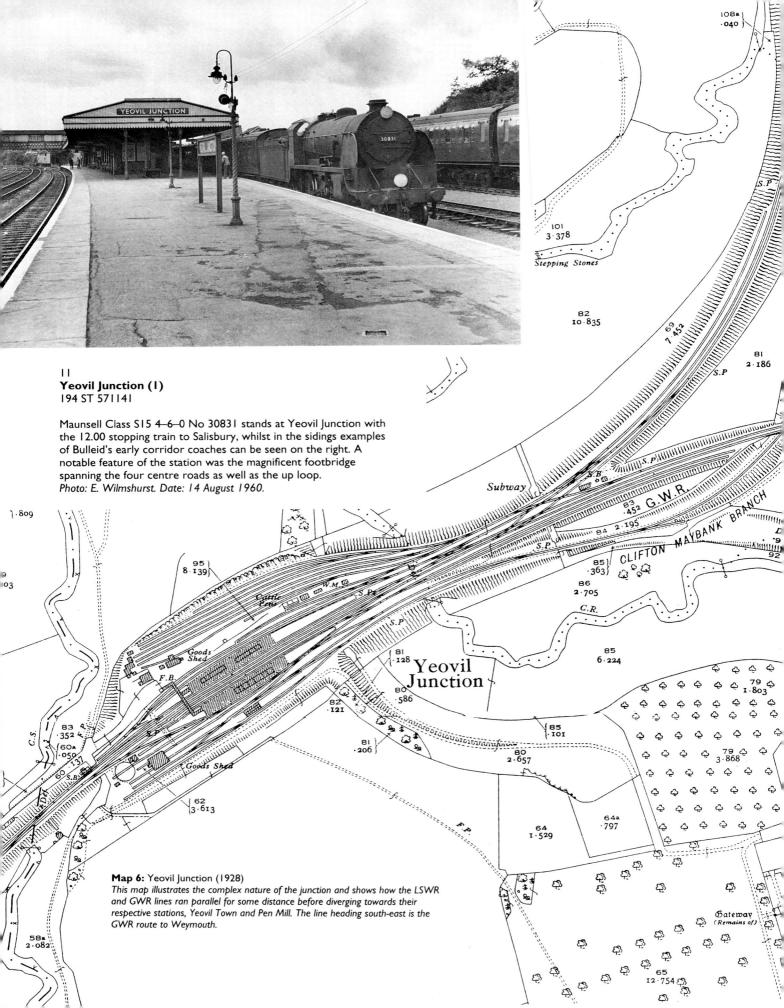

11

Yeovil Junction (1)
194 ST 571141

Maunsell Class S15 4–6–0 No 30831 stands at Yeovil Junction with the 12.00 stopping train to Salisbury, whilst in the sidings examples of Bulleid's early corridor coaches can be seen on the right. A notable feature of the station was the magnificent footbridge spanning the four centre roads as well as the up loop.
Photo: E. Wilmshurst. Date: 14 August 1960.

Map 6: Yeovil Junction (1928)
This map illustrates the complex nature of the junction and shows how the LSWR and GWR lines ran parallel for some distance before diverging towards their respective stations, Yeovil Town and Pen Mill. The line heading south-east is the GWR route to Weymouth.

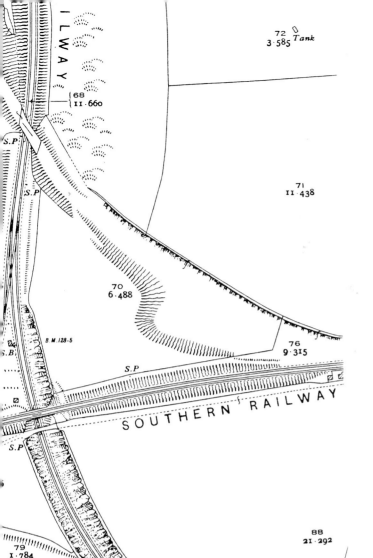

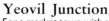

Yeovil Junction

For a market town with a moderate population of approximately 10,000 people in the nineteenth century, despite being an agricultural centre and a base for the leather industry, Yeovil boasted no fewer than three stations and a halt. Situated just over a mile to the south of the town, Yeovil Junction was the busiest between Salisbury and Exeter. Originally the station was provided with an overall roof that covered much of the two island platforms, but after a major rebuild between 1907-9 these were set wider apart allowing four roads though them, with loops to the outer faces. The inner platform faces were used by main line trains, whilst two through roads were provided for non-stop services. The outer face on the up side was mainly used by stopping trains and an auto-train, which shuttled between here and Yeovil Town station a couple of miles away. The equivalent on the down side was used for shunting purposes only. Moderately extensive yards were created around the junction at the east end of the station, whilst on the south side of the platforms, the GWR's Clifton Maybank branch terminated. This was used for the transfer of goods, but the lines were not originally connected because the GWR arrived here in 1864 as broad gauge; however, it was converted to standard gauge ten years later. The Clifton Maybank branch closed in 1937 and the main yard closed for general goods on 5 April 1965, but remained open for private coal deliveries, seasonal sugar beet traffic and engineers' trains.

Apart from the absence of one line and the footbridge, not much has changed here except the modern lighting and new platform faces constructed to handle the Class 159 units.

Looking all its 27 years, Class 47 No 47706, in Scotrail livery, waits to restart from platform 1 with the 09.45 Exeter St David's service to Waterloo. Direct access to platform 1 from the west was provided in 1975, but until then platform 2 had been used for both up and down trains, following the singling of the line in 1967. Today up trains use platform 1, whilst down services use the other face; however, both lines are reversable in the event of point or signal failures. *Date: 11 September 1992.*

Yeovil Junction (2)
194 ST 570141

West Country class Pacific No
34098 *Templecombe* passes
through Yeovil Junction with a
down freight for Exeter, whilst
N class 2–6–0 No 31833 waits
in the down loop. No 34098
was rebuilt in February 1961 and
withdrawn from service in June
1967, when based at Eastleigh. It
was finally scrapped by
Buttigieg's, Newport, Gwent, in
August 1968. No 31833 was not
so long lived: it was withdrawn
22 months later in February
1964 and scrapped at Eastleigh
two months after.

Much of the elegant
footbridge is seen to advantage
in this worm's eye view of the
station. *Photo: E. Wilmshurst.
Date: 28 April 1962.*

With a low winter's sun making
photography difficult, Class 47
No 47707 *Holyrood* is about to
leave platform 2 with the 13.15
Waterloo–Exeter Service. The
station looks positively naked
without its footbridge, which has
been truncated as far as the
platform which is still in use.
The former down platform is no
longer used, except the building,
now deprived of its canopy,
which is occupied by the
section's permanent way
engineers. The former down
lines constitute no more than
sidings accessed from points at
the east end of the station,
which are sometimes utilised by
engineers' trains and the
occasional steam locomotive
using the 70ft vacuum operated
turntable, which is still in situ at
the south western corner of the
complex. *Date: 24 February 1993.*

1986 saw the introduction of steam specials on the line. On this
occasion Class 7P Pacific No 70000 *Britannia*, having hauled a train
from Andover, is about to use the turntable prior to setting off on
its return journey. The amount of interest these special steam
workings create is shown by the number of people crowding on the
platform in the background. Adjacent to the turntable is the former
Clifton Maybank goods shed built by the GWR when the branch
opened in 1864. *Date: 20 March 1993.*

13
Yeovil Town (joint LSWR/GWR) station (1)
183 ST 556158

When opened, on 1 June 1861, the station was operated jointly by the GWR and LSWR. The best view of it was from Dodham Bridge, a structure built over the line at the west end of the station for the benefit of pedestrians wishing to gain access to Summer House Hill. Here the photographer has an excellent panoramic view of the station and shed, which has a variety of classes in evidence. Both unrebuilt and rebuilt Bulleid Pacifics are represented: the three seen here are Battle of Britain class No 34051 *Winston Churchill*, West Country class No 34091 *Weymouth* and Merchant Navy class 35004 *Cunard White Star*, which is the rebuilt locomotive. In the station is No 6435 0–6–0PT working the Yeovil Junction shuttle. The station closed to passengers on 2 October 1966 and entirely on 9 October the following year, but the shed remained open to house the Pen Mill–Junction DMU until the service was withdrawn from 6 May 1968. *Photo: Peter W. Gray. Date: 13 June 1964.*

There is not much to say about a car park; suffice to note that the remains of the station were demolished several years ago to make way for it. Dodham Bridge was also a casualty and has not survived. However, the tree on top of Wyndham Hill signifies that this is the same location, as does the bridge in the background carrying Newton Road, which leads to Yeovil Junction about a mile and a half away. Much of the GWR trackbed beyond the bridge towards Pen Mill has been made into a pedestrian way, which is widely used by local residents. About half of the old LSWR curve to a point where it crosses the River Yeo is overgrown; but from there to where it converges with the GWR Weymouth line, it forms part of the Yeovil golf club's course. In fact, one of the tees has been built on an elevated section of the trackbed!

Fortunately, West Country Pacific No 34051 survives cosmetically restored and is part of the National Collection. The other two Bulleids were not so lucky: No 34091 was withdrawn three months after the photograph was taken and scrapped in February 1965, whilst No 35004 survived until February 1966, having been taken out of service in October 1965. *Date: 28 January 1993.*

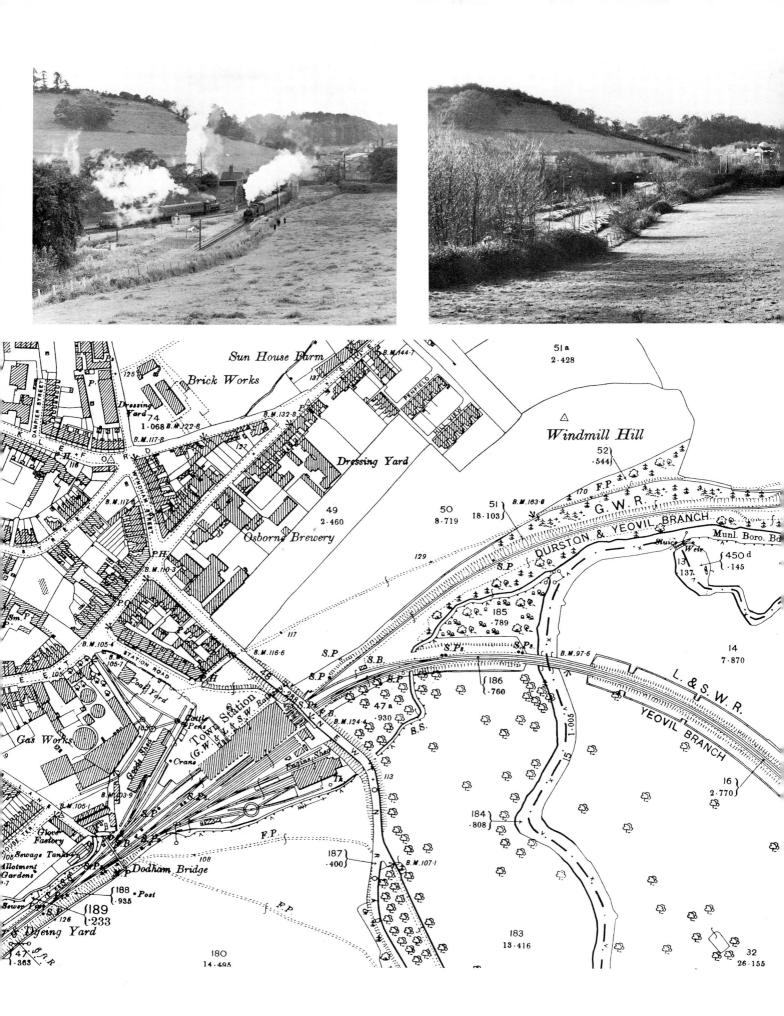

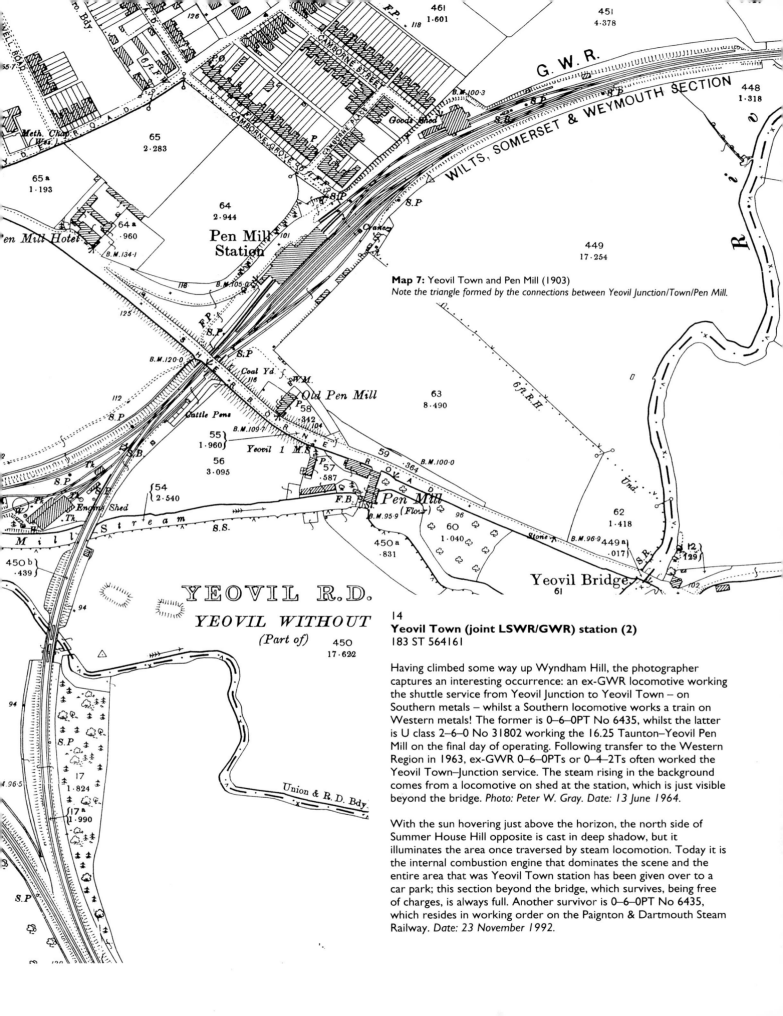

Map 7: Yeovil Town and Pen Mill (1903)
Note the triangle formed by the connections between Yeovil Junction/Town/Pen Mill.

14
Yeovil Town (joint LSWR/GWR) station (2)
183 ST 564161

Having climbed some way up Wyndham Hill, the photographer captures an interesting occurrence: an ex-GWR locomotive working the shuttle service from Yeovil Junction to Yeovil Town – on Southern metals – whilst a Southern locomotive works a train on Western metals! The former is 0–6–0PT No 6435, whilst the latter is U class 2–6–0 No 31802 working the 16.25 Taunton–Yeovil Pen Mill on the final day of operating. Following transfer to the Western Region in 1963, ex-GWR 0–6–0PTs or 0–4–2Ts often worked the Yeovil Town–Junction service. The steam rising in the background comes from a locomotive on shed at the station, which is just visible beyond the bridge. *Photo: Peter W. Gray. Date: 13 June 1964.*

With the sun hovering just above the horizon, the north side of Summer House Hill opposite is cast in deep shadow, but it illuminates the area once traversed by steam locomotion. Today it is the internal combustion engine that dominates the scene and the entire area that was Yeovil Town station has been given over to a car park; this section beyond the bridge, which survives, being free of charges, is always full. Another survivor is 0–6–0PT No 6435, which resides in working order on the Paignton & Dartmouth Steam Railway. *Date: 23 November 1992.*

2
SUTTON BINGHAM–SEATON JUNCTION;
CHARD, LYME REGIS
AND SEATON BRANCHES

15
Sutton Bingham station
194 ST 550115

Named after the small hamlet nearby and nestling close to a large reservoir, built in the early 1950s, Sutton Bingham would have gained more custom from East Coker, about a mile away. This view looking westwards shows that the station is much the same as when it was built. The main difference is that both the main building on the right and the shelter on the down platform have lost their canopies. Sutton Bingham became a halt on 1 August 1960 and closed entirely on 31 December 1962. The signal box shut on 14 February 1965. *Photo: R. M. Casserley. Date: 16 July 1958.*

This approximate viewpoint shows very little of the station left; only remnants of the up platform survive. Three miles west of here, there is no sign of the sidings at Hardington, which were taken out of use on 7 February 1937, but the railway land is still identifiable. *Date: 4 September 1992.*

16
Crewkerne station
193 ST 454085

Situated on the south-eastern outskirts of the town, about a mile from the centre, the station sported a large main building on the up platform. Crewkerne was also provided with a goods shed and sidings off the end of the up side, with further sidings opposite.

Pictured here, Class S15 4–6–0 No 30827 has arrived with an up stopping train; it obscures a small 12-lever wooden signal box which was replaced when a new 24-lever one opened on 6 November 1960. Goods traffic ceased to be handled here on 18 April 1966 when the yards were closed. The down platform was taken out of use on 7 May 1967, following singling of the line. *Photo: R. C. Riley. Date: 26 July 1958.*

In this view Crewkerne's platform was in the process of being extended and reconstructed, in preparation for the arrival of the new Class 159 South Western Turbo units. The redundant signal box which had replaced the original wooden structure is seen to good advantage. The main building has lost its chimneys, but still retains a dignified appearance. The patience of the passengers standing on the platform was surely being tried, as the scheduled train was running at least forty-five minutes late, due to the failure of a Class 33 locomotive! *Date: 31 July 1992.*

17
Chard Junction station
193 ST 340048

Originally called Chard Road, a title which it carried until 1872, it became a junction on 8 May 1863, when the LSWR opened a branch to Chard 2½ miles away; thenceforth the station was named Chard Junction. From 1917, as a wartime economy measure the branch was operated by the GWR, which had constructed its own from Taunton to the town. A large milk factory was set up adjacent to the line in the 1930s by the Wilts United Dairies and sidings were provided in April 1937 to handle the considerable amount of traffic it generated. Although general freight traffic was not nearly so great as handled by the former GWR lines from the West of England, the Southern route made up for it in milk: in 1957, some eighteen million gallons were transported from the factories here, Semley, Sherborne and from Seaton Junction.

Rushing through Chard Junction is Merchant Navy Pacific No 35006 *Peninsular & Oriental S.N. Co* with the SO 11.45 Waterloo–Ilfracombe service, which ran non-stop between Templecombe and Sidmouth Junction. *Photo: E. Wilmshurst. Date: 11 July 1964.*

The railway no longer enjoys the milk traffic it once handled and to all intents and purposes ceased from April 1980: Chard Junction lost its main source of revenue in one fell swoop. Despite the rail connection being still in place, all the milk from here now goes by road tanker. Chard Junction had closed to passengers on 7 March 1966 and lost its general goods handling facilities some five weeks later on 18 April. Another casualty had been the branch from Chard, which shut to passengers from 10 September 1963 and completely on 2 May 1966.

The scene of dereliction is evident in this view taken from the remnants of the former down platform. The buildings on the opposite platform were demolished during the 1980s and not a trace remains. Chard Junction is now just a passing loop on the line; a small signal box on the east end of the up platform controls this section and the crossing gates. Seen travelling at speed through the old station is NSE-liveried Class 47 No 47711 with the 11.15 ex-Waterloo. *Date: 4 September 1992.*

The loop was used at 11.40 on 31 July 1992 when Class 47 No 47706 was spotted hauling a failed Class 33 on the 09.45 service from Exeter. No 47714, running on time with the 08.35 ex-Waterloo train, was put into the down loop to await the passing of the up service – which was over an hour late. Note the old goods shed awaits a new tenant and lies empty. Part of the milk factory can be seen on the left in this view taken from the derelict up platform. The branch platform and bay on the right form part of a coal yard.

COMMENT: I sometimes used this station when returning to Farnborough from leave some thirty-two years ago. This necessitated a change at Yeovil Junction and then Woking, before backtracking on a down local. I find it sad to see the decay here, but there are moves to have the station reinstated and an embryonic pressure group has been formed. I wish them luck.

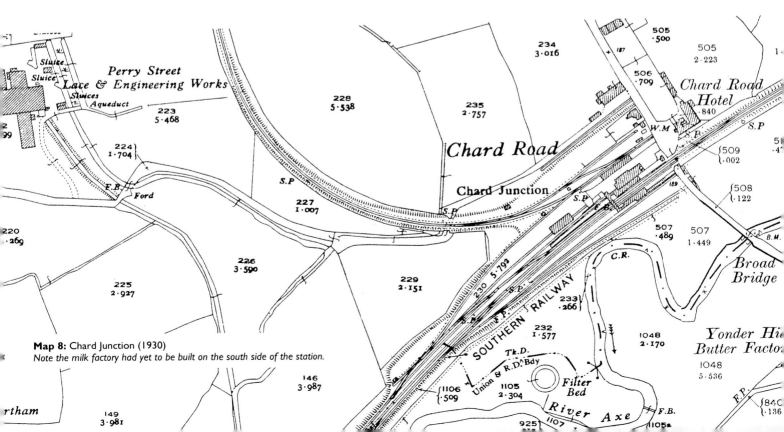

Map 8: Chard Junction (1930)
Note the milk factory had yet to be built on the south side of the station.

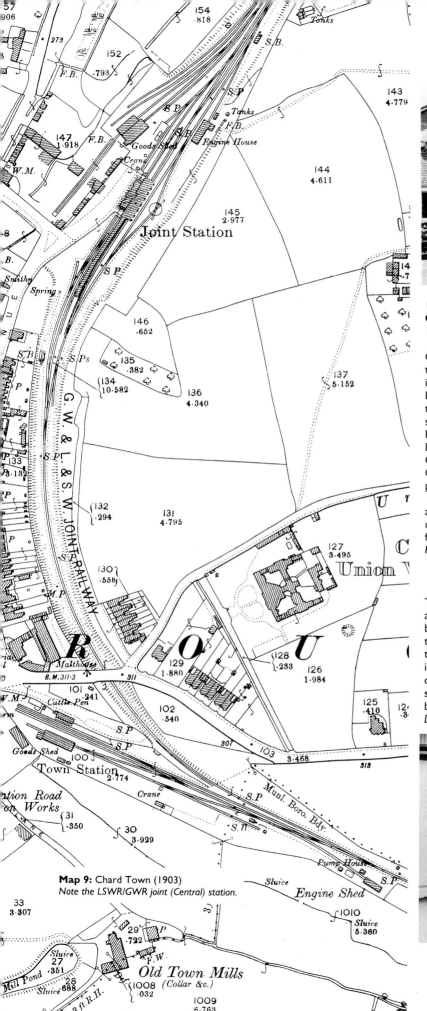

18
Chard (LSWR) branch – Chard Town station
193 ST 330086

Chard was to be disappointed, for it expected to be connected to a trunk route connecting the English and Bristol channels. In the event it was only served by two branch lines, by far the shorter was the LSWR's to Chard Road (Junction). Situated at the east end of the town, this station opened on 8 May 1863 for passenger traffic. The second branch, the Bristol & Exeter's (GWR's) from Taunton via Ilminster, arrived to a joint station on 11 September 1866. The LSWR had used powers gained for the construction of a loop from Chard Town station to the canal basin to reach Chard Joint (later Central) station, by which time the almost derelict canal had been purchased by the B&E and promptly closed.

Chard Town closed to passengers on 1 January 1917, but survived as a goods depot until 18 April 1966. This photograph shows it in use as such a few years before closure. The last passenger service from Chard Central to the junction was on 8 September 1963.
Photo: R. C. Riley. Date: 6 July 1960.

There is no trace whatsoever of Town station. This shot from approximately the same position, shows the south end of a Bass brewery distribution depot built on the site some years ago. With the exception of the parapets of the bridge carrying the A30 over the former loop-line, there is no evidence of a railway in this immediate vicinity, which is largely given over to industrial development. However, south of the town, one can still see the odd section of the trackbed towards Chard Junction. The Central station building survives and one of its users is a taxi firm.
Date: 9 March 1993.

Map 9: Chard Town (1903)
Note the LSWR/GWR joint (Central) station.

19
Axminster station (1)
193 SY 292981

The line closely followed the Axe valley from Clapton, south west of Crewkerne, before reaching the town on its western side close to the river. Axminster was blessed with a station which complemented the quality of the carpets manufactured in the adjacent factory. The grand scale of the main building, like all of Sir William Tite's Gothic creations on the line, exuded the confidence the Victorians had in their enterprises.

This superb photograph is how many would like to remember the line as it was in the halcyon days when steam still ruled supreme. Standing against the down platform is West Country class No 34030 *Watersmeet* working the 12.36 Salisbury to Exeter local service,

whilst 2–6–2T No 41320 waits in the bay having been detached from a Lyme Regis branch train. *Photo: Peter W. Gray. Date: 2 November 1963.*

The station building has lost much of its tall chimneys, which were shortened in the late 1960s. The line was singled through here on 11 June 1967 and the up platform became redundant. Now it is partly covered by weeds and scrub. The remaining platform has recently been extended and the building, despite once being threatened with demolition, is currently undergoing an extensive programme of refurbishment.

Entering the station on a dull winter's afternoon – a complete contrast to the one in 1963 – is Class 47 No 47701 *Old Oak Common Traction & Rolling Stock Depot* with the 16.22 from Exeter to Waterloo. *Date: 16 February 1993.*

The Lawn

849
·509

F.B.

FP

852
13·828

856
7·484

854
1·060

S.P.

F.P.

BM.103·88

109

850
1·061

851
·451

WESTERN ROAD

847
{·223

908
3·114

Slui

BM.104·76

S.P.

S.P.

895
10·916

BM.79·45

Bow Bridge

76

898
1·158

Site of
ROMAN ROAD

896
1·812

F.P.

F.P.

897
3·136

95

Tk

Tank

S.B.

Station

Goods
Shed

Cattle
Pens

Cr

Cr

903ᵃ
·620

903
·597

902ᵃ
·660

902
·615

Saw Mills

W

WHIT POT LANE

ROMAN ROAD

904
·322

907
3·834

Allotment
Gardens

913
{·162

905
3·860

Hakes Farm

BM.136·44

136

909
·389

911
·696

W

4·200

S.P.

900
1·739

901
·644

899ᵃ
·200

947ᵃ
·252

Old
Clay
Pit

Old
Clay
Pit

948ᵃ
3·684

949
14·568

S.P.

948
3·954

F.P.

956

956ᵃ
3·662

**20
Axminster station (2)**
193 SY 292981

This view taken from an open window on the glazed footbridge looking towards Exeter and the carpet factory, features rebuilt West Country No 34048 *Crediton*, arriving in the rain which had set in, with the 15.20 Exeter to Templecombe local, whilst No 41320 runs around its branch train. Axminster station became a junction on 24 August 1903 when the Lyme Regis branch opened.

This vantage point shows how trains for Lyme Regis starting from the bay platform were immediately faced with a 1:80 climb round a sharp curve to cross over the main line, before the branch rose steeply at 1:40 for about a mile. The 4¼-mile heavily graded climb, much of it at 1:40 to the summit at Combpyne, was a severe test for locomotives and their crews. *Photo: Peter W. Gray. Date: 2 November 1963.*

This is the same view today – and taken on a suitably dismal afternoon in the rapidly failing light. The carpet factory remains untouched by the passage of time, but the changes to the station and branch line are all to obvious. The platform's new extension is seen to good advantage. *Date: 16 February 1993.*

COMMENT: *The footbridge having been removed presented the photographer with some difficulty in assuming the same vantage point. However, with the help of adapted television aerial masts to loft a camera, this was done – and I hope with reasonable effect. My efforts brought looks of astonishment from the station staff!*

Map 10: Axminster (1905)
Note the flyover for the Lyme Regis branch and also its connection with the down main line.

Lyme Regis branch

The steeply graded 6⅓-mile Lyme Regis branch opened on 24 August 1903 after a long gestation period of over thirty years, although it had been first proposed in 1845. At first the revenues were poor, which resulted in the operating company, the LSWR, taking over the line from the Axminster & Lyme Regis Light Railway from 1 January 1907. It became famous as the stomping ground of the LSWR Class 415 4-4-2 Adams Radial tanks that worked the branch from 1913 until 1960. The mainstays were Nos 30582 and 30584; but No 30583 (erstwhile 488), which had worked on the East Kent Railway, to whom it had been sold in 1919, joined them when it was transferred to the line in 1946. Over the years various locomotive trials were carried out, which also included the ex-GWR 1400 series 0-4-2s, but were generally unsuccessful and the Adams tanks were not replaced until 1960 when Ivatt Class 2 2-6-2Ts were introduced. From 1963, DMUs took over most of the services during the two years the line remained open. The branch closed on 29 November 1965 – even though it was said to be making 5% clear profit, not counting through ticketing sales. In 1970, work commenced to lay a 15in gauge miniature railway at Combpyne, but lack of financial resources led to the abandonment of the scheme after 1½ miles had been laid.

**21
Lyme Regis branch – Combpyne station**
193 SY 301923

The station was located near the summit of the branch and was the only intermediate one built on the line. Until 1930, when they were removed, it possessed a goods loop and a 14-lever signal box. However, the loop was then converted into a long siding and the loading dock remained. Although passengers were few, the station handled quite a variety of freight and produce, but goods services were withdrawn on 5 December 1960.

Leaving the station for Lyme Regis is No 30584, one of the three fabled LSWR Class 415 4-4-2 Adams Radial tanks introduced to the line in 1913 to cope with the tight curves, for which they were eminently suited and gave 47 years of sterling service on the branch, outlasting the class of 71 by around thirty-three years. *Photo: R. C. Riley. Date: 8 July 1959.*

The former station house has been converted into a dwelling, but the platform no longer survives and the area it once occupied has been made into a lawn, forming part of a large garden. However, the loading dock is still in place, but is obscured by the ocean-going yacht seen here propped up on chocks. No 30584 was withdrawn from service in February 1961 and scrapped at Eastleigh Works during the following December. *Date: 19 August 1992.*

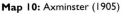

22
Lyme Regis branch – Cannington Viaduct
193 SY 310921

The 10-arch viaduct was the major structure on the line and one of the earliest examples built by 'Concrete Bob' McAlpine. This viaduct was always marred aesthetically by the fact that the west abutment and first pier subsided due to the excessive vertical load placed on the sandy foundations; it was necessary to construct a jack arch in the third span to prevent further settlement. As a consequence, the west end of the viaduct always had a 'drooped' appearance to it.

In this marvellous panorama taken from the side of a hill in the valley which the viaduct dominated, 2–6–2T No 41216 appears to puff contentedly along the side of the hill opposite with a one-coach train for Axminster. *Photo: Peter W. Gray. Date: 27 February 1965.*

Some things change, whilst others do not: there is very little evidence to suggest that the line is not still in place, for there are only limited amounts of scrub along the trackside and the viaduct stands as securely as ever at the head of the valley. The farm appears not to have been altered one iota; only some trees have succumbed, but the one cast in shadow on the extreme left of the picture acts as a good reference point for the observer. The trackbed is due to be made into a public footpath which will eventually lead over the viaduct and beyond. *Date: 14 January 1993.*

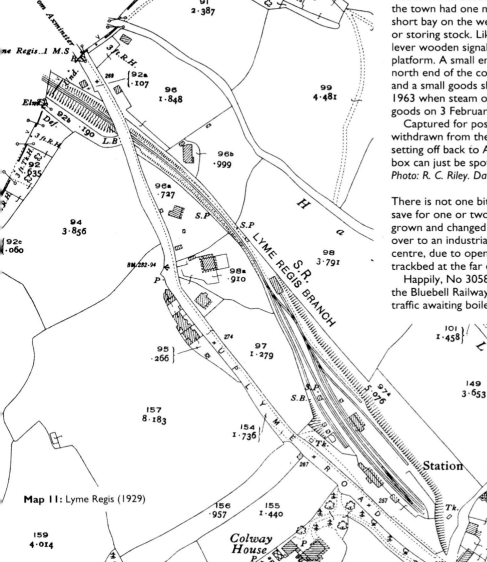

Map 11: Lyme Regis (1929)

23
Lyme Regis branch – Lyme Regis station
193 SY 335925

The terminus situated at 250ft above sea level at the north end of the town had one main platform face with a run-round loop, but a short bay on the west side was also provided for one-coach trains or storing stock. Like the one at Combpyne, Lyme Regis had a 14-lever wooden signal box, which was situated just off the end of the platform. A small engine shed was located near the points at the north end of the complex, which was also provided with two sidings and a small goods shed. The engine shed closed on 4 November 1963 when steam operation ended on the branch and the yard for goods on 3 February 1964.

Captured for posterity by the photographer shortly before it was withdrawn from the branch, No 30583 runs around its train prior to setting off back to Axminster. In the background, the small signal box can just be spotted between the locomotive and carriage.
Photo: R. C. Riley. Date: 14 July 1960.

There is not one bit of evidence that a station ever existed here, save for one or two trees that can be identified, although they have grown and changed shape over the years. The site has been given over to an industrial estate comprised of small units, whilst a medical centre, due to open at the end of 1993, has been built on the trackbed at the far end.

Happily, No 30583 escaped the cutters' torch and is a stalwart of the Bluebell Railway; at the time of writing, it was currently out of traffic awaiting boiler repairs. *Date: 14 January 1993.*

24
Seaton Junction (1)
193 SY 249965

Until the opening of the Seaton branch on 16 March 1868, the main line station, originally opened on 18 July 1860, was named 'Colyton for Seaton', but then became 'Colyton Junction' until it was renamed 'Seaton Junction' in July 1869. It was extensively rebuilt and widened from 1927–8, which allowed two through lines to be laid, with loops to the extended platforms. The large station house on the up side was retained and had been constructed to a standard LSWR design common to the route. Considerable milk traffic from Express Dairies was handled here from the adjacent depot. The yards closed on 18 April 1966, but coal deliveries continued until 8 May the following year and milk for a short period after. The station, as with others on the route, had closed from 7 March 1967.

Unrebuilt West Country class No 34104 *Bere Alston* rushes through Seaton Junction with an up working to Portsmouth. Note

the tall lower quadrant signals with repeater arms, which aided visibility on the approach to the station. The nearest of the two footbridges provided access to the down platform and that of the Seaton branch, whilst the other was constructed to carry a public footpath across the railway. *Photo: R. C. Riley. Date: 11 July 1959.*

Looking absolutely immaculate in its freshly-painted NSE livery, Class 33 No 33114 *Ashford 150* thunders past the disused station with the 12.17 service from Exeter to Waterloo. Out of the four tracks, only the up through line remains, although the former up loop was used as a siding until the 1980s. Although the fabric is in poor condition and requires considerable sums of money spent on it, the station building is rented out to a variety of small businesses, including an antiques restorer. The former milk depot in the background is now occupied by an engineering company.

The Crompton diesel-electric suffered a disastrous generator fire a few months later on 4/5 January 1993 and was subsequently withdrawn from service. *Date: 21 July 1992.*

25
Seaton Junction (2)
193 SY 248965

Standing on the public footpath bridge at the end of the station the photographer has a good view of the signal box, opened on 3 April 1928, and also the junction with the Seaton branch, together with the goods sidings situated at the west end of the station. Here S15 No 30847 hauls a long up freight past the yard, whilst Class N15 No 30455 *Sir Launcelot* waits to restart with the 12.46 Salisbury–Exeter local service. *Photo: E. Wilmshurst. Date: 17 June 1949.*

Looking in the other direction from the public footbridge spanning the main line and the former Seaton branch platform, Class 47 No 47583 *County of Hertfordshire* tears through Seaton Junction with the 11.15 service from Waterloo. The former Express Dairies milk depot is on the left. *Date: 16 February 1993.*

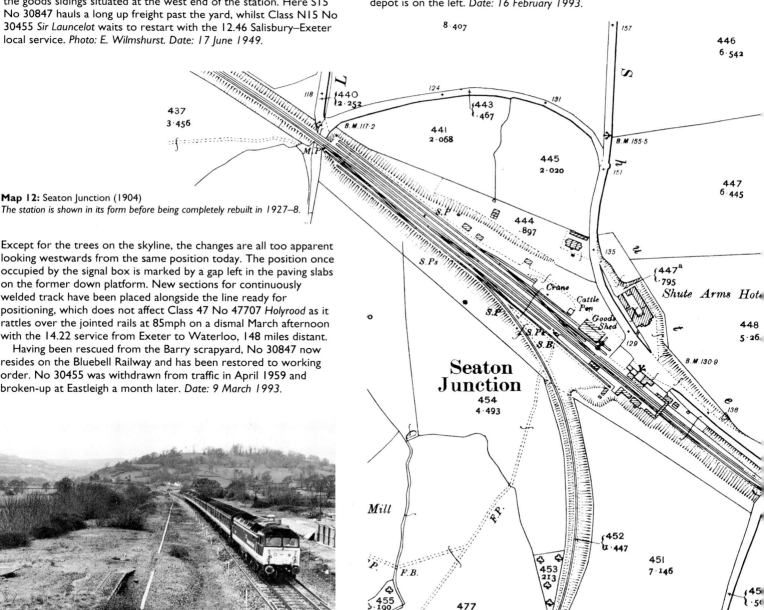

Map 12: Seaton Junction (1904)
The station is shown in its form before being completely rebuilt in 1927–8.

Except for the trees on the skyline, the changes are all too apparent looking westwards from the same position today. The position once occupied by the signal box is marked by a gap left in the paving slabs on the former down platform. New sections for continuously welded track have been placed alongside the line ready for positioning, which does not affect Class 47 No 47707 *Holyrood* as it rattles over the jointed rails at 85mph on a dismal March afternoon with the 14.22 service from Exeter to Waterloo, 148 miles distant.

Having been rescued from the Barry scrapyard, No 30847 now resides on the Bluebell Railway and has been restored to working order. No 30455 was withdrawn from traffic in April 1959 and broken-up at Eastleigh a month later. *Date: 9 March 1993.*

Ivy Batten, the lady at the lineside

In recent years, Ivy Batten, an elderly lady who lived in a small bungalow nestling Umborne Brook near the line on Honiton bank, became well known to locomotive crews, for she waved, without fail, at every passing train. Crews responded by sounding the locomotive's hooter in a return greeting. This became a tradition and any new crews 'learning the road' were unofficially told what was expected of them when Ivy was spotted. Sadly, a few years ago, she was found murdered in her own home. When her untimely fate became known to BR staff, what had become a tradition came to an abrupt end. Some time after, Pat Lambert wrote to the Regional Manager at BR and said that she and other local residents missed the sounding of the locomotives' horns and would it be acceptable if she were to wave at the trains, so they could resume the practice. No objection could be seen, so the crews happily obliged whenever she was spotted. 'Auntie Pat', as drivers affectionately know her, can still be seen waving at every passing train today – and all in the memory of the late Ivy Batten.

So she passed over, and the trumpets
sounded for her on the other side.

After John Bunyan (1628–88)

Standing just off the west end of the down platform, the photographer had a good chance to capture both a main line and a branch working in one frame. The Seaton platform on the right was first used on 13 February 1927, before which date trains had to reverse into a down bay. On this misty autumn day, West Country class Bulleid Pacific No 34030 *Watersmeet* departs with the 12.36 stopping train from Salisbury to Exeter Central, whilst ex-GWR Class 64xx 0–6–0PT No 6412 waits at the branch platform with a train from Seaton. By this date the 0–6–0PTs had been introduced to the branch following the line's transfer to the Western Region. The signal box closed on 11 June 1967. *Photo: E. Wilmshurst. Date: 26 October 1963.*

The two footbridges are still very much in evidence, and the length of the one carrying the footpath can be judged well. The platform and branch line face are overgrown with scrub, providing a haven for innumerable rabbits.

Although its former haunt is succumbing to the passage of time, No 6412 is alive and well having been restored to running order, and can be seen hard at work on the West Somerset Railway, from Minehead. *Date: 27 February 1993.*

Seaton branch and Seaton tramway

The Seaton & Beer Railway, authorised on 13 July 1863, opened without ceremony on 16 March 1868, having being leased to the LSWR on 8 March 1867, the agreement being signed on 31 December following. The 4¼-mile branch ran from Seaton Junction, through Colyton and Colyford to a station at Seaton built on the west bank of the River Axe. The branch had flourished in earlier times, but in latter years with the Beeching axe poised to fall on unprofitable lines, and although the summer passenger traffic was sometimes considerable (through coaches ran from Waterloo until 1963), the lack of it in winter meant that the branch was not viable and it closed on 7 March 1966.

It is still possible to travel by public transport along the bank of the Axe from Seaton to Colyton, for on 28 August 1970 the Seaton & District Tramway commenced operations. The 2ft 9in gauge line uses replica trams built to approximately two-thirds full scale. Some of them had previously operated on the line that ran on the Crumbles at Eastbourne, which had closed in 1969.

27
Seaton branch – Seaton Junction (4)
193 SY 249963

Running tender-first, U class 2–6–0 No 31792 leaves Seaton Junction with the Seaton portion of the 09.00 from Waterloo. The curvature of the platform can be judged well in this view taken from the embankment on the east side of the line. The lattice construction of the finial-topped LSWR signals gave them an appearance of quality, unlike those sometimes constructed by the Southern Railway, which often were constituted of two rail sections bolted together to form the post. The goods yard seems depressingly empty of custom, apart from the odd coal truck and two tanker wagons. The 2–6–0 was withdrawn just over a year later in September 1964.
Photo: Peter W. Gray. Date: 3 August 1963.

The long public footpath bridge is the only pointer to this being the same location, for even the trackbed has been wiped off the face of the earth – literally! The embankment on its west side has been bulldozed into the cutting and the field is now more or less how it might have been in the 1860s. Although largely covered with scrub, part of the platform is still exposed beyond the second fence line. A pipeline was recently laid through here, which accounts for the temporary double fencing. *Date: 14 January 1993.*

Seaton branch – Colyton station
193 SY 252940

The 12.50 (SO) Seaton Junction–Seaton trains stands at Colyton before setting off to Colyford, its next stop. DMUs were introduced to the branch on 4 November 1963, having displaced steam.

The station was built on rising ground just east of the River Coly, with the attractive village similarly situated on its west bank. A small goods yard with two sidings and a brick-built shed were provided for freight handling. The small signal box which was situated on the north end of the platform was taken out of general use on 4 April 1922, but used as a ground frame until 4 November 1958. It was subsequently demolished and substituted by a two-lever ground frame. The goods yard closed on 3 February 1964 – the day the

station also became unstaffed. By the time this photograph was taken, the sidings had already been lifted (19 May 1964), as illustrated by the rail chairs stacked on the left.
Photo: Andrew Muckley/Ian Allan library. Date: 5 September 1964.

The station building and a few artefacts, like the fire bucket hooks, remind one of previous days, but all else has changed: now trams run to here; Colyton is the northern terminus of the Seaton & District Tramway, having reopened on 8 March 1980. The shades over the windows seem rather incongruous on the old building, but the whole scene is a worthy attraction for tourists. Here tram No 12 leaves for Seaton and is about to pass a Ruston Class 48DL locomotive made redundant after being used during the construction work on the line. *Date: 21 August 1992.*

29
Seaton branch – Colyford station
193 SY 254926

The station was modest compared with its neighbours and only constituted to be designated a halt in reality. A wooden booking office-cum-crossing keeper's cottage was built at the north end and the station was provided with a simple wooden shelter, but a fine gentlemen's cast-iron urinal was installed to the rear of the platform! There were no goods handling facilities in the form of sidings or shed.

By the time this shot was taken, the cottage had been demolished and supplanted with a concrete slab wall. A DMU enters Colyford with the 12.15 (SO) train to Seaton on the last day of the summer service. *Photo: Andrew Muckley/Ian Allan library.*
Date: 5 September 1964.

When the tramway was constructed to here in 1973, the old station was demolished and all that remains, apart from the tall telegraph pole on the left, are the concrete platform posts . . . and the gentlemen's urinal, not seen in this view! In 1980 driver-operated lifting barriers were installed and trams were able to cross the A3052 road, enabling them to reach Colyton to where the line was extended. Here the 1963-vintage tram No 2, based on the Metropolitan Tramway's design and in red and cream livery with gold lining, leaves Colyford for Colyton and is about to cross the main road. The tramway is busy at the height of the season and the passing loop built here comes into its own. *Date: 21 August 1992.*

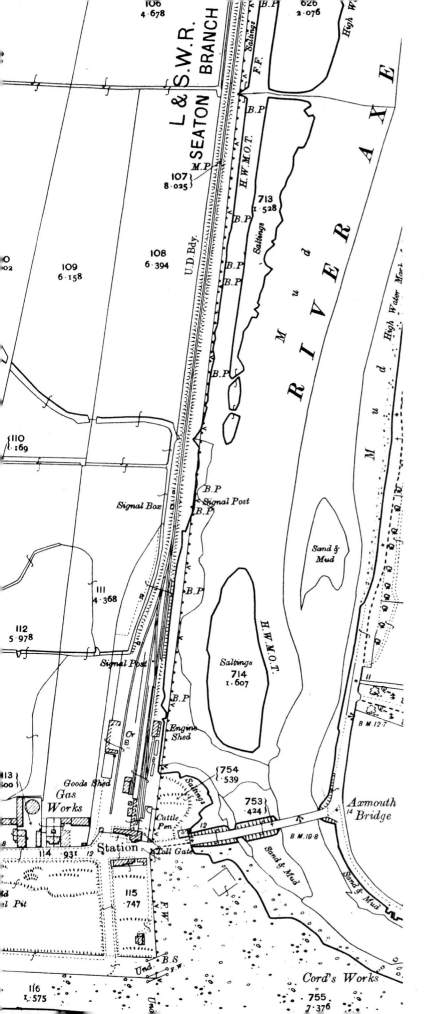

30
Seaton branch – Seaton station
193 SY 251902

The terminus was situated near to Axmouth Bridge, a structure built in 1877 by the Seaton & Beer Railway over the River Axe in order to attract custom from the area immediately to the east, although a toll had to be paid to cross it until 1907. The original Italianate structure of the station was demolished and replaced with a concrete Art Deco design by the Southern Railway which totally rebuilt it in 1936; it came into use on 28 June that year. A lengthy island platform, partly covered by a canopy extending from the concourse provided some degree of shelter for passengers. A long siding and modest goods shed were located on its west side; and of a similar length, a long run-round loop on the east also provided access to a small engine shed situated near the south end of the station. This was replaced in 1935–6 after the original wooden building became undermined due to the erosion of the river bank. The goods yard closed on 3 February 1964.

This photograph shows Seaton a few months before closure: all the signalling and points had been removed from the branch, and the shed stands forlornly empty. A DMU waits at the weed-strewn platform before departing with a train for Seaton Junction.
Photo: Ronald A. Lumber. Date: 15 October 1965.

There is nothing left on the site to remind one that a station ever existed here. A Racal electronics factory and car park now occupies much of the area, whilst the Seaton & District Tramway's terminus has been constructed at the north end. Very careful study will reveal a building on the left which was part of Mear's boatyard on the west bank of the River Axe. *Date: 27 February 1993.*

Map 13: Seaton (1905)

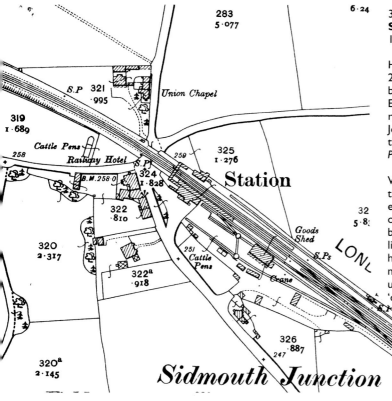

31
Sidmouth Junction
192 SY 098990

Having just left Sidmouth Junction and the main line, ex-LMS Class 2 2–6–2T No 41307 and BR Class 4 2–6–4T No 80042 round the bend at the start of the branch with the 12-coach 11.45 Waterloo–Exmouth train. Soon the train will pass under the main A30 trunk road before following the course of the River Otter to Tipton St John's, where the train will be split and the locomotives will take the two portions to Sidmouth and Exmouth respectively.
Photo: Peter W. Gray. Date: 10 August 1963.

Were it not for the cottage on the right, it would be difficult to see that this was the same spot. The most obvious change is the enormous amount of building development that has taken place over on the other side of the former main line, as well as the bungalows built on the extreme left. The track formation of the branch now lies underneath a tangle of ground cover and bushes. It is quite clear how the disappearance of individual mature elm trees lost in the mid-1970s has had a detrimental effect on the landscape; unfortunately their place seems to have been taken by various 'quick-grow' varieties. *Date: 7 December 1992.*

Map 14: Sidmouth Junction (1905)
Note the turntable in fork of junction.

Sidmouth branch and Exmouth branch via Tipton St John's
Following the passing of an Act in June 1871, the line from Feniton to Sidmouth opened on 6 July 1874 as a branch of the LSWR, whilst the Budleigh Salterton Railway was authorised on 20 July 1894 and opened as a branch from Tipton St John's on 15 May 1897. The connection between Budleigh Salterton and Exmouth was completed by the LSWR and opened in June 1903. Both these branches closed to passengers on 6 March 1967.

32
Ottery St Mary station
192 SY 093951

The station was situated in the Otter valley about a half-mile west of the town centre. A passing loop was provided and was extended in 1936 to cope with longer holiday trains, but the station was built with two platforms of reasonable length as seen here in this view looking north. The substantial modern-looking signal box was built in 1955 to replace a smaller one which had been situated on the opposite side of the line; it also controlled the level crossing. Coal traffic was handled here until 8 May 1967, exactly two months after

passenger services were withdrawn. *Photo: Andrew Muckley/ Ian Allan library. Date: September 1964.*

Only the former station building and the goods shed, hidden behind the main building, still survive. The station building was used until recently as a youth centre run by the Social Services Department of Devon County Council. The trackbed adjacent to the station area has been tarmacked and is used as a car park, but is reasonably distinct on the south side of the B3174 road. Two miles further on, the 55yd-long viaduct across the River Otter still stands today, as do many other bridges on the branch. *Date: 7 December 1992.*

33
Tipton St John's station (1)
192 SY 092918

BR Class 4 2–6–4T No 80059 arrives at Tipton St John's on the 17.25 Sidmouth Junction–Sidmouth train, whilst in the yard No 80035 has arrived from Sidmouth and will form the 17.41 to Exmouth.

The neat layout of this country station is evident from this atmospheric shot. Until the opening of the Budleigh Salterton Railway on 15 May 1897, Tipton St John's was only a passing point on the Sidmouth line; but as a junction it was a busy place – especially on summer Saturdays – when long through trains from Waterloo were divided here and as many as fifty trains a day called at the station. During the 1950s and 1960s, Tipton St John's was one of a number of country stations in the West Country where camping coaches were located in the summer, providing cheap holiday accommodation; here was usually just one sited in a siding behind the main building. *Photo: Peter W. Gray. Date: 30 June 1963.*

The station building survives in much the same form and now makes a very cosy dwelling. The owner has ensured the canopy is kept in good order and has enhanced it with 'saw-toothed' fascia boards, as was common with other station designs. Only a portion of the former up platform remains under the canopy and to the shed constructed just beyond. The down platform was demolished some time ago and its remains bulldozed across the site, after which topsoil was brought in to enable a lawn to be created on the trackbed. *Date: 19 January 1993.*

Tipton St John's station (2)
192 SY 092918

The junction of the Sidmouth and Exmouth branches can be judged well in this shot taken from the station footbridge, which had lost its roof in the mid-1950s, and shows BR Class 3 2–6–2T No 82011 arriving from Sidmouth, whilst a train from Exmouth waits at the signal in the distance.

Sidmouth trains starting from the station at Tipton St John's were immediately faced with a steep climb at 1:45 for nearly one-and-a-half miles, before dropping at 1:54 for a mile and almost into the terminus at the seaside town. Conversely, trains for Exmouth had an easy run on the slightly falling gradient for about a half-mile beyond East Budleigh. After a short stretch of gently rising gradients, the line climbed steeply for nearly three-quarters of a mile at 1:50 before the

station at Budleigh Salterton, which was built on a level section, was reached. *Photo: S. C. Nash. Date: 3 August 1959.*

Careful study of the same scene today will reveal the surviving level crossing gateposts; but only the one on the right was visible in the original shot, with the 33-lever signal box obscuring the other from the camera. The only other clue to the location is the hillside on the extreme left of the photograph which is readily identified, but several mature trees and some hedgerows have been felled or grubbed out.

Tipton St John's, like many other small villages in the area, has seen considerable development over the years and the houses built on the former trackbed at the point of the junction testify to this. The bridge on the Sidmouth branch seen in the distance in the 1959 view survives today, but the trackbed towards it is now covered by trees. *Date: 19 January 1993.*

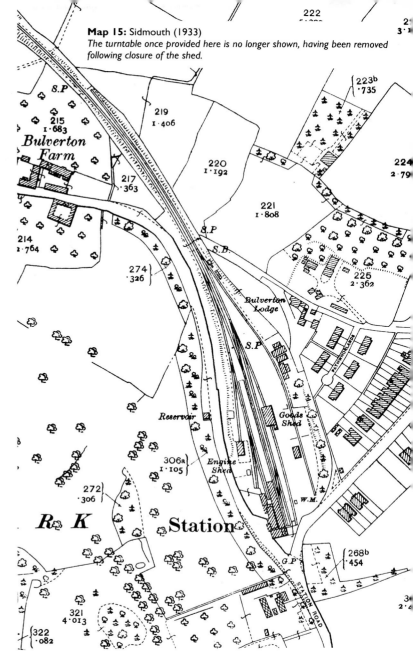

Map 15: Sidmouth (1933)
The turntable once provided here is no longer shown, having been removed following closure of the shed.

35
Sidmouth branch – Sidmouth station
192 SY 121887

The terminus, located on the north-west outskirts of the town about a mile from its centre, was situated on a hillside 200ft above sea level. This photograph shows the layout clearly: the canopied island platform, the eastern side of which could accommodate seven coaches and the western side five, is flanked by an engine shed, which replaced a wooden one destroyed by fire in 1900, but was not used as such after the mid-1930s. On the other side of the platform, a substantial goods shed was provided, which remained in use until general goods traffic ceased on 6 September 1965; the line closed to passengers on 6 March 1967, whilst coal traffic was handled until the following May and remained an important revenue for the line. The substantial station building is seen in the background. The sturdy LSW wooden gantry finial-topped signal posts in the foreground complete the setting. *Photo: R. C. Riley. Date: 13 July 1960.*

When viewed from the same vantage point today the changes are obvious: the site has been given over to industrial use. The unit in the foreground is used by a building services and design company, which also uses the site of the former signal box and trackbed as a materials store. The goods shed and much of the yard is used by a builders' merchant, whilst the former engine shed is occupied by an engineering company, as is the unit which now largely obscures it. The main station building is occupied by a builder and the remainder has been split into several smaller units, with others adjoined to it being purpose built. The trackbed back towards Tipton St John's is still quite well defined and most of the bridges survive.
Date: 19 January 1993.

The station building today is still very much as it was in Victorian days. Entrance to the platform was once gained via a door under the smaller canopy on the right. *Date: 21 August 1992.*

36
Newton Poppleford station
192 SY 089898

Set just east of the village it
served on the west bank of the
River Otter, the station opened
on 1 June 1899, over two years
after the opening of the line. A
short goods siding was provided,
but the yard was reasonably
spacious; pedestrian access to
and from it and the platform
was made via a barrow crossing
at the north end of the station.
Facilities for freight were
withdrawn on 27 January 1964
and the siding was lifted the
following year. The station
became unstaffed after 16
August 1965 and closed
altogether on 6 March 1967.
The track was recovered during
1968, but was delayed by severe
flooding of the River Otter on
10 July.

Here 2–6–2T No 41321
arrives at Newton Poppleford
with the 11.08 Tipton St John's–
Exmouth service. This seemingly
idyllic portrait probably sums up
perfectly all that appeared
romantic about small country
stations in their latter years:
paraphernalia from previous
decades stands on the platform
as a reminder of better and
busier days. Typically, the
station looks devoid of
customers, a situation which
was to sound the death knell for
it and hundreds like it in the
1960s. *Photo: Peter W. Gray.
Date: 10 August 1963.*

The station has been wiped off
the face of the map; not a trace
remains, save the gatepost of
the goods yard entrance. Even
the steel-spanned bridge from
which the original shot was
taken has been demolished to
allow widening of the A3052
road, which – even in winter –
seems busy. In the three
decades separating the
photographs, it is quite
noticeable how large the tree
has grown in the centre
background and its canopy has
started to envelop the trackbed,
much of which is still quite
evident north of this point
towards Tipton St John's.
Date: 21 August 1992.

37
East Budleigh station
192 SY 077851

Set between the two, the station was geographically closer to Otterton than East Budleigh, but possibly to avoid confusion with Ottery St Mary, it was so named. However, the prefix 'East' was not added until 27 April 1898. A small goods loop and cattle loading dock were provided at the south end of the station, not visible in this view looking north from the platform. This also provided a stabling point for camping or – as they euphemistically became known latterly – 'holiday' coaches. As suggested by the sign, East Budleigh was also the alighting point for the nearby Bicton Gardens and the 18in gauge Bicton Woodland Railway set in the grounds of Bicton House, which became an agricultural college. Much of the equipment for the narrow gauge line of almost two miles came from the Woolwich Arsenal Railway. *Photo: Andrew Muckley/Ian Allan library. Date: September 1964.*

At first glance there has not been much change – apart from two windows put into the end wall – but the main building has been tastefully converted into the most delightful home. The platform is well maintained, as is the canopy, which provides an open sun lounge! The trackbed has been made into a lawn, as has the goods yard and they form part of a well-tended, beautifully kept garden. Although obscured by trees in this view, the road bridge survives and carries very much more traffic than it did in 1964. The Bicton railway and gardens are still popular attractions in the summer months, as is the nearby historic Otterton Mill, which has been restored to working order and is about a quarter-mile from the old station. *Date: 26 October 1992.*

38
Budleigh Salterton station (1)
192 SY 065825

There is no shame in a boast extolling the virtues of one's town and region – especially when it is spelt out in painted pebbles flanked by broken lobster pots! Over the years the station staff had changed the message, but not the theme. Having just disgorged its passengers, BR Class 3 2–6–2T No 82042 on the 13.34 Exmouth–Waterloo service stands bunker first under the 1903-built footbridge at Budleigh Salterton before leaving for East Budleigh and Tipton St John's. *Photo: Peter W. Gray. Date: 15 August 1964.*

Map 16: Budleigh Salterton (1903)

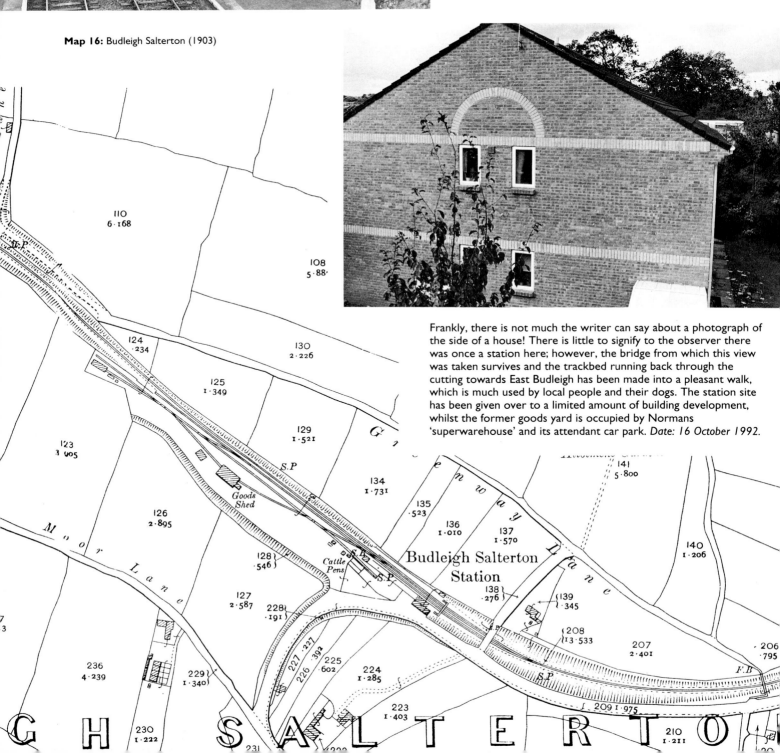

Frankly, there is not much the writer can say about a photograph of the side of a house! There is little to signify to the observer there was once a station here; however, the bridge from which this view was taken survives and the trackbed running back through the cutting towards East Budleigh has been made into a pleasant walk, which is much used by local people and their dogs. The station site has been given over to a limited amount of building development, whilst the former goods yard is occupied by Normans 'superwarehouse' and its attendant car park. *Date: 16 October 1992.*

39
Budleigh Salterton station (2)
192 SY 065826

A general view of the station which shows the main building to good effect. The approach to the station from Newton Poppleford was made through a curved cutting, which can be seen beyond the road bridge in the background.

The station was a terminus until the completion of the extension to Exmouth on 1 June 1903. It was provided with a fairly extensive yard and commodious goods shed; this remained open until 27 January 1964. To house the branch locomotive, originally a small

engine shed, measuring 50ft x 18ft, was built at the western end of the yard, which remained in service for some years after the Exmouth extension opened. *Photo: Andrew Muckley/Ian Allan library. Date: September 1964.*

The obvious reference point today is the house on the left, which still bears the scar on its end wall as evidence of a repair carried out many years ago and which appeared in the 1964 shot. The photograph was taken from a piece of waste ground adjacent to the supermarket car park and shows the other end of the fairly recent housing development that now covers the site.
Date: 16 October 1992.

40
Littleham station
192 SY 019813

Built on a sharp curve a half-mile from the village and on the outskirts of Exmouth, Littleham could boast all the accoutrements necessary for a complete station: it was provided with a passing loop, two platforms, signal box, crossing gates, plus a spacious sidings and attendant goods shed. The latter is not visible in this view and was situated behind the platform shelter on the right seen beyond the tall LSWR starter signal in the foreground. For many years prior to closure, the sidings also played host to camping coaches in the summer months. Like Budleigh Salterton, the goods yard closed on 27 January 1964, followed three years later by the station, on 6 March 1967 – just two months after this photograph was taken. *Photo: E. Wilmshurst. Date: 7 January 1967.*

The only reminder of former days is the station master's house, which stands among a development of houses and bungalows built some twenty years ago. Many of these provide sheltered accommodation for the elderly. Some of the trackbed beyond what is now Jarvis Close has been made into a footpath and is a pleasant local amenity. Conversely, on the other side of the road – and behind the camera's view – further housing development has taken place over the years and hardly a trace of the railway remains. *Date: 26 October 1992.*

41
Exmouth station
192 SY 000812

Exmouth welcomed its first train on 1 May 1861. The station was sited near the mouth of the River Exe on its east bank and located in Imperial Road – later called Station Parade. In 1924 a new terminus building was constructed just to the rear of the original and was opened on 20 July that year. The old building was then demolished enabling a large forecourt to be sited at the front of the new one, which had an imposing façade of classical proportions.

This view taken from the balcony of the 70-lever signal box shows M7 0–4–4T No 30676 busy shunting a van alongside platform 4 and also gives a good impression as to the generous layout of the station together with a portion of the yard. Following land reclamation from the sea in the mid-1920s, the latter was enlarged and in addition a new goods shed was built. Behind the goods shed was a short branch to the nearby docks, which itself had several sidings. Note the engine shed visible to the rear of the locomotive: rebuilt in 1927, it normally had an allocation of four engines. Also noteworthy are the two fine LSWR gantry signals at the end of the platforms, but its lower quadrant arms had been replaced with the upper type used by the SR. *Photo: R. C. Riley. Date: 13 October 1959.*

This shot taken from the same spot probably sums up how rationalisation is taken to the extremes. Today only a single track runs into Exmouth's one remaining platform face and a new relief road occupies much of the former station's area. The run down had commenced during the 1960s: the shed closed on 8 November 1963, after DMUs were introduced on most Exeter services. Rail traffic to the docks ended in December 1967 and the signal box closed a few months later, on 10 March 1968. By the early 1970s, following the removal of all but the single track against platform 4, the station site was a scene of dereliction and neglect. During this period the imposing viaduct that once carried the line from Budleigh Salterton over the outskirts of the town was demolished, even though reservations were expressed about the safety of the houses almost underneath the structure. The old terminus building, much admired by many, was wantonly demolished and a new transport interchange, a modern design of modest proportions incorporating a bus station, was built in 1975 and came into use on 2 May 1976. This building abutted the former platform 2, which was reinstated in shortened form and the remaining line was slewed adjacent to it from platform 4.

Despite the station's lack of grandeur, Exmouth enjoys good rail services to Exeter as well as to Barnstaple and Paignton. On weekdays, according to the winter timetable of 1992/3, it sees no fewer than twenty-four train movements in each direction – one roughly every half hour. This is increased slightly in summer. Even when stopping at all intermediate stations, a train journey only takes some twenty-two minutes from Exmouth into Exeter city centre; so many people, especially commuters and shoppers, find it quicker to travel by rail rather than by car. Here the Class 150 Sprinter unit No 150219 leaves Exmouth with the 14.45 service to Paignton. *Date: 7 December 1992.*

Exmouth branch via Exmouth Junction

The line from Exeter to Exmouth remains open and is still very much in use. This dates from an Act passed on 12 July 1858 to permit the construction of a branch to Topsham from the planned LSWR main line, which was extended and opened to Exmouth on 1 May 1861. The southern section followed part of the Exmouth & Exeter's proposed broad gauge route which was to have been from Exminster to Exmouth (and previously planned by Brunel), for which an Act had been passed on 2 July 1855. However, it was not built – probably due to the enormous cost of a bridge needed to span the Exe estuary – and the LSWR persuaded the company to build a narrow gauge line, sharing Queen Street station in Exeter. From the outset the branch was operated by the LSWR, which eventually absorbed the company.

Map 17: Exmouth (1933)
Note the docks branch sweeping past the goods shed and also the line from Budleigh Salterton, which curved in from the east over the viaduct ending at Exeter Road, just out of view on the map.

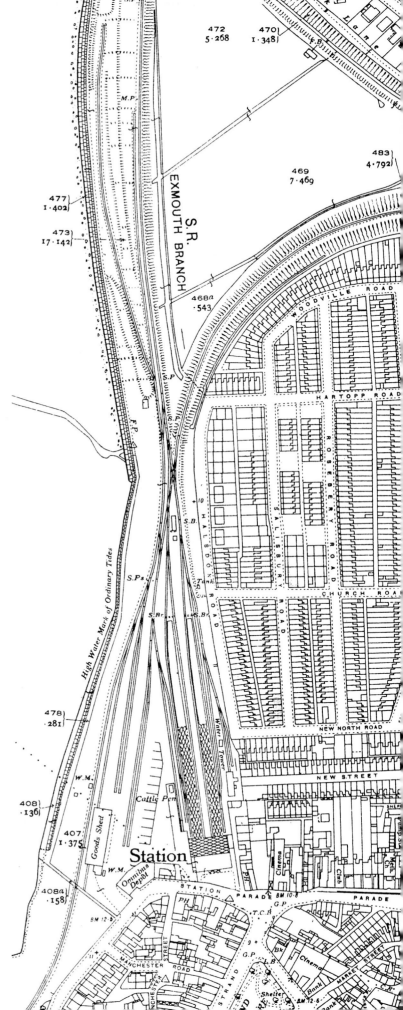

Lympstone station
192 SX 989843

BR Class 4 2–6–4T No 80038 leaves Lympstone with the 17.45 from Exmouth on a fine summer's afternoon. Note the rather untidy trackside in the foreground and the torched remains of an LSWR signal post lying abandoned on the ground. The signal box had closed the year before on 16 September 1962. Set near the heart of the village and built in a cutting, the station of modest proportions was originally equipped with a goods loop and a short siding to a cattle loading dock. The sidings were taken out of use on 4 April 1960 and removed sometime after. Until the outbreak of the Second World War quantities of shellfish were also loaded onto passenger trains here. *Photo: Peter W. Gray. Date: 7 July 1963.*

The station has lost its remaining buildings and now only has a small shelter provided on the platform. However, it is well patronised and most trains stop here, with the exception of five up and one down during a weekday in the winter timetable. Here Class 150 Sprinter No 150221 leaves Lympstone with the 15.45 Exmouth–Paignton service. The next stop – only two minutes' travelling time – is Lympstone Commando, a halt opened on 3 May 1976 for exclusive use by those serving at the adjacent Royal Marines commando training centre. *Date: 28 April 1993.*

COMMENT: *Quite surprisingly, three trips had to be made here due to camera malfunctions and difficult lighting conditions experienced before this uninspiring comparison was obtained!*

43
Woodbury Road/Exton Halt
192 SX 981863

Up to 15 September 1958 the station was named Woodbury, after the village some two miles away, then it became Exton until 28 February 1965 when it was renamed 'Exton Halt', reverting to 'Exton' on 5 May 1969 after staffing ceased. A commanding view across the Exe estuary is had from the railway line here, alongside which it runs for some distance either side of the station. In this study, which also shows the remains of the original booking hall and waiting room, Warship class diesel-hydraulic No D858 *Valorous* is in charge of a Swindon 75-ton steam crane, which has been brought in to help transport gas main equipment for laying a pipeline across the River Exe. *Photo: Ronald A. Lumber. Date: 16 November 1969.*

Although not a direct comparison, this view taken from the south end of Exton shows a modern chalet bungalow built alongside the original station house, which became the 'Silver Fox' restuarant for a time, but is now a private dwelling. The platform has been provided with a small shelter, which is adequate save when the biting winter gales blow fiercely across the estuary! Sprinter unit No 153374 stops at Exton with the 11.45 Exmouth service to Exeter St David's. *Date: 4 March 1993.*

COMMENT: *My photograph was taken prior to any archive shot being acquired of Exton, therefore it will have to suffice as a comparison study!*

44
Topsham station
192 SX 967883

BR Class 3 2–6–2T No 82025 enters Topsham with the 16.00
Exeter Central–Exmouth. The grand design of Sir William Tite's
station building can be appreciated in this study. Due to the number
of commuters using the line, by World War I it was necessary to
construct double track from Exmouth Junction to the town, but
with the gradual decline of traffic the track was singled in February
1973. Topsham was equipped with a moderately extensive yard and
sizeable goods shed, which were located behind the platform on the
down side of the line with access to the sidings via points at the
south end of the station. Also, access via trailing points was gained
to a 700yd-long branch, which curved from the line westwards
through 90°, and which was constructed to a wharf on the Exe
estuary for the purposes of being able to transfer goods from ships
unable to proceed further up the river. It opened on 23 September
1861 – and one principal commodity handled in the 1930s was
considerable quantities of guano from South America! The branch
was closed in 1957 and lifted the following year. The goods yard
officially closed on 4 December 1967, but some sidings remained
for private use and the shed survived well into the 1980s.
Photo: H. B. Priestley. Date: 1 September 1958.

Today the station still has two platforms in use and is the only
passing point on the branch. Here Sprinter unit No 150236 stands in
the station with the 12.15 ex-Paignton service to Exmouth, whilst
No 150253, having got the road, has just left with the 13.15
Exmouth–Exeter St David's.
   Although cement rendered and no longer sporting its canopy, the
main station building survives in private use, but has been segregated
from the platform by railings. Closed on 30 January 1988, when
colour light signals became operational, the old 23-lever signal box,
now let as an office, still stands near the road crossing, which has
been equipped with lifting barriers, installed in 1973.
Date: 7 December 1992.

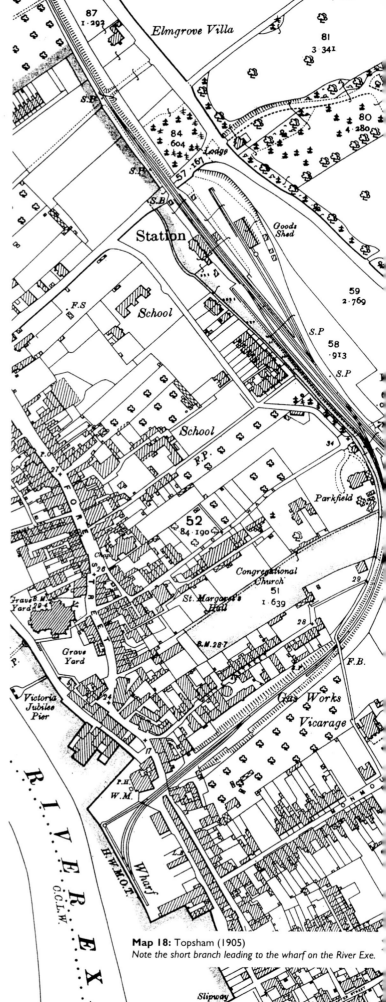

Map 18: Topsham (1905)
Note the short branch leading to the wharf on the River Exe.

45

Polsloe Bridge Halt
192 SX 921934

Together with Clyst St Mary and Digby Halt to its south, Polsloe Bridge first opened on 31 May 1908 on doubling of the line to Topsham. Set high on an embankment near a busy road junction in the eastern suburbs of Exeter, this modest halt was rebuilt and extended in 1927 using standard concrete components fabricated at the nearby Exmouth Junction works. Here the 11.15 local service from Exmouth to Exeter Central rolls into Polsloe Bridge, headed by BR Standard Class 3MT 2–6–2T No 82010. The locomotive remained in service until withdrawn in April 1965 and was scrapped at Bird's, Morriston, in October that year. *Photo: Brian Morrison. Date: 11 May 1958.*

Apart from the absence of the shelter on the down platform and singling of the line, nothing very much has altered, except the motive power: living up to its name, Sprinter unit No 153355 speeds past Polsloe Bridge Halt at 13.34 with the 13.15 Exmouth–Exeter St David's service.

Scheduled to be opened during the summer of 1994, a station is planned to be built adjacent to a new retail development between Polsloe Bridge and Topsham, not far from the site of the former Clyst St Mary and Digby Halt, which was closed on 27 September 1948. Although not finalised at the time of writing, it is likely to be called either Exe Vale Halt or Sowton Halt and is understood to be a joint venture between the local authorities, British Rail and Tesco, who are to build a new supermarket near the site of the former Digby Hospital. *Date: 7 September 1992.*

4
HONITON–EXETER CENTRAL

46
Honiton station
193 ST 164003

Having built up speed on the falling 1:90 gradient from Honiton Tunnel, Merchant Navy 4–6–2 No 35010 *Blue Star* thunders through Honiton with the 10.15 ex-Waterloo to West of England train.

The station, situated fairly near the centre on the south side of the town, was similar in design to those at Crewkerne and Axminster. The main building on the down side was adorned with a large canopy and ornate fretwork, but the shelter on the up side had no such trimmings. A small goods shed was located on the down side at the west end of the station. Sidings were provided on both sides to handle the town's commercial traffic, which included timber from an adjacent yard. Goods facilities were withdrawn in 1967, the same year the line was singled. *Photo: E. Wilmshurst. Date: 11 July 1964.*

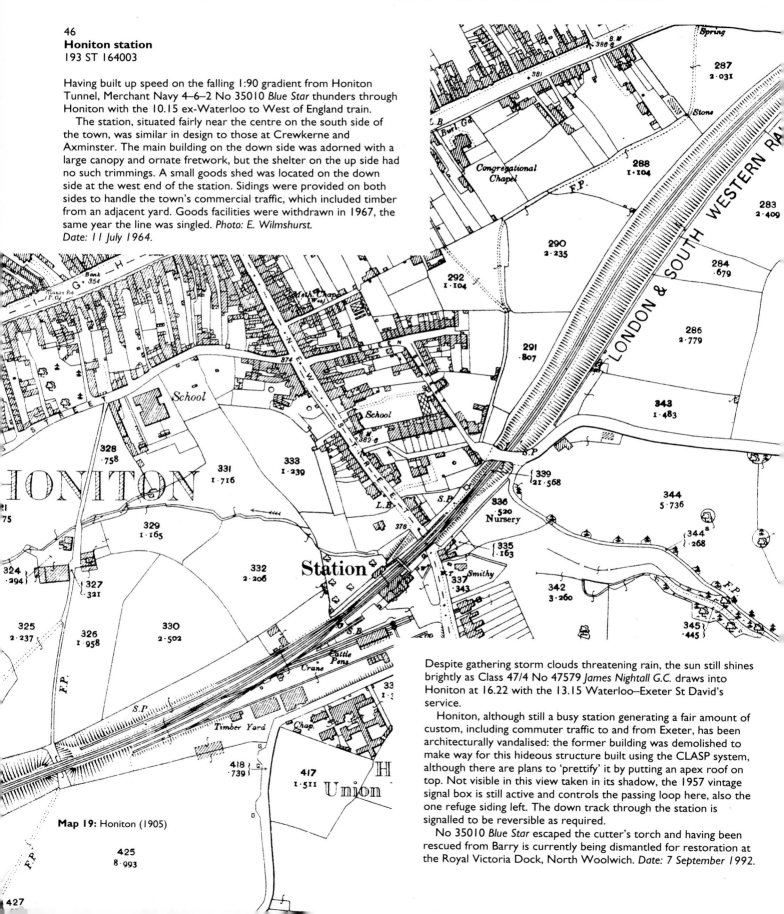

Map 19: Honiton (1905)

Despite gathering storm clouds threatening rain, the sun still shines brightly as Class 47/4 No 47579 *James Nightall G.C.* draws into Honiton at 16.22 with the 13.15 Waterloo–Exeter St David's service.

Honiton, although still a busy station generating a fair amount of custom, including commuter traffic to and from Exeter, has been architecturally vandalised: the former building was demolished to make way for this hideous structure built using the CLASP system, although there are plans to 'prettify' it by putting an apex roof on top. Not visible in this view taken in its shadow, the 1957 vintage signal box is still active and controls the passing loop here, also the one refuge siding left. The down track through the station is signalled to be reversible as required.

No 35010 *Blue Star* escaped the cutter's torch and having been rescued from Barry is currently being dismantled for restoration at the Royal Victoria Dock, North Woolwich. *Date: 7 September 1992.*

47
Sidmouth Junction
192 SY 099990

A good view of Sidmouth Junction from the minor road bridge east of the station near milepost 159 shows the extensive sidings associated with it. The branch to Sidmouth and Exmouth can be seen curving away southwards on the left.

Rebuilt Battle of Britain class Pacific No 34109 *Sir Trafford Leigh-Mallory* makes light work of the six-coach 15.25 (Sundays) Exeter–Yeovil train, leaving nothing for the fireman to do except take a well-earned breather on this hot summer's day, as he leans from the cab. *Photo: Peter W. Gray. Date: 21 July 1963.*

There is precious little to associate this scene with the former: the trackwork is rationalised to the bare minimum and the site of the former junction has been fenced off. Feniton's platform can just be made out in the distance. Although it is largely screened behind cypress trees, which have been planted on the north side of the line, it is quite noticeable how much housing development has taken place in the village over recent years.

Having restarted on time at 10.04 from Feniton, Class 47/7 No 47711, in NSE livery, gathers speed as it passes milepost 159 with the 09.45 Exeter St David's–Waterloo service on a chilly winter's day. *Date: 19 February 1993.*

Sidmouth Junction (Feniton station)
192 SY 096993

The layout of Sidmouth Junction station is superbly portrayed in this study by Dick Riley and shows Merchant Navy class Pacific No 35026 *Lamport & Holt Line* about to leave with the 10.30 Exeter Central–Waterloo train, whilst BR Class 3 2–6–2T No 82018 waits in the bay with a train for the branch line. Apart from normal branch line services, carriages for the seaside towns of Sidmouth and Exmouth were detached from some through trains here and then hauled separately to their destinations from Tipton St John's, where they were split, including a portion of the fabled 'Atlantic Coast Express'.

Just visible over the carriages on the left is the goods yard's 5-ton crane. The substantially built goods shed and station master's house give an air of permanence, which sadly would not last many years longer. Goods facilities were withdrawn on 6 September 1965. *Photo: R. C. Riley. Date: 6 July 1961.*

The station remained open until 6 March 1967 – exactly a year after nine intermediate stations between Salisbury and Exeter closed – but, like a Phoenix rising from the ashes, it reopened on 3 May 1971 as 'Feniton', by which time extensive residential development was

taking place immediately to the north of the railway. Tickets were issued from the small gate box on the down side until 1974, when an office was provided on the platform after the old buildings, including the former goods shed, were demolished.

Today only the former down platform is in use – albeit in rebuilt form, but the old up one is extant, as seen in this comparison view which shows Parcels-liveried Class 47/7 No 47717 leaving with the 09.45 Exeter St David's–Waterloo service. *Date: 23 February 1993.*

Class 47/7 No 47703 *The Queen Mother*, in charge of the 07.50 Basingstoke–Exeter St David's train, departs from Feniton with an impressive column of black smoke issuing from its exhaust. The platform had recently been rebuilt to accommodate the Class 159 units. *Date: 23 February 1993.*

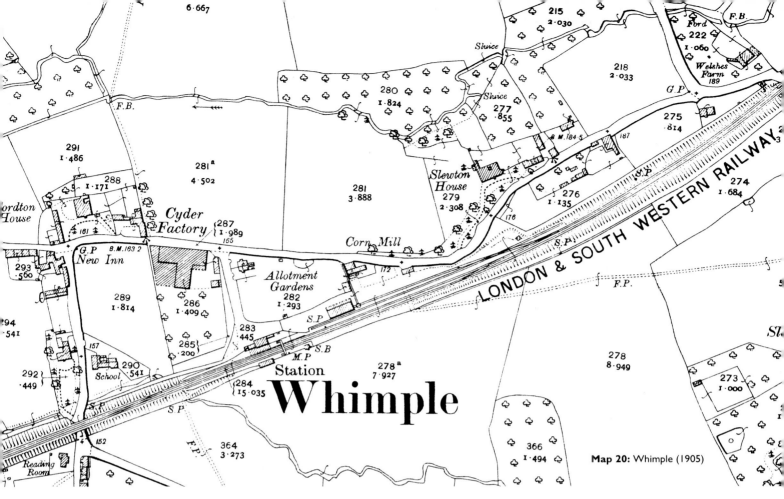

Map 20: Whimple (1905)

49
Whimple station
192 SY 046973

A general view of Whimple taken from the down platform looking east towards Sidmouth Junction. A notable feature here was the monkey-puzzle tree, seen behind the station building. The village became synonymous with cider making and was the home of the famous factory of Henry Whiteway & Co. The factory generated custom for the line, probably reaching a peak in the 1930s: a figure has been suggested that 30,000 tons of freight, which included apples, casks and cider were handled annually in the sidings. These were used until 1989, when Whiteway's production moved elsewhere, although they had closed for general goods traffic on 4 December 1967. When the line was singled on 11 June that year, the up road was retained to provide access to the goods yard, but passengers had to cross the bridge to the down platform in order to catch trains. The station was staffed until 5 October 1970, after which date tickets could be obtained in the mornings from a hut near the footbridge on the down platform. *Photo: Andrew Muckley/ Ian Allan library. Date: September 1964.*

Despite the fact that the former up line and sidings were taken out in 1990 and the goods shed demolished the following year, this is a last glimpse of the station as it was, albeit on a rainy day. Shortly after this photograph was taken, the footbridge was removed and down side platform demolished. This was during the course of a £117,000 improvement scheme involving the reconstruction of the up platform, which was raised and extended forward to meet the line. Other work included new station lighting, the provision of a passenger shelter and some limited forecourt landscaping. In this view the blocks used in the platform's reconstruction are seen stacked ready for the contractors to start work.
Date: 24 August 1992.

On 19 February 1993 a small re-dedication ceremony was held at Whimple, attended by local councillors, railway officials and guests, to mark its reopening after the platform was rebuilt. Class 159 South Western Turbo unit No 159004, then brand new, was used to take invited guests from Exeter to Honiton and return, stopping at Whimple *en route*. Standing on the reconstructed platform in the foreground admiring the three-car Class 159 unit is Colin Marsden, Modern Traction Editor of *Railway Magazine*.

COMMENT: I arrived here only to photograph the train at the rebuilt station; but on asking for a press release, was invited along for the ride by Richard Burningham, Network SouthEast's public relations manager, who kindly arranged to drop me back here, although the train was not scheduled to stop on the return journey from Honiton to Exeter. British Rail earned plenty of Brownie points from me that day!

50
Broad Clyst station
192 SX 992952

Located a mile or so south from the village it served, the station was of a standard design; but the down platform, upon which the main building was situated, was somewhat shorter than the other, as seen in this view looking west. Broad Clyst had a goods shed and a small yard with sidings on the down side; in addition the Civil Engineers' department established a permanent way depot on the up side of the line to the east of the station. The yard closed for freight on the 6 September 1965 and the station to passengers on 6 March 1966.
Photo: Andrew Muckley/Ian Allan library. Date: September 1964.

This view obtained by standing on a small step ladder and reaching over the fence, which now segregates the station building from the line, only depicts remnants of the up platform; the one on the down side no longer survives having been demolished some years ago. The station building is occupied by SW Land & Planning estate agents, valuers and surveyors, whilst the goods shed is occupied by a bookbinding and printing company. Sandwiched between it and the former station building, a small row of industrial units has been built over recent years, providing local employment.
Date: 24 August 1992.

51
Pinhoe station
192 SX 964941

Exmouth Junction (83D) shed Battle of Britain class Pacific No 34080 *74 Squadron* stands at Pinhoe with the 11.02 Exeter Central–Salisbury local. Pinhoe opened on 30 October 1871, some ten years after the line, as the buildings would suggest, being different from those constructed at other stations. Like Sidmouth Junction, Pinhoe was one of the casualties when the SR line was downgraded to a secondary route and it was closed on 6 March 1966.

The station was reopened for a trial period on 16 May 1983 by Tony Speller, the MP for North Devon, who had introduced an amendment to the Transport Act of 1962, which allowed the reopening of stations, but in the event of it being a failure, could be closed again without any undue formal procedure.

No 34080 was withdrawn one month after this photograph was taken and subsequently cut up at Bird's, Morriston, Swansea, the following December. *Photo: Ronald A. Lumber. Date: 18 August 1964.*

The former station master's house still has the same upstairs window open as 28 years before! However, other things have changed: no longer do the platforms have any buildings and the concrete footbridge, fabricated by the concrete works at Exmouth Junction, has been removed. The trial period of opening was obviously successful, for the station is still reasonably well patronised, especially by commuters using the three up and four down trains which stop here each weekday during peak hours. This train, the 12.17 from Exeter St David's to Waterloo, with Class 47 No 47708 *Templecombe* in charge, was not one of them and tears through the station at speed! *Date: 7 September 1992.*

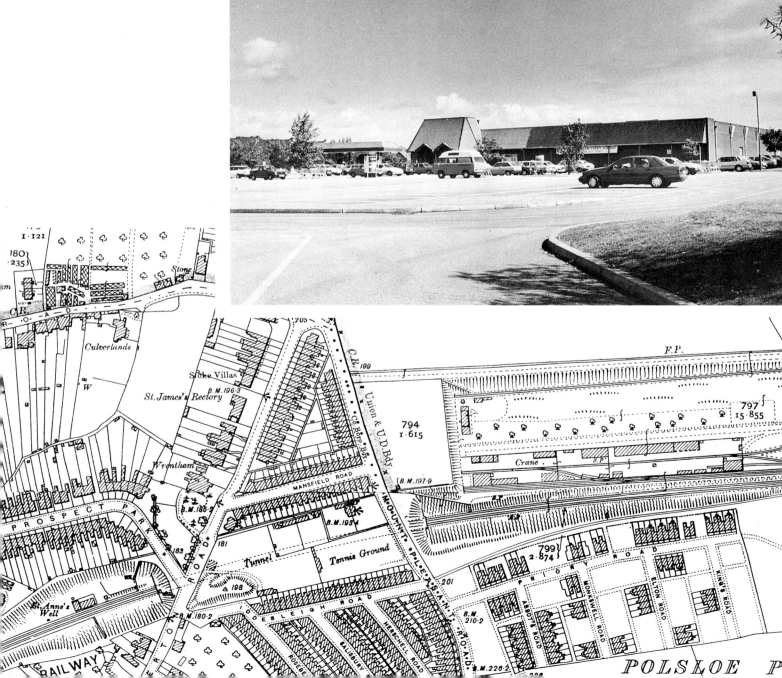

52
Exmouth Junction shed
192 SX 938937

The shed was opened on 3 November 1887, having replaced a smaller one at Exeter Queen Street (later Central) station. The first structure of light steel and corrugated iron cladding became very dilapidated by the mid-1920s. It was replaced with a much more substantial concrete building, completed by 1929, which was cast by the company's adjacent works and had twelve shed roads with a lifting shop attached. The shed was coded 72A until 9 September 1963, when it became 83D; it was closed to steam on 1 June 1965 and completely on 6 March 1967.

This view of the MPD shows several classes of locomotives in residence: those identified are Light Pacifics Nos 34031 *Torrington* and 34069 *Hawkinge*; Drummond T9 No 30712; BR 2-6-2T No 82018; S15s Nos 30841 and 30844. Also on shed is an Adams Class O2 tank and a third Light Pacific. *Photo: R. C. Riley. Date: 5 July 1957.*

After the shed closed, it stood empty for many years until 1970, when it was demolished; the site then lay derelict until 1979 when a supermarket was built. This scene, taken from about the same position as Dick Riley's photograph in 1957, shows how vastly different things are today: a Leo's supermarket and car park cover the area where the steam leviathans from another age once stood. The points of reference are the roofs of the houses on the extreme left of the picture. Maunsell S15 No 30841 has been preserved and once carried the name *Greene King*; it is still in traffic – but on the North Yorkshire Moors Railway. *Date: 7 September 1992.*

The adjacent repair shops are still occupied by the Civil Engineers' Plant department of British Rail. This view inside one of the shops shows Derby's experimental Austrian-built Plasser automatic track and top aligning (ATTA) machine No 73271 in temporary residence. *Date: 7 September 1992.*

Map 21: Exmouth Junction/shed (1905)
The engine shed is shown in its original form, before being replaced by a concrete structure in 1929; the track layout was also altered considerably.

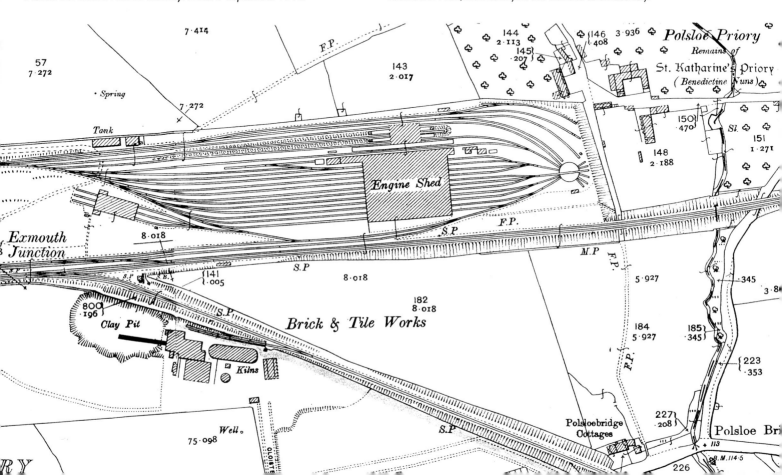

53
Exmouth Junction coaling plant
192 SX 937936

The large concrete coaling plant alongside the shed at Exmouth Junction was a feature which dominated the skyline in the locality. Merchant Navy class Pacific No 35007 *Aberdeen Commonwealth*, seen working the 'Devon Belle' in its third season of operation, passes the coaling plant. No doubt it will be returning here for replenishment, having been detached from the 'Belle' at Exeter Central, where two West Country classes will take over the Ilfracombe and Plymouth portions of the train, into which it will be divided. For many years No 35007 was shedded at Salisbury, where it eventually ended up in store after being withdrawn in July 1967. *Photo: H. C. Casserley. Date: 8 July 1949.*

Working the 11.15 Waterloo–Exeter St David's service, Class 47 No 47710 *Capital Radio's Help a London Child* passes the site of the former coaling plant which was demolished around 1970 together with the shed, now the location of the Leo's supermarket visible in the background. The initial attempts to blow up the coaling tower were not successful, leaving it with a decided list! A subsequent attempt succeeded.

The eight-road down side marshalling yard on the right has been lifted and now the site is littered with sleepers, which have been left to rot. *Photo: Ian Hitchcock/author's camera. Date: 7 September 1992.*

COMMENT: With two trains due to pass here within a couple of minutes of one another – and the need to capture both workings without having to scramble across the line – my lookout and escort, Ian Hitchcock, BR's assistant maintenance supervisor from the adjacent Civil Engineers' Plant depot, kindly offered to take this photograph with one of my cameras from the other side of the tracks – which he managed with considerable accuracy!

54
Exmouth Junction
192 SX 937937

Having just emerged from the 263yd Blackboy Tunnel in the background, immediately passing the site of Mount Pleasant Road Halt (closed on 2 January 1928), Battle of Britain class Light Pacific No 34062 *17 Squadron*, with an up express, breasts the summit to cross the junction with the Exmouth branch, hidden from view behind the train. The up side marshalling yard and sidings for the adjacent concrete works are on the right in the background. Both up and down yards were a hive of activity, where as many as 60 goods trains a day were assembled or broken-up. Exmouth Junction was the SR's main freight distribution point to and from London and the 'withered arm'. *Photo: R. Russell/Ian Allan library. Date: c1958.*

In charge of the 14.22 Exeter St David's service to Waterloo, Class 47 No 47710 *Holyrood* powers up the slope from the tunnel to pass the junction. Apart from the siding on the right having been slewed slightly, it is not obvious in this view that there have been many changes to the track layout. The concrete works site is occupied by Western Fuels, which has built a large coal concentration depot there and it utilises a few of the sidings that once constituted the 10-road marshalling yard. Sadly, movements are only a fraction of what they used to be here and the majority are by the Civil Engineers' department, who use the sidings for storage. *Date: 7 September 1992.*

55
St James' Park Halt
192 SX 926934

The halt, situated in a cutting between Blackboy Tunnel and Exeter Central, was built almost in the shadow of Exeter City football ground. St James' Park opened as Lion's Holt Halt on 26 January 1906; its name was changed on 7 October 1946.

Returning to Waterloo from Exeter Central, Lord Nelson class 4–6–0 No 30861 *Lord Anson* passes St James' Park Halt with an SCTS special working. This was probably the last occasion that a 'Nelson' worked from Exeter – a rare occurrence in any event. No 30861 was withdrawn a month later at Eastleigh, where it had been

shedded over the previous years and was scrapped there in the following November. *Photo: Ronald A. Lumber.*
Date: 2 September 1962.

Not quite such a special event, but nevertheless, with the demise of locomotive-hauled workings on the former LSWR route, this scene will be history by the time this book is published. Parcels-liveried Class 47 No 47717 is captured by the camera at precisely the same spot as it accelerates through St James' Park Halt with the 14.22 Exeter St David's–Waterloo service on a very dull October day, making photography extremely difficult. The halt has not changed in the past thirty years or more. Only some Exmouth trains use it today. *Date: 26 October 1992.*

56
Exeter Central – Howell Road (1)
192 SX 922933

Shortly after passing St James' Park Halt in the cutting beyond the bridge in the background, Battle of Britain class 4–6–2 No 34052 *Lord Dowding* approaches Exeter Central with the 12.27 Portsmouth & Southsea–Plymouth Sunday working. Note the restaurant car and a 'Tavern' car in the siding. The latter were introduced in 1949 and their interiors designed to resemble a public house, but the narrow windows made them seem claustrophobic. They were not deemed a success with the travelling public and were soon withdrawn from service; some were reconstructed with conventional large windows. *Photo: Michael Mensing. Date: 14 June 1959.*

The carriage sidings where the 'Tavern' car once stood have been lifted and a lineside building has been erected. Passing through with the 7Z52 engineers' working on a cold Sunday is Class 37 Co-Co diesel-electric No 37146, having deposited its train of ballast between Chard and Yeovil Junction, where a programme of replacing and cleaning was being carried out. It would work the empties up to Meldon the following day. *Date: 28 February 1993.*

57
Exeter Central – Howell Road (2)
192 SX 922932

This scene is how many will wish to remember Exeter Central in its heyday, as Merchant Navy class Pacific No 35023 *Holland-Afrika Line* leaves the station with the up 'ACE'. Although the coaches are of mixed stock and livery, the gleaming condition of the locomotive would suggest it has recently left the Eastleigh works after being rebuilt a few months before in February. The train obscures the up platform of the station which was extended beyond the bridge in the background carrying New North Road; also out of the picture is the carriage shed situated on the extreme left, although its shadow can be seen. Note the livestock wagons in the siding behind the signal box. *Photo: R. C. Riley. Date: 5 July 1957.*

One supposes in years to come this scene will also be remembered with affection – at least for its subject motive power. The sun skulking behind a cloud makes the same aspect seem dull by comparison. Here Class 47 No 47701 *Old Oak Common Traction & Rolling Stock Depot*, with a train of mixed NSE and BR blue-and-white livery Mk2 stock, accelerates hard with the 14.22 Exeter St David's working to Waterloo. It passes the graffiti-covered disused 'A' box, which closed on 6 May 1985 when the station became controlled by the Exeter power box located at St David's; since then it has occasionally been used as an instruction room. It is obvious in this view how the track at what was originally known as the Queen Street yard has been rationalised here over the last quarter-century. *Date: 1 March 1993.*

58
Exeter Central (Queen Street) station
192 SX 921931

The LSWR's route to Exeter was completed in 1860 and a terminus sited in the centre of the city abutting Queen Street on its west side, after which it originally took its name. Queen Street station, which was also in the lee of Rougemont Castle, had a covered roof which made it appear rather dark and gloomy, although this was altered over its life. The station underwent a total rebuild, which started in 1931 and was completed two years later opening officially on 1 July 1933, whence it was given its current name.

The view from the concrete footbridge at the east end of the station afforded the photographer an excellent panorama across the complex. In this study of Exeter Central, seen in its definitive state with two through roads, all platforms operational and busy goods yard, West Country class Light Pacific No 34038 *Lynton* leaves with an up train from Plymouth. The ex-LBSCR Class E1/R 0–6–2T banker, which helped the Pacific up the 1:37 gradient from St David's, has been detached and awaits the return to the lower station for another similar duty. The Fyffes' banana depot in the yard on the right became a well known feature of Exeter Central; however, the yard closed to general goods traffic on 4 December 1967, but a Blue Circle Cement terminal remained until January 1990. *Photo: John Robertson. Date: 5 August 1955.*

The buildings on the skyline show how Exeter has developed over the past years, whilst at the station the two through roads no longer survive and were subsequently lifted after they were taken out of use: the up side on 9 November 1969 and the other on 21 October 1984. Some effort has been made to fill their place and flower tubs have been placed in the gap they left. The goods yard sidings have been lifted, but one remains adjacent to the up bay platform, which is no longer used. The canopy on the down platform has been shortened to less than half its original length.

Driver Dave Walker at the controls of Parcels-liveried Class 47 No 47703 *The Queen Mother* puts on a show for the benefit of the photographer and makes a spirited start from the station with the 08.10 Exeter St David's–Waterloo service, whilst driver leader Steve Drabwell, laden with some of the author's camera equipment, stands on the platform looking on. The railway enthusiast leaning out of the front coach also seems to be appreciating the healthy bark of the Sulzer's exhaust. Soon this sound will be rare on the line and will not be heard, with the exception of a Class 47's occasional use on engineers' trains or enthusiasts' specials. *Date: 14 April 1993.*

COMMENT: *Being the possessor of a two-day cab pass for photographic purposes, I was able to ride from St David's to here in the cab of No 47703. Since the stop was scheduled only for two minutes, a quick dash up the footbridge was necessary to acquire this shot in order not to delay the working, which I managed to avoid!*

59
Exeter Central – St David's Tunnel
192 SX 918929

Leaning over the parapet of the bridge carrying Queen Street, the photographer had a good view of the 1:37 incline from St David's, which opened on 1 February 1862, linking the two stations. West Country 4–6–2 No 34014 *Budleigh Salterton*, with steam sanders on helping to maintain traction, pounds up the final few yards to Central station with a midday departure for Waterloo. The banker can be seen in the rear having just emerged from the 184yd St David's Tunnel. Besides being used for storing stock, the sidings on the left were also used by engines waiting to be attached to the Plymouth, North Cornwall and Ilfracombe portions of trains that had been split in the station. Note the wagon turntable providing access to the timber yard on the right and the trap siding on the up line to prevent runaways. A further two were sited beyond the tunnel. *Photo: Ronald A. Lumber. Date: 30 September 1951.*

Cars now invade the area once occupied by sidings, which were removed in February 1970. The trap siding on the up side survives, but the crossover points do not. Seen descending the incline towards the tunnel and Exeter St David's is Class 150 Sprinter No 150234 with the 14.03 Exeter Central–Crediton shuttle service. The chances are that it will return from there at 14.35 with very few passengers at this time of day. *Date: 1 March 1993.*

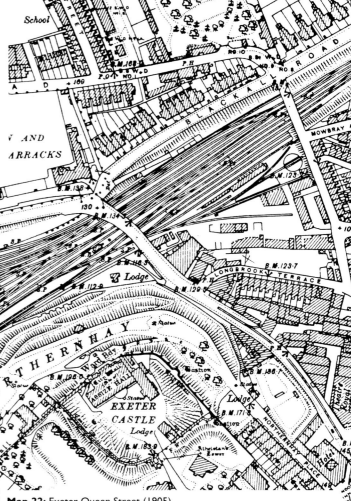

Map 22: Exeter Queen Street (1905)
This plan shows the station before reconstruction in the 1930s, after which it was renamed Exeter Central.

60
Exeter St David's station (1)
192 SX 911932

This superb study taken from the end of the GWR's down platform shows ex-LSWR T9 4–4–0 No 30708 heading West Country class 4–6–2 No 34034 *Honiton* standing on the up side of the centre island platform with the 'Atlantic Coast Express'. After negotiating the junction at the end of the station, they would immediately be faced with the stiff 1:37 climb built on a curve to Exeter Central station nearly three-quarters of a mile away.

When combined with trains on the GWR route, such workings as this added to the richness Exeter St David's could offer the observer, for there was seemingly no end to the types of locomotives that could be seen here. The spectacle of up SR trains starting from the station, which were usually banked, was always stirring. A variety of banking engines were employed over the years and amongst those classes used ex-LBSCR E1/R 0–6–2Ts,

Drummond M7 0–4–4Ts, SR Z class 0–8–0Ts; the latter were replaced towards the end of steam by Maunsell W class 2–6–4Ts.
Photo: R. C. Riley. Date: 29 August 1954.

Although the station has not changed very much, with the exception of the removal of the centre through road, the types of motive power have: standing at platform 3, where the up 'ACE' once waited, Sprinter No 153327 has arrived with the 15.45 Exmouth–Paignton service, whilst waiting at platform 1 to leave with the 16.22 service to Waterloo is Class 47 No 47708 *Templecombe*, soon to be withdrawn from the route.

Today the trackwork has been modified to permit Waterloo, Exmouth and Paignton trains to arrive or depart from either platforms 1 or 3, but it is normal practice for up trains to use platform 1 and platform 3 for down services. Those on the ex-GWR line utilise platforms 4–6, with one or two exceptions on a day when the station is busy and platform 3 is used for Plymouth-bound trains.
Date: 23 February 1993.

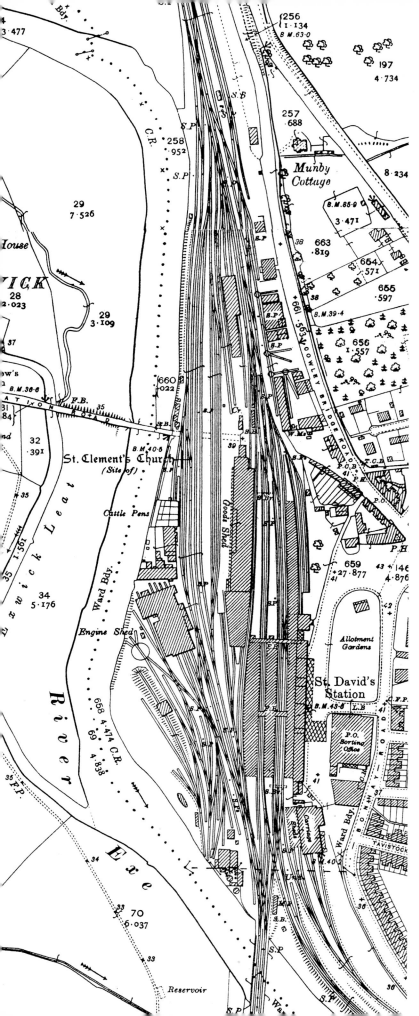

61
Exeter St David's station (2)
192 SX 911934

This excellent study taken at the north end of St David's shows a
typical Southern working as West Country class No 34032
Camelford approaches the station with a train for Waterloo, whilst Z
class 0–8–0T No 30957 waits in the refuge siding on banking duties.
There was plenty of interest for the photographer at this end of the
station, which included the elegant Exeter 'Middle' box, the goods
shed beyond and the busy level crossing on Station Road which
required a permanent lookout. This was provided at the behest of
the local authority, who contributed to all or part of the man's
wages. *Photo: John Scrace. Date: 14 September 1959.*

Having arrived with the 13.15 service from Waterloo some minutes
before, Class 47 No 47583 *County of Hertfordshire* moves out of the
station to deposit its train in a siding on the right beyond the goods
shed, in what is now known as 'New Yard', where run-round
facilities exist. Later it will form the 17.38 return working with the
same locomotive, which will have been detached to wait at the sub-
shed in the interim.
    The same view from the north end of the station is no longer
such an inspiring sight, as 'Middle' box has been demolished
following the re-signalling of St David's and the track rationalisation;
however, 'West' box, once sited near the River Exe bridge, has been
saved and removed to the Crewe Heritage Centre. The goods shed,
an original B&E building, in the background, survives without a real
use, but a level crossing lookout is still employed. There are long
term plans to build a flyover to carry Station Road across the line at
this point, which will eventually obviate the need for such lookout
duties. *Date: 23 February 1993.*

Map 23: Exeter St David's (1932)
Note the Southern (ex-LSWR) line sweeping in from the south-east.

Exeter Riverside

With the recent withdrawal of the occasional fertiliser trains to
Lapford, the only freight workings on the former SR lines west of
Exeter to and from the Riverside goods yard are the Meldon Quarry
ballast trains which use the sidings here prior to being despatched,
either loaded or returning as empties. Seen at first light on a chilly
Monday morning in an otherwise deserted yard, apart from an 08
shunter in the distance, Class 37 No 37197 waits to leave with a
short train of empty Dogfish wagons for Meldon.
Date: 1 March 1993.

COMMENT: On learning that some workings to and from Meldon Quarry were being discontinued, Network SouthEast not having renewed a contract, and with my desire to record on film these trains, I was lucky enough to be granted a cab pass, which enabled me to make two trips up the former Southern main line – now worked as a branch – as far as the quarry, where it terminates. Although the dawn promised good weather on this occasion, by the time we left Meldon it took a dramatic turn for the worse, as will become apparent later in the book!

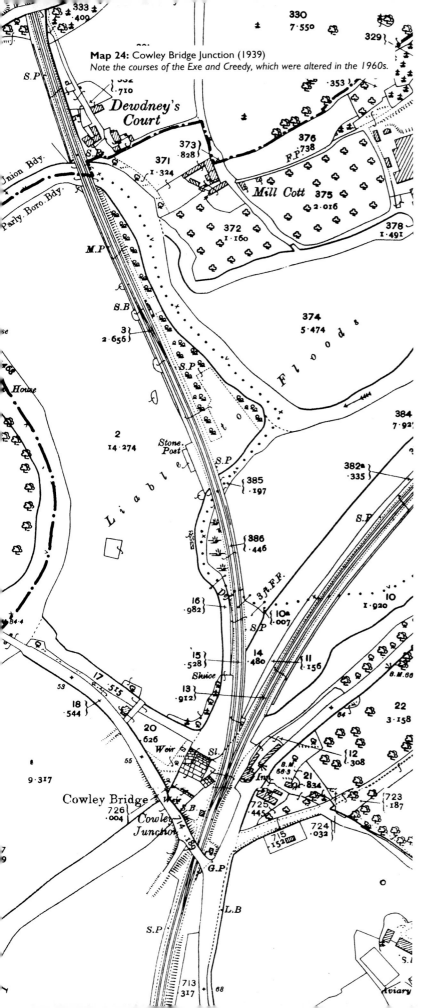

Map 24: Cowley Bridge Junction (1939)
Note the courses of the Exe and Creedy, which were altered in the 1960s.

Cowley Bridge Junction
192 SX 909953

The junction marked the divergence of the Southern from the GW main line. From this point the Southern's territory westwards was dubbed 'The Withered Arm' by T. W. E. Roche in his book of that title, first published in 1967, which was of his reminiscences of its lines west of Exeter. However, perhaps it would have been fairer to describe the North Cornwall line and the Bude branch as such, for the Southern's route to Plymouth was constituted to be its main line.

Seen cautiously negotiating the junction, which had a permanent speed limit of 20mph imposed, West Country Light Pacific No 34104 *Bere Alston* with the 16.02 Plymouth–Waterloo train joins ex-GW metals and passes Cowley Bridge signal box. The lower quadrant up home signals in the background behind the train are of GWR design, installed in 1943 when the junction was resignalled following the construction of the Riverside yard. *Photo: S. C. Nash. Date: 9 June 1960.*

Here a pair of Civil Engineers' Class 33 Cromptons, Nos 33118 and 33002, with the 11.20 Meldon Quarry–Tonbridge ballast train, have been halted at the signals near the bridge over the River Exe, whilst Railfreight Distribution Class 47 No 47288 passes the junction on the ex-GWR main line with a mixed train of wood for paper making (which had been delivered by road from Eggesford) and returning unloaded 'Cartic' transporter wagons. Earlier these had carried a consignment of cars to Exeter on behalf of Silcock's Car Transporter Company from Alexandra Dock Junction, Newport, to Premier Transport's sidings at St David's. *Date: 24 March 1993.*

Cowley Bridge Junction/flood relief scheme
Although the Southern line was effectively singled west of the junction on 28 November 1965, two tracks remained on the iron bridge over the River Exe. At that time it had also become necessary to alter the courses of the Exe and Creedy near their confluence in connection with the anti-flood schemes planned for the area. This entailed the reconstruction and resiting of the river underbridges west of the junction, some of which were eliminated. This work lasted until early 1967, during which time a single track connection with the main WR line was created, variably using the up or down SR line. This extended to the Upton Pyne road underbridge about a half-mile distant, where a temporary signal box controlled the return to double track to Crediton. When the work was completed, a permanent point was put in for the purpose just beyond the river bridge near the junction. This arrangement lasted until resignalling and singling of the line under the Exeter MAS scheme on 15 December 1984, then the junction was simplified.

This view taken from the cab of Class 37 No 37197, on a Meldon Quarry–Riverside working, shows to good advantage the current layout of Cowley Bridge Junction. Beyond the A377 Crediton road bridge, upon which a photographer is seen poised with his camera, are the points on the GW up road, which provide access to the Riverside sidings; the crossover to the GW down side is used for North Devon line workings. *Date: 1 March 1993.*

63
Newton St Cyres station
192 SX 880989

The station was the only intermediate one on the Exeter & Crediton Railway and situated about a half-mile from the village at the hamlet of Sweetham, just north of the River Creedy. The main station buildings were on the up side and of wooden construction. A small siding and cattle loading dock were provided on the down side.

This post-steam era shot shows Hymek No D7011 passing Newton St Cyres with the 16.00 Exeter St David's–Ilfracombe service. The station is largely intact with the exception of the siding and the tall LSWR down starter signal. The siding had closed on 12 September 1960 and was lifted in December 1962.
Photo: Ronald A. Lumber. Date: 12 September 1970.

With long shadows cast by a setting sun, Class 33 No 33046 passes Newton St Cyres with the 7V84 train of empties from Eastleigh for Meldon. With the line having been singled to Crediton in December 1984, today only the up platform remains in use and the station is purely a request stop for trains on the North Devon line. The usable platform is rather too low for the modern Sprinter units and passengers have to take quite a step when alighting from or boarding a train; this would require considerable funds to rectify, but because of the low usage of the station would not be justified on cost grounds. Recently local residents mounted a vigorous protest involving the local media at the suggestion that trains would no longer call here, but at the time of writing there are no plans to discontinue services. *Date: 23 February 1993.*

64
Newton St Cyres
192 SX 880989

Looking west from the road bridge near the station, N class 2–6–0 No 31836 drifts down the 1:305 grade towards Newton St Cyres with a short up freight. Note the guard leaning out of his brake van at the rear, taking advantage of some fresh air on this hot summer's day. The houses are in the hamlet of Sweetham, which also has a pub nestling close to the line near the road bridge. No 31836 was withdrawn four months later and stored at Exmouth Junction until it

was moved to Eastleigh, where it was broken-up in April 1964. *Photo: Peter W. Gray. Date: 23 August 1963.*

Having just passed under the road bridge, Class 37 No 37098 charges up the slight grade towards Crediton with a short train of empties for Meldon Quarry. The section of single track over which it is travelling is of continuous welded rail, but ends just ahead of the locomotive and reverts to jointed lengths, which are in a poor condition further round the bend at Codshead Bridge, giving a rough ride to ballast train crews. *Date: 25 March 1993.*

65
Crediton station
191 SX 841995

Although the line to Crediton was completed in 1847 it did not open for another four years as broad gauge, due to a prolonged argument over the gauge. In the end a compromise was reached and one track remained as broad gauge whilst the other was narrowed, but the latter initially had no station at Exeter to go to and therefore was unused! Crediton remained as an outpost of the broad gauge until its demise in 1892. Because it is set almost a mile south of the town centre, the station became less convenient for local journeys as bus services developed in the twentieth century. An unusual steel-framed goods shed clad in corrugated iron with an arched roof was sited on the up side at the east end of the station, together with the main yard, which was quite complex and included a wagon turntable; sidings were also provided on the down side. The goods yard closed for general traffic on 4 December 1967.

N class 2–6–0 No 31853 passes Crediton on a Monday morning with the 09.33 Padstow to Waterloo service. The locomotive was withdrawn a month later and stored at Exeter St David's MPD, before being sent to Bird's, Morriston, Swansea, where it was scrapped the following December. *Photo: Ronald A. Lumber. Date: 17 August 1964.*

The fabric of Crediton station has largely remained unchanged over the years. Class 150 Sprinter No 150249 waits to depart with the 12.35 service to Exeter having arrived 45 minutes before with the 11.15 service from Exmouth. This working is part of a recently created 'park and ride' service to and from Exeter, but on this occasion there were no customers for the return journey. If ever there was a case for reinstating a service to Okehampton, this would be it, as the Sprinter would have just enough time to get there and back – Meldon workings permitting! *Date: 3 November 1992.*

At the east end of the station the goods shed has been isolated from the line by a fence and forms part of a small industrial estate built on the site of the up yard. Recently the shed burnt down and only its skeleton remains. Only two sidings have been left in place on the down side for the civil engineers. This view was taken from the cab of Class 37 No 37141 on its way to Meldon. *Date: 14 April 1993.*

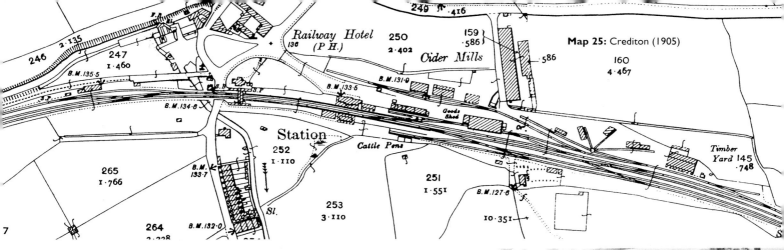

66
Crediton signal box
191 SX 840995

Besides its main signalling function, the LSWR wooden signal box of 1875 vintage controlled the gated crossing over a minor road at the west end of the station. Approaching the crossing with the 08.48 Padstow–Exeter Central is N class 2–6–0 No 31855. The locomotive was not destined to remain long in service, for like its stable mate in the previous view, it was withdrawn the next month and suffered the same fate.
Photo: Ronald A. Lumber. Date: 17 August 1964.

The signal box exterior remains unaltered and is the last of its design and vintage in active use, although its internal equipment has been changed with electric signalling installed and operates as a fringe box to Exeter. Crediton became a junction on 17 October 1971, when the crossover, seen in this view, was the point from which the double tracks were operated as two separate lines, with the former up road for the North Devon line and the down side for the Meldon branch. Lifting barriers replaced the gates in 1974 and when the line was singled ten years later, Crediton became a long crossing loop with points installed about a half-mile east of the station, so the two platforms could also be used.

Here the driver of Class 153 Sprinter No 153380, working the 12.30 Barnstaple–Exmouth, hands the single line token to signalman Eric Stone before proceeding to the station. *Date: 3 November 1992.*

67
Yeoford station
191 SX 783989

The station opened on 1 August 1854 as part of the broad gauge North Devon Railway. Later it became important as an interchange station between the North Devon and Plymouth lines, due to its proximity to Coleford Junction. The line to North Tawton opened on 1 November 1865 and was doubled between Coleford and Crediton on 16 May 1877. The station had three platform faces, the down side being an island and was used for interchanges. The wooden buildings, although adequate, were not palatial. In addition, a cattle loading dock and extensive sidings with a long loop were provided on the down side for the transfer and re-marshalling of freight. The yard closed on 10 February 1964, whilst the tall signal box, situated on the west side of the bridge, shut on 18 August 1968. Passenger services to Okehampton ceased on 3 June 1972.

This east-looking view of Yeoford from the adjacent three-arched road bridge shows it still largely in its definitive form, although the yard had closed by this date. A two-car DMU leaves Yeoford with an Exeter–Barnstaple train. *Photo: Ronald A. Lumber.*
Date: 9 March 1968.

Trains still call at Yeoford, but on request and only use the former up platform. The station has been shorn of its buildings, except the small wooden structure on the former up platform; in addition, all the sidings and down bay loop have been removed. The North Devon or 'Tarka' line is on the left, whilst the Meldon branch is on the right, upon which Railfreight Distribution Class 47/0 No 47079 darts under the bridge and passes the disused island platform with a train of 19 loaded Turbot wagons from Meldon – although the first was empty, probably being designated a 'green card' vehicle: faulty, but able to be hauled. Earlier, the locomotive had taken a train of some 40 unladen wagons to Meldon: according to signalman Eric Prouse at Crediton, one of the longest he had recently seen on the branch. *Date: 14 April 1993.*

68
Yeoford
191 SX 783989

Battle of Britain class 4–6–2 No 34062 *17 Squadron* approaches Yeoford with the Okehampton–Surbiton Car Carrier. This was the last year that the motorail service ran, after being introduced in 1960 enabling holidaymakers to beat the notorious traffic jams, particularly around Exeter. The track layout on the west side of the bridge adjacent to the tall signal box, which is just out of view on the left, is seen to good advantage in this aspect; one of the sidings has already been lifted, judging by the sleepers left on the trackbed. The Light Pacific, rebuilt only five years before, had only a few days left in service, for it was withdrawn the same month and was later

scrapped by Bird's, Bridgend, between January 1965 and June 1966. *Photo: Peter W. Gray. Date: 20 June 1964.*

This comparison study taken on a hazy evening with the sun too far round, making photography somewhat challenging, shows that only the two branch lines are left today: the remaining sidings were lifted after the box closed in 1968. Having dropped off one passenger, two-car Sprinter unit No 150249 has just restarted from Yeoford with a 'Barnie' train, as Barnstaple workings are affectionately known to local railwaymen. This one is the 17.30 service from Exeter. Note the church on the horizon, which is that in Colebrooke and adjacent to Coleford Junction on its east side at the bottom of the hill around which the Meldon branch also circumnavigates. *Date: 14 April 1993.*

Coleford Junction
191 SS 775001

When the Devon & Cornwall Railway opened on 1 November 1865, the junction, a mile from Yeoford, marked its divergence point from the North Devon line. The track from Crediton to here and beyond was doubled in the late 1870s as part of the LSWR's improvement of the route to Plymouth; the North Devon line to Copplestone was doubled from here on 4 November 1883. The weatherboarded signal box of 1877 vintage had 13 levers to control the signals, junction and crossover, which was needed when engineers required possession of a line. Seen passing the junction at 17.30 is N class 2–6–0 No 31859 on a long up freight from Barnstaple. Like the previous members of the class featured in this chapter, it was soon to be withdrawn from service and was only to last another six months. *Photo: Ronald A. Lumber. Date: 26 March 1964.*

The signal box and junction closed on 17 October 1971, when both lines were singled and the connection between them removed. Today only remnants of the stone base of the box remain, which is seen partly in deep shadow.

On its second return trip of the day to Meldon with driver Albert Reed in charge, Class 37 No 37141 storms rounds the 20-chain radius curve with a Meldon–Eastleigh ballast working, and passes the site of the former junction. *Date: 14 April 1993.*

The former junction seen from the cab of Class 37 No 37141 on its first trip of the day shows clearly how the two lines diverge. *Date: 14 April 1993.*

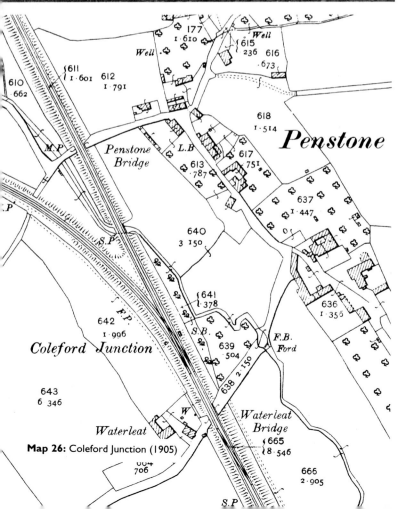

Map 26: Coleford Junction (1905)

70
Bow station
191 SX 714999

Opened on 1 November 1865 as Nymet Tracey when services started on the section to North Tawton, the station was the first on the Devon & Cornwall Railway. Later it took its name from a village over a mile away to the north. Because of its isolated position, it is questionable whether it ever enjoyed good custom regarding passenger traffic; however, it had a small yard with a moderately sized stone-built goods shed to compensate!

This study of Bow taken from the up platform towards the end of its operational life shows the substantial station building the down side. By this date Bow had a distinctly dilapidated look to it, with flaking paint on the platform shelter and rusting iron fencing. *Photo: Andrew Muckley/Ian Allan library. Date: April 1964.*

With only the single line for the Meldon branch passing the down platform, the up side has a look of total abandonment, with the edging slabs having been lifted and left untidily along its length. The shelter and concrete station sign survived until recently, but the latter was removed as a souvenir. The station building is a private dwelling and the owner runs an antique business from there. The former yard and shed is owned by a company specialising in salvaged roofing materials. *Date: 29 January 1993.*

During a snowstorm, Bow looks even more bleak from the cab of Class 37 No 37197 returning to Exeter Riverside with 15 loaded wagons from Meldon. *Date: 1 March 1993.*

71
North Tawton station
191 SS 665000

Like Bow, the station was not best placed to attract custom and was a mile south of the village it served. Although identical in design to that at Bow, the main station building here was positioned on the up side. North Tawton was built on an undulating four-mile straight stretch of line on a 1:80 gradient, which eased to 1:264 through the station.

When through services ceased from Plymouth in 1968 and the line closed between Bere Alston and Okehampton, a DMU shuttle service was instituted between the latter and Exeter, which survived until 3 June 1972. Here, a DMU passes North Tawton *en route* to Okehampton. Note how the line rises steeply from the station towards the summit, reached at the occupation bridge on the horizon. *Photo: Andrew Muckley/Ian Allan library. Date: April 1971.*

The station buildings survive, the main one as two private dwellings which have been fenced off from the line, whilst the former goods yard is occupied by a transport and a cable laying company. The road bridge was removed some years ago and a new one built to allow more headroom for heavy goods vehicles; also, before the opening of the new A30 dual carriageway and Okehampton bypass, the road here formed part of a holiday diversion route. During this period the footbridge was removed to Ropley on the Mid-Hants Railway, where it has been re-erected and is in public use. With the new road bridge installed, the track level had to be raised accordingly and now is above the platform height, as can be seen here. *Date: 29 January 1993.*

It is plain to see how the track level has been raised above the platform level at North Tawton when viewed from the cab of Class 37 No 37141, as it drifts down the 1:80 gradient and passes over the new bridge. Note how the line dips beyond the station and then climbs towards the western horizon at 1:77. *Date: 14 April 1993.*

72
Sampford Courtney station
191 SX 627986

The station opened in 1867 as Okehampton Road, but subsequently was named Belstone Corner, only to be changed again in 1872 to Sampford Courtney, after a village over a mile-and-a-half to the north! Situated in such an isolated position, it was hardly placed to attract much custom. The station building was much more modest that those at Bow and North Tawton, as can be judged from this photograph, which shows 3DMU (LA309) on the 18.30 Okehampton–Exeter St David's service at Sampford Courtney. Yes Tor can be seen in the background standing at 2,028ft above sea level. *Photo: Ronald A. Lumber. Date: 25 May 1970.*

The platforms survive intact together with the shelter on the down side, but the main building has been demolished. Note that one of the posts from the station sign still stands in the undergrowth, as does the lineside hut near the site of the goods yard, which is now occupied by a joinery company. With the day being rather dull and overcast, Yes Tor is obscured from view. *Date: 29 January 1993.*

COMMENT: *This comparison is hardly stimulating, especially without a train, but with Meldon ballast workings not always running to schedule, one might be faced with at least a two-hour wait or more to capture one on film. This I was not prepared to do on such a miserable day in failing light – sorry!*

Okehampton station

The railway arrived at Okehampton on 3 October 1871, just a year before the Devon & Cornwall Railway was fully absorbed by the LSWR. The station was constructed 750ft above sea level on the slopes of East Hill, bordering Dartmoor to the south side and high above the town, about a half-mile from its centre. The easterly approach to Okehampton was made on a stiff 1:77 gradient, which continued for some distance beyond the station, although it was built on a short level stretch. With the opening of the North Cornwall line and the Bude branch, it was to become an important junction town, for it was not only an interchange station, but a dividing and joining point for trains, particularly the 'Atlantic Coast Express'.

Although the through route to Plymouth was severed to Bere Alston from 6 May 1968, scheduled DMU shuttle services continued to operate from Exeter and Okehampton until 5 June 1972, when they were withdrawn. Later, the West Devon Borough Council sponsored a series of charter trains in 1985 and 1986 as extensions of the Exmouth–Exeter services. Although they were quite popular, they lost money and were not repeated in 1987; however, a few enthusiasts' specials have since run to Okehampton on occasions.

Recently British Rail has again looked into the possibility of reopening the station, but has estimated £10–15,000 is required just to make the station safe, as the roof is in a dangerous condition. The chances of regular train services to Exeter are slim because of lack of demand brought about by the improved road infrastructure – also the station is not conveniently sited in the town. Limited services for Dartmoor walkers and tourists may be possible if support is forthcoming from the local councils and other interested parties.

73
Okehampton station (1)
191 SX 594944

A panorama of Okehampton taken from the goods yard shows BR Standard Class 4 No 75025 standing by the 70ft turntable, which was built in 1947 to handle larger locomotives; adjacent to it is the water tower and out of the picture on the right is the engine shed. This was a subsidiary of Exmouth Junction, which in latter years housed a small allocation of T9s, Ivatt 2–6–2Ts and Ns for interspersed workings to Plymouth, Bude, Padstow and back to Exeter. Waiting at the station with the up 'Brighton' is BR Type 4 Bo-Bo diesel-hydraulic Warship D815 *Druid*, then five years old, emitting almost as much steam from its heating boiler as the 4–6–0 on this chilly winter's day. The tall upper quadrant repeater starting signal is off and soon the Warship will move out of the station and roll down the 1:77 grade. For the next 25 miles it will have an easy task requiring little effort, for it is mostly downhill to Exeter, apart from one or two short sections. *Photo: Peter W. Gray.*
Date: 2 January 1965.

Just over 28 years later two diesels of a different type but of the same vintage are spotted at Okehampton, again on a January day: with the foreground cast in deep shadow, Civil Engineers' Class 33s Nos 33108 and 33019 *Griffon* are caught in a shaft of sunlight as they trundle through the station with the 11.20 Meldon–Tonbridge ballast working. Although the station is largely intact and the goods shed survives, the engine shed has been demolished along with the turntable and water tower, and little evidence remains of them ever being there. Many of the sidings in the goods yard have been lifted, but a few remain for use by the civil engineers.
Date: 18 January 1993.

Map 27: Okehampton (1905)

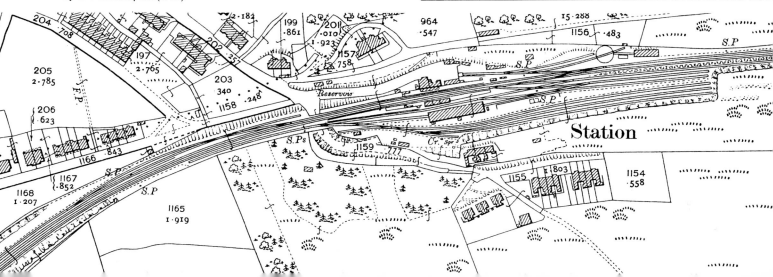

Station

74
Okehampton station (2)
191 SX 593944

The station building (rebuilt in brick in the 1930s) was located on the up side, providing all the necessary facilities including waiting rooms, ticket office and lavatories, plus a parcels and left luggage office. At the west end a covered footbridge of lattice construction gave access to the down side and the bay platform for the North Cornwall line and Bude branch trains.

This photograph, taken a month before closure, shows a DMU at Okehampton with a train for Exeter. These were employed on the shuttle service between the two towns after the through route from Bere Alston and Plymouth was shut. *Photo: E. Wilmshurst. Date: 6 May 1972.*

Today the station appears as if caught in a time warp; its general fabric is reasonable, but the roof badly needs attention and many of the slates are in danger of falling off. The yellow and green paint is flaking, allowing the rust to take hold on some of the steel work, but it will be many years before it is eaten through. The former down line is retained as a siding for occasional use by engineers' trains – which is a rare occurrence.

After a two-hour wait, a working that is sadly no longer is captured on camera for posterity, for it and all other Network SouthEast ballast trains were withdrawn a matter of days after this photograph was taken. Class 33 D6308 (No 33008) *Eastleigh*, painted in original green livery, passes Okehampton with the 11.20 Meldon to Tonbridge. *Date: 30 April 1993.*

75
Okehampton station (3)
191 SX 592944

A view from the west end of the station shows a double-headed short up goods as it drifts round the bend to pass through Okehampton with Ivatt 2–6–2T No 41317 and N class 2–6–0 No 31406 in charge. In the bay, BR Class 4MT 2–6–4T No 80042 waits with the 13.30 service to Bude. The station sign is receiving attention and gets a good clean from a member of the staff. Obscured from view behind the goods train is the signal box.

The Mogul was withdrawn a month later and was broken-up at Bird's, Bynea, in December the same year. The others had not long to remain in service either, but survived the year – just.
Photo: Peter W. Gray. Date: 4 August 1964.

Even with winter's lighting making photography extremely marginal, there appears to be little change at this end of the station either; apart from a siding and set of points taken out and the signals removed, it is not hard to imagine a Bude branch train still calling here. The station sign so lovingly cleaned has also gone with only the posts remaining, but the signal box still stands and is used as a storeroom.

The absence of a train in this shot was due to the fact that there were no further workings to or from Meldon scheduled in daylight hours, and the infrequency of these passing through the station will be the general situation if new contracts are not forthcoming soon.
Date: 18 January 1993.

76
Okehampton station (4)
191 SX 591945

This is more like it! Battle of Britain class No 34058 *Sir Frederick Pile* of Exmouth Junction shed enters Okehampton with a down express for Plymouth, whilst in the background a Padstow train is seen waiting in the bay behind. Having climbed 25 miles from Exeter, with grades of up to 1:76, the Pacific still has three miles to go before the summit, 950ft above sea level, is reached in a cutting at Prewley Moor, near Sourton Down just beyond Meldon Viaduct and the junction. Soon after starting from the station, it will be faced with a stiff climb at 1:77 up to the quarry, and after crossing the viaduct the grade will steepen to 1:58 for a few chains. *Photo: P. H. Wells. Date: 20 May 1952.*

With no train standing in the station a clear view is to be had of the goods shed; although most of the windows are broken it remains in reasonable shape. Today the main station building on the up side is occupied by Devon Training for Skills (DFTS), a training agency, and Lion Designs, who make 'furniture for plants'. Looking through the station, one can see how steeply the line drops away at the far end beyond the remaining sidings, which are on level ground. There are no points at the east end and access to the sidings is gained from the west side. *Date: 18 January 1993.*

This is what Dartmoor weather can do even in spring time! Seen from the cab of Class 37 No 37197, Okehampton looks positively bleak with a covering of snow, which had been falling for less than one hour. Nevertheless, this aspect taken from the locomotive gives a good impression of the state of preservation of the station. Long may it continue to remain so. *Date: 1 March 1993.*

COMMENT: *For the purposes of photography – and at my request – the driver slowed the locomotive to no more than a slow walking pace through the station, despite a 539-ton load trying to push us down the gradient; but in the excitement, the 'then and now' shot I wanted failed miserably because I had incorrectly adjusted the camera to compensate for the bad lighting. Pity!*

77
Okehampton military sidings
191 SX 587942

A few chains around the bend west of the station and, being in proximity of Okehampton Camp, sidings were installed for troop trains, the handling of military equipment and vehicles using the Dartmoor ranges. The sidings were also used between 1960–4 for a motorail service which ran to and from Surbiton, introduced during the summer season enabling holidaymakers to beat some of the notorious traffic jams in the West Country, particularly the Exeter bypass. On occasions they were also utilised to hold ballast trains.

Brush Type 4 No D1911 (Class 47 TOPS No 47234) passes the

sidings at 14.00 with a down empties for Meldon.
Photo: Ronald A. Lumber. Date: 1 May 1969.

Without any train in view this is probably not one of the most interesting shots, but it illustrates how things have changed: the military no longer need to transport vehicles or guns by rail to the ranges; it would take too much time when compared to the ease of road travel today, and fuel is not so scarce as it was during the war years, so the sidings were removed some time ago. The prefabricated hut in the background is an Air Cadet squadron's headquarters. No 47234 is still in service and currently painted in Railfreight Distribution livery. *Date: 18 January 1993.*

Meldon Quarry Ltd

Dating from 1897, Meldon Quarry has been a supplier of ballast to the railways for almost a hundred years. It produces hornsfels, sedimentary rocks modified by heat and pressure and metamorphosed to a slaty material, which is extracted adjacent to the granite intrusion of Dartmoor. The material is hard and durable, which is ideal for railway ballast, particularly for use with high speed track. It is estimated that there are at least 300 million tons in reserve and Meldon could supply ballast well into the next century. Since 1989 it has operated as a 'stand alone' company, a wholly owned subsidiary of British Rail, but in a recent announcement by the Government is currently up for sale under the railway privatisation programme.

Recently, up to six trains a day were loaded and despatched from the quarry. The wagons are marshalled under the loading point by a Class 08 shunter, which creeps under the loading conveyor. The contracts with Network SouthEast and the Western Region were for 300–350,000 tons per annum, but because of the high cost of rail transport in uneconomically small load capacity wagons, NSE found it cheaper to acquire ballast from Foster Yeoman's Glensander quarry near Oban in Scotland and to ship it down to the South Coast, then transport it to where it was required. As a consequence the contract with NSE was not renewed, which resulted in MQL's workforce of 50 being halved; and from the introduction of the 1993 summer timetables, all ballast trains to Tonbridge, Eastleigh, Hoo Junction and Woking ceased. At the time of writing Meldon are committed to supplying InterCity, Reading, with 100,000 tons and Regional Railways Civil Engineers, Exeter, with 60,000 tons per annum; additionally, there are other contracts in the offing, which might increase the requirement for ballast.

As the quarry borders Dartmoor National Park, there have been severe planning restrictions imposed on it and with environmental considerations it is unlikely to be allowed to expand much beyond its current limits. However, there has been a slight relaxation in planning policy which now allows up to 75 lorry trips a day; the previous limit was 37. The quarry requires considerable investment if it is to remain viable. One option is to install a mobile crusher which would obviate the need for much of the heavy plant used; and since the fixed primary crusher, set high on a pinnacle in the middle of the complex, has to be taken down in 1995, it will release several million tons of material upon which it has been sitting. This may well be the opportunity to make the quarry much more competitive and therefore an attractive proposition for a would-be purchaser.

Although trains have been as few as one per day in the early summer of 1993, these are likely to increase as demand dictates. With the withdrawal of the NSE contract and the Class 33s used, most trains are currently hauled by Class 37s, but some Class 47s have been used. Lately InterCity have chartered 102-ton Foster Yeoman KEA and JXA wagons with a carrying capacity of 75 tons, which have been loaded at the quarry, making it more economic to transport ballast by rail, so there is still a glimmer of hope that the branch line to Meldon might be retained for some time to come.

Meldon Quarry at work

COMMENT: Being granted a cab pass on two occasions, I took the opportunity to record on film Meldon Quarry at work and the following photographs are just a few of those taken on both trips, which were made in a Class 37 locomotive. Space precludes the inclusion of more.

(i)
A general view of the quarry showing the marshalling yard and the resident shunter No 08937, which is at work dragging wagons under the loading conveyor. *Date: 13 November 1992.*

(ii)
A driver's eye view from Class 37 No 37197 shows the end of the Meldon branch, the headshunt of which is seen swinging away from the redundant viaduct in the background beyond the Class 08 shunter. The Class 37 which has uncoupled from its train and moved forward, waits for the points to be swung prior to reversing into a siding, enabling No 08937 to collect the wagons, which it will then manoeuvre under the loading conveyor. Being the first working on a Monday morning, the Class 37 will have to wait to have its wagons filled before returning to Riverside with them. The normal practice is to leave a train of empties and return with one that has already been loaded. *Date: 1 March 1993.*

(iii)

The 15-wagon train comprised of Dogfish containers is dragged under the loading conveyor by the Class 08. The horizontal lights showing on the signal near the control cabin indicate to the shunter to stop; when they are angled at 45° the locomotive reverses until the next wagon is positioned correctly for loading. Note that it has just started to snow. *Date: 1 March 1993.*

(iv)

Having had its 15 wagons loaded, the Class 37 is reunited with its train and prepares to leave the quarry for Exeter Riverside in what is by now a blizzard, which all but obliterates it from the camera's view! The shunter's shed can just be made out on the left. *Date: 1 March 1993.*

(v)

Some six weeks later the weather was totally different, being hot and sunny. Having been uncoupled from its 655-ton train of empties comprised of Seacow, Sealion and Turbot wagons, Class 37 No 37141 runs past to move further down the quarry sidings before coupling up to an already loaded train of 993 tons for Tonbridge. *Date: 14 April 1993.*

78
Meldon Quarry
191 SX 566924

Meldon as seen from a passing train, which was the 19.45 Plymouth–
Exeter DMU service and shows a USA 0–6–0T quarry shunter
lurking in its shed, beyond which are the wagon loading hoppers.
Note the primary crusher's building perched on the hill in the
middle of the quarry works. *Photo: Ronald A. Lumber.*
Date: 10 July 1965.

The same aspect shows how the track has been rationalised
somewhat today. Shunter No 08937 moves slowly back along the
headshunt towards the viaduct as it helps load a ballast train. When
the track layout was modified the opportunity was taken to
rationalise pointwork to the shed and it had its westerly end blocked
up and the other side opened, which also had the benefit of giving
some measure of protection against the severe gales which tend to
blow in that direction. In winter, this could cause havoc to the
shunter's diesel fuel which could freeze, rendering it useless!
Although there have been some alterations to the quarry plant, the
primary crusher's building is still identifiable.
Date: 13 November 1992.

79
Meldon Quarry Halt
191 SX 566924

This snapshot taken from a passing train is a bonus, as photographs of the tiny halt at Meldon are extremely rare. It has been written that this was constructed for the benefit of quarrymen's wives who wished to go shopping in Okehampton. North Cornwall trains would stop on a Saturday to pick them up, but equally it was used by workmen travelling from the town to work. Standing behind the down platform with a coach attached is a faithful servant of the quarry in the form of its shunter, G6 0–6–0T DS3152 (BR No 30272). Photo: H. C. Casserley. Date: 20 August 1954.

The former compressor house survives and is used as a store, but there is no sign of the halt which was demolished many years ago, probably before the track layout was altered in the late 1980s. The headshunt can be seen sweeping to the left of the viaduct. Note the old vehicle entrance road to the quarry behind the former compressor house, which was superseded many years ago. Date: 12 November 1992.

80
Meldon Viaduct (1)
191 SX 565923

The viaduct, built on a curve of 30 chains and situated 199 miles from Waterloo, was without doubt the most prodigious on the line. Its spindly-looking steel structure of six 86½ft spans built on stone plinths strode a deep ravine through which the West Okement river ran, rising some 120ft at its highest from the valley floor. Built in two parts, the intertwined supports were brought about by the doubling of the line in 1879 and account for the slight differences in construction. The low parapets accentuated its height and the views had from a train were most spectacular, giving a glimpse of Dartmoor on its south side and a sweeping vista of Yes Tor, 2,028ft above sea level; on the other side, the views to the north were almost unlimited. A permanent 20mph speed limit was imposed on trains crossing the viaduct.

Having reduced its speed, West Country class No 34030 *Watersmeet* drifts over the viaduct with the 08.30 Padstow–Waterloo portion of the 'ACE', whilst Battle of Britain Light Pacific No 34064 *Fighter Command* stands on the down line shunting hoppers into the quarry sidings. It has been suggested that it was not usual practice to allow two moving trains to pass on the viaduct, but on this occasion, one was stationary! Photo: B. Haresnape/Ian Allan library. Date: 3 June 1959.

The former up line over the viaduct was retained as a quarry headshunt until the late 1980s, whilst back in the early 1970s the down side was decked in steel plating and used by lorries crossing from the quarry transporting stone to Meldon Reservoir, then under construction and completed in 1972. Today the viaduct's steel structure remains in reasonable condition, although the wooden decking is suspect in places, as is the inspection walkway underneath, and the structure has been fenced off to prevent people walking across. In recent years it has been used by members of the public for bungee jumping and service personnel for abseiling. British Rail has offered the viaduct for sale for a token sum and the Property Board is open to sensible offers from those willing to maintain the listed structure. Note the present day headshunt in the foreground, which ends at buffers just out of the picture on the left. Date: 13 November 1992.

81
Meldon Viaduct (2)
191 SX 562922

A month before its withdrawal from service, N class 2–6–0 No 31855, with the 09.00 Waterloo–Plymouth train, has just crossed the viaduct and is about to enter the cutting through which the line steepens to 1:58 for a short distance. Prewley Moor summit at 950ft above sea level is 1½ miles distant and will be reached soon after passing the junction for the Bude branch and North Cornwall line. Notice the short breakaway siding in the foreground and the quarrymen's cottages on the right. *Photo: Peter W. Gray.*
Date: 4 August 1964.

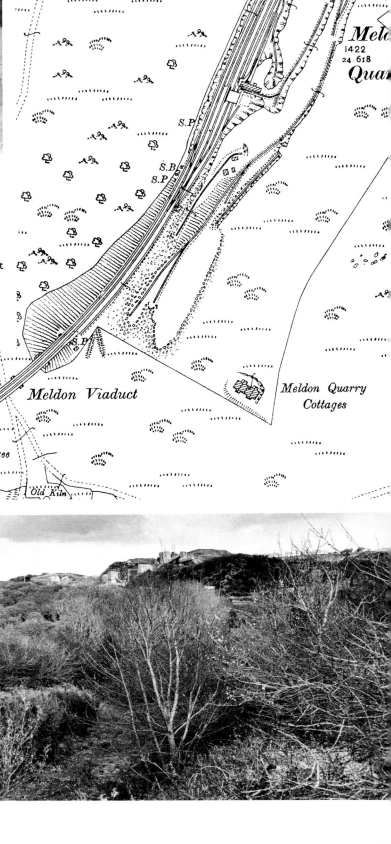

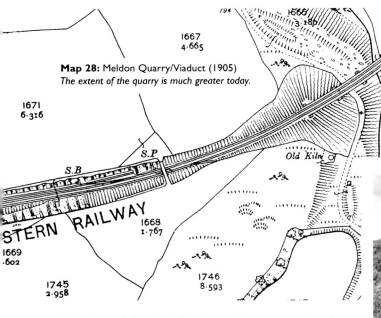

Map 28: Meldon Quarry/Viaduct (1905)
The extent of the quarry is much greater today.

The viaduct is barely visible through the trees and scrub which have grown on the banks. The trackbed, although overgrown to some degree, is still passable and remnants of the tarmac road, laid in the early 1970s for reservoir traffic, still remain. It is interesting to note the changes made to the quarry buildings over the years. The cottages are exactly the same, but are obscured from view in this shot taken from the same location.
Date: 12 November 1992.

82
Meldon Junction
191 SX 560922

The camera captures a rarely photographed location: the junction as seen from the cab of a DMU working the 10.05 Okehampton–Bude service shows the layout well, although by this time the up line had been taken out of use, as the sand barrier indicates. The main line to Plymouth swings left towards Prewley Moor summit, whilst the Bude and North Cornwall line bears off to the right. Adjacent to the signal box is a wooden level crossing to a small stand on the other side used for the exchange of tokens when coming off the branch, which closed a few months later on 1 October.
Photo: Ronald A. Lumber. Date: 5 March 1966.

Although the spot where the photograph was taken is now in the middle of a gorse bush, the rest of the trackbed is reasonably clear and the remnants of the tarmac surface laid by the reservoir contractors keep it that way. The temporary road swung left just after the bridge and was connected to the public highway there. The cottage on the left has been extended considerably, which is why it appears to be out of proportion to the former scene; it was empty and up for sale at the time of this visit. The trackbed towards Plymouth is still well defined and most of the structures remain in place, although a small occupation underbridge leading on to the moor near Prewley Farm has been demolished.
Date: 12 November 1992.

83
Bridestowe station
191 SX 523873

From Meldon Junction the line curled around the north-western extremities of Dartmoor, passed over Prewley Moor Summit in a cutting and swept downhill following the contours of Sourton Tors before crossing Southerly Viaduct, then it wove its way in a south-westerly direction, leaving Great Links Tor on its left before arriving at Bridestowe (originally St Bridget's Stowe), which opened on 12 October 1874. Bridestowe (pronounced briddystoe) station was about a mile-and-three-quarters from the village it served. The station building on the up side was of typical LSWR design, but the down platform was only provided with a simple shelter. Always a pleasing sight at Bridestowe were the banks covered with rhododendrons. A 5¾-mile standard gauge branch line, opened in 1879, ran from the Okehampton end of the down platform to Rattlebrook Peatworks on Dartmoor, but this closed around 1925 and was lifted in 1932; throughout its active life the trains were horse-drawn.

Two days before closure a 2+1 DMU arrives at Bridestowe with an Exeter–Plymouth service. The Rattlebrook Peatworks branch diverged to the right of the concrete hut at the far end of the station. Great Nodden and Great Links Tor in the background are partly shrouded in haze. The goods sidings on the up side beyond the station have already been removed, following the withdrawal of freight facilities on 5 June 1961. *Photo: Ronald A. Lumber. Date: 4 May 1968.*

The platforms have been filled in to make a lawn and the station house has been extended; in addition, the goods yard forms part of the garden and the shed survives in good condition. The concrete footbridge from which this study was taken is also in good condition, as is the platform shelter on the down side, although it needs a lick of paint. Of amusement is the very contented-looking cat sitting on its nest in the conservatory; its owner also offers bed and breakfast accommodation which is very popular with walkers during the holiday season. Despite it being a dull autumn afternoon, the moors stand out clearly on this day, where Southerly Viaduct still stands as surely as ever – but will it ever see the passing of another train over its granite arches? *Date: 13 November 1992.*

84
Lydford station (1)
191/201 SX 501828

Opened on 1 June 1865, the first railway to reach Lydford was the South Devon's broad gauge which extended its Tavistock branch to Launceston, 19 miles distant. The LSWR's extension from Okehampton arrived in 1874 and access to Plymouth was gained by a third rail added to SD's original line. This was obviously a far from satisfactory arrangement and when the Plymouth, Devonport & South Western Junction Railway (PDSWJR) opened its own route from Devonport on 2 June 1890, it gave the LSWR, a capital holder in the company, who worked the line from the start, the independence it craved.

Lydford seen in its last days: on the right the GW (ex-SDR) line and much of the wartime junction, built in 1943, which connected the two, have recently been lifted, although some of the sidings still remain. These were installed for housing Government stores as a measure of protection against the bombing of Plymouth. A Plymouth-bound DMU leaves at 18.40 with a service from Exeter during the last few days of operation. In the background the church on Brent Tor stands out on the horizon, whilst the slopes of Gibbet Hill are on the left. *Photo: Ronald A. Lumber. Date: 27 April 1968.*

Taken on a dismal January day, the same view is depressing to say the least: the trackbed between the platforms, which are gently crumbling away, is now a soggy mess overgrown with reeds and bushes. Gorse has pervaded much of the area, but the site of the wartime junction and sidings still remains reasonably clear, being well grazed by rabbits. The church on Brent Tor acts as a good reference point between these comparisons. The trackbed south towards Brentor station is still well defined and the one intermediate overbridge survives. *Date: 18 January 1993.*

COMMENT: An indelible part of my memory is of a visit to Lydford Gorge as a boy and I can remember with startled amazement catching the sight, fleetingly glimpsed through trees, of a plume of pure white steam accompanied by the sound of a train as it passed high above us in the gorge and audible above the roar of a cascading waterfall; but I cannot recall whether it was on the Southern line or the GW's Launceston branch. Looking at the map today, I rather think it must have been the latter! In my youthful ignorance, I had not realised that both lines passed so close to this most beautiful spot, which seemed as remote from the outside world as one could get. Today it is owned by the National Trust and is well worth a visit.

85
Lydford station (2)
191/201 SX 501827

This photograph, taken a year later than the previous view, finds the station lying derelict but complete apart from the GW track and the goods shed at the far end, which stood in the fork where the two lines diverged. It also shows the proximity of the two stations: the GWR's is on the left with its own station building, whilst that of the LSWR is on the right. It is interesting to note how the GWR's down side was connected with the LSWR's up platform; the latter's station master's house is on the right. Seen in the distance under the concrete footbridge are the LSWR railwaymen's cottages. The GW line closed to passengers 31 December 1962, but although the yard closed to goods on the same date, the line was retained for freight movements to Launceston until it too was closed completely on 28 February 1966. Goods traffic on the former LSWR line ceased on 7 September 1964 and was closed to passengers on 6 May 1968, with the through route to Plymouth cut. Track removal took place between October and December 1969. Photo: Ronald A. Lumber. Date: May 1969.

Although they all survive in derelict form to a certain extent, in this view only a fraction of the LSWR's up platform can be made out in the undergrowth. Some signal rodding has escaped the scrap men and a few remnants can be found along the trackbed through the former station. The trees in the background can readily be identified, although they have grown in the 24 intervening years. Much of the trackbed north of here is overgrown, but virtually all the bridges and viaduct at Lydford remain. Date: 18 January 1993.

COMMENT: This was a most uncomfortable photograph to take, as it was achieved by backing into a gorse bush and holding its branches back with various limbs to achieve this relatively clear view of the former station!

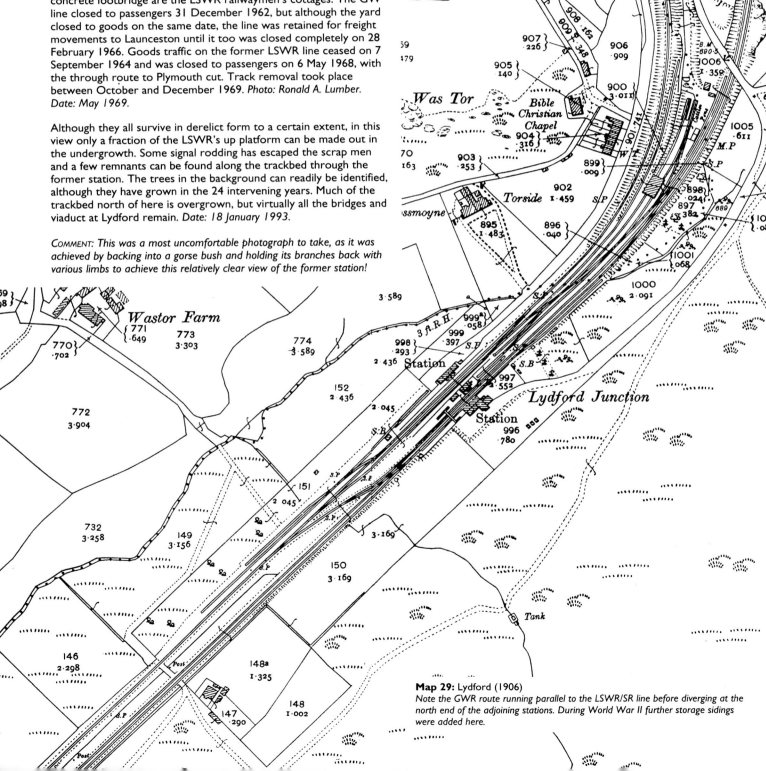

Map 29: Lydford (1906)
Note the GWR route running parallel to the LSWR/SR line before diverging at the north end of the adjoining stations. During World War II further storage sidings were added here.

110

Brentor station
191/201 SX 485811

After leaving Lydford the line dropped at 1:75 for about a mile-and-a-half before Brentor was reached, having run close to and parallel with its GWR rival. The station's main building was on the down side with a stone-built platform shelter opposite, immediately behind which the GWR line ran. The latter did not have a station here but its own, Mary Tavy and Blackdown, was a little way down the line towards Tavistock. Brentor opened for business on 2 June 1890 and closed on the same date as Lydford (SR); however, freight had ceased to be handled in the yard on 4 April 1960.

A north-looking view towards Lydford shows the large stone-built station house with the platform shelter opposite. Of interest are the two bridges, the one on the left being that of the GW line constructed with a steel span, whilst the LSWR's was more substantially built of stone.
Photo: Andrew Muckley/Ian Allan library.
Date: July 1966.

The present day view does much credit to the former station's owner, who bought the property in 1989, the same year as the the bridges were removed and the road widened. Although the area between the platforms has been filled in, forming a lawn, and an ornamental pond installed, the buildings have been beautifully restored and are in excellent condition. The down platform sports a few railway artefacts and both station signs are still in situ, but not seen in this view. An ongoing programme of restoration and improvements will ensure that it signals its heritage for many years to come.
Date: 18 January 1993.

Brentor station today as seen from the new road.
Date: 18 January 1993.

1 (Opposite)
Yeovil Town station
183 ST 562159

Drummond M7 0-4-4T No 30129 stands at Yeovil Town with a two-coach push-pull set used on the shuttle service from Yeovil Junction. The trees on Wyndham Hill in the background testify as to the location of this close-up shot of the station, which was near the town centre and therefore more readily accessible than the other two, particularly Yeovil Junction, situated about one and a half miles distant by road from here. *Photo: R.C.Riley. Date: 6 October 1962.*

There is no positive description one can really give to a large municipal car park, except that this is the same place where the M7 once busied itself between the two stations. The bridge and Wyndham Hill in the background, which still supports trees on its summit, provide the links to these vastly different views.
Date: 14 August 1992.

2
Seaton Junction
193 SY 250963

On a very busy Saturday at the height of the summer holiday season, Merchant Navy No 35026 *Lamport & Holt Line* passes Seaton Junction with an up portion of the 'Atlantic Coast Express'. On such a Saturday as this, the famous multi-portioned train ran to the West Country from Waterloo as four separate trains: 10.35 to Bude and Padstow; 10.45 to Seaton and Lyme Regis; 11.00 to Ilfracombe and Torrington; finally, the 11.15 to Plymouth, Padstow and Bude. *Photo: R.C.Riley. Date: 11 July 1959.*

3
Sidmouth station
192 SY 120888

Drummond Class M7 0–4–4T No 30044 approaches the signal box at Sidmouth with a train from Sidmouth Junction. With the driver peering over his shoulder, the fireman is about to hand the token to the signalman before the train enters the station. The signal box was usually adorned with roses and other blooms; its neat appearance was often mirrored by many others on the system at the time. This was so much part of the railway scene, where well-tended stations and signal boxes reflected the pride that some railwaymen had in their work; but often it was a way to pass the time when movements were few and far between on some branch lines. *Photo: R.C.Riley. Date: 28 July 1958.*

4
Broad Clyst station
192 SX 992952

Making a fair amount of smoke, Maunsell S15 class 4–6–0 No 30824 enters Broad Clyst with a pick-up freight for Salisbury. The station was equipped with a substantially built goods shed and fairly modest sidings on the down side. In 1896 the Civil Engineer established a yard just east of the station on the up side, which later became a permanent way pre-assembly depot and had long sidings. Broad Clyst seems at its best here, and the sunshine highlights all the trappings of a complete country station on a busy main line, like the tall repeater signal adjacent to the box and also the goods shed with loading gauge on the left. *Photo: R.C.Riley. Date: 6 July 1961.*

Running late with the 12.28 Bank Holiday Monday service from Exeter St David's to Waterloo, a Class 47, believed to be No 47707 *Holyrood*, rushes through Seaton Junction, now only a shadow of what it was. The one remaining track has recently been replaced with continuous welded rail in this section. *Date: 3 May 1993.*

Comment: After two fruitless visits here with an ailing camera, I was determined to get things right. This shot was supposed to be the precursor to the one I wanted, and in the event it turned out to be the last frame, so it was subsequently impossible to identify the locomotive's number. Just to rub salt into the wound, the processors attached a joining strip to the end of the film, covering some of the transparency's area! C'est la vie.

A dull day is not ideal for taking colour photographs and helps make this scene seem even less interesting than it might do otherwise, for the area now forms part of a design and construction company's yard, which is stacked with a range of building materials. The trackbed provides access to the site, which at least is kept tidy. There is not much to indicate this is the same position, except for the trees on the right, which have grown and altered in shape considerably; however, the line of the horizon and the telegraph pole on the left in the middle distance indicate that this was the same location Dick Riley visited some thirty-five years before. *Date: 17 March 1993.*

Class 47 No 47715 *Haymarket* passes the remains of the station at speed with the 12.17 service from Exeter St David's to Waterloo (in steam days, Broad Clyst was always regarded as one of the speed high spots – but in the down direction!).

No longer do the artefacts of this attractive country station seen in the original photograph survive, apart from the goods shed on the extreme left, which is now used as an industrial unit and is generally in good condition. Note the factory unit adjacent to where the signal and its box once stood. This scene is all too familiar on the route where the railway has been fenced in and allowed just enough space to operate as a single line, whilst all the surrounding land it once owned has been sold off as 'surplus to requirements'. *Date: 28 April 1993.*

5
Exeter Central station
192 SX 922932

Salisbury (72B) shed King Arthur class 4–6–0 No 30452 *Sir Meliagrance* eases its five-coach train comprised of one maroon and four in 'blood and custard' livery, out of the down bay platform at Exeter Central, passing the busy Exeter Central 'A' box with a stopping train to Salisbury. The axle loading of the 4–6–0s prevented them from working west of Exeter.

The King Arthur was to remain in service for another two years before being withdrawn in August 1959 and scrapped at Eastleigh two months later. *Photo: R.C.Riley. Date: 29 July 1957.*

6
Cowley Bridge Junction
192 SX 908954

West Country class No 34002 *Salisbury*, which has just branched off the GW main line at Cowley Bridge Junction, is seen going westwards on Southern metals on its way to Barnstaple with the 16.21 service from Exeter Central. This evocative shot taken as it passes over the River Exe, swollen with muddy waters after a period of heavy rain, is a portent of how easily the line could be flooded here, which on occasions caused much disruption to traffic on this and the GW line. *Photo: Peter W.Gray.*
Date: 16 March 1963.

7
Lydford
191 SX 503830

Viewed from the overbridge just north of the adjoining stations, the divergence of the GWR branch and the LSWR main line can be gauged well, as can the wartime sidings on the left. Although the goods shed was accessible from both lines, the linking of the two systems here could not constitute a junction; however south of the stations the two were joined during the last war and the junction came into use on 15 November 1943. The ex-GWR line was closed a few months before this photograph was taken, having shut entirely on 28 February; the track had been lifted by the spring of 1968. *Photo: Bernard Mills.*
Date: July 1966.

Hardly an inspiring sight by comparison: having worked the 08.35 service from Waterloo earlier in the day, Class 159 DMU No 159004 departs with the 14.22 service from Exeter St David's, scheduled to arrive in the capital just over three and a half hours later at 17.54. The once-busy Exeter Central 'A' box now lies empty and is covered in graffiti, a sight that is now so common up and down the land on railway buildings and structures. The trackwork has been rationalised considerably through here and apart from the two running lines only a few engineers' sidings remain, which are rarely used today. *Date: 28 April 1993.*

With the river in a much more tranquil mood on a pleasant spring day, a one-car Class 153 Sprinter unit with the 12.30 Barnstaple–Exmouth service is seen in the same position, but already has crossed the Exe on a new bridge constructed since 1963. The original was demolished and a new one resited a few chains further west from the junction, along with another which was also rebuilt. The Exe's course was altered to alleviate flooding at this point, which is also the confluence with the River Creedy. The SR line was singled here and over the junction on 28 November 1965. *Date: 28 April 1993.*

Taken in typical Dartmoor weather on a dull and overcast day, the scene looks even more depressing than perhaps it would on a sunny day. Apart from a farm track on the ex-GWR branch, scrub covers much of the site and the remains of the two stations are hidden from view, as is a riding academy located on the site of the wartime storage sidings. Note the end of the cottage on the right and how the trees have grown beyond. *Date: 21 April 1993.*

8
Brentor station
191 SX 486812

Battle of Britain class No 34109 *Sir Trafford Leigh-Mallory* passes Brentor with the up 'Brighton'. Although the station was situated on a short level stretch, the line rose at 1:75 north of it for about a mile, before Lydford was reached on another level section; but there would be a further 6½ miles climb before the summit was reached in a cutting at Sourton Down, which meant there was still some hard work ahead.

Note the GWR branch on the right: it ran under a bridge built alongside that of the Southern's. *Photo: L.F.Folkhard/Colour Rail. Date: 1961.*

9
Tavistock (Bannawell Street) Viaduct
191/201 SX 478745

On the Wednesday before closure a DMU, forming the 16.24 Tavistock–Bere Alston school special, crosses the viaduct at the south end of the station and is about to pass under the minor road bridge spanning the cutting taking the line almost clear of the town. School trains were always well patronised right up until the withdrawal of services a few days later.

Of note are the LSWR lattice signals, particularly the tall up starter with repeater arm, visible in the background beyond the station. Bathed in sunlight, the 1,450ft Cox Tor on Dartmoor stands out well in the distance. *Photo: Bernard Mills. Date: 1 May 1968.*

10
Gunnislake station
201 SX 437711

Class 2 2–6–2T No 41345 waits at at Gunnislake with a train for Plymouth. The sidings on the left were reasonably extensive to handle a variety of goods over the years, and after the demise of mineral traffic between the wars, market garden produce was despatched in great quantities from both here and Calstock. *Photo: Bernard Mills. Date: October 1963.*

The sun's reluctance to shine does not detract from the fact that it is easy to see that the station building, now a private residence, is well cared for today by its owner who is a railway enthusiast. The buildings are restored as near to the original specification as practical, as is the station sign on the left, which signifies a link with its illustrious past. An ongoing programme of improvement, both to the house and the extensive garden, which also takes in the former GWR trackbed, will keep its sentinel busy for a long time to come! *Date: 21 April 1993.*

Whilst the foreground and Cox Tor in the distance are in shadow, the viaduct and station site are caught in the last light of a sunny autumn evening. Council and privately owned dwellings have been built where the station once stood, so if proposals come to fruition to connect Tavistock once again to the rail system, a parkway station will have to be sited on the south-west outskirts of the town and will not reach the viaduct, therefore it is unlikely that it will ever see the passage of a train again. *Date: 8 September 1992.*

Sprinter unit No 150241 has arrived with the 16.25 train from Plymouth North Road; soon it will depart with the 17.20 return service.

Although the ex-PDSWJR station lacked any pretentious buildings – even in its heyday – it has certainly been reduced to the minimum today, with only a small shelter standing on the platform. With plans to move the station slightly to the south of the main A390 road, not even this is destined to remain long.
Date: 21 April 1993.

11
St Budeaux (Victoria Road) station
201 SX 446581

Within the previous few minutes, West Country class No 34104 *Bere Alston*, has passed through the station of the village after which it was named. After dipping under the GWR line, it rushes through St Budeaux Victoria Road with a train for Plymouth Friary. Shortly it will cross Ford Viaduct before diving under the GWR again as it passes through the first of two tunnels before emerging at Devonport (King's Road) station. *Photo: R.C.Riley. Date: 28 August 1961.*

12
Devonport (King's Road) station
201 SX 459549

This time rebuilt West Country class No 34104 *Bere Alston*, seen working the 14.25 ex-Plymouth Friary service to Waterloo, passes through the former LSWR terminus and is about to sweep round the sharp curve at the end of the station before entering Devonport Park Tunnel.

When the PDSWJR's line from Lydford arrived in 1890, the station ceased to be a terminus and the west end wall's glazing was breached to allow the passage of trains. *Photo: R.C.Riley. Date: 30 August 1961.*

13
Devonport – Paradise Road bridge
201 SX 462550

With a long up freight for Nine Elms, West Country Bulleid Pacific No 34024 *Tamar Valley* passes under the bridge carrying Paradise Road across the Southern main line and swings round the bend to pass through Devonport (King's Road) station. The freight will probably be worked forward by another engine which will take over from Exmouth Junction, where No 34024 is allocated. *Photo: R.C.Riley. Date: 28 August 1961.*

With the down line having been removed after singling in 1968, there is no chance of seeing a train in the same position today, so a general view of the station shorn of all its buildings, save a small modern shelter on the former up platform, will have to suffice! At least the footpath railings on the left have been painted red to brighten things up. Ford Viaduct was demolished in 1986, but the LSWR's two tunnels passing under Devonport survive.
Date: 29 April 1993.

From the same vantage point today there is nothing to see that was once familiar in 1963. The main building of the Plymouth College of Further Education dominates the foreground. Although one can walk on the remaining few yards of the trackbed, upon which students are currently creating a wildlife conservation area, to Devonport Park Tunnel, entrance has been barred by strong steel gates placed on its southern portal. *Date: 29 April 1993.*

Comment: In order to take this photograph, I press-ganged two students into holding down the branch of the tree in the immediate foreground so some view of the building could be obtained; and because of my bad back, they kindly helped me up and down the embankment as well!

Thirty-two years later no train is going to pass under the Paradise Road bridge – at least not with the Plymouth College of Further Education's building in the way! Even after this period, soot from locomotives' chimneys still adorns the arches of the bridge, which generally remains in good condition. To the rear of the building seen here, students undergoing instruction on various building trades' skills learn their craft in a compound under the shadow of the bridge. *Date: 29 April 1993.*

14
Devonport – Paradise Road
201 SX 463550

Adams Class O2 0–4–4T No 30193, on
station shunting duties, is seen from the
Paradise Road bridge at work on sidings
leading to the goods yard situated
immediately to the south side of
Devonport (King's Road) station. It was at
this point that the branch to Stonehouse
Pool Ocean Quay was also gained.
Photo: R.C.Riley. Date: 30 August 1961.

15
Devonport Junction
201 SX 467553

BR Standard Class 4MT 2–6–4T No
80036 runs bunker first past
Devonport Junction with a train for
Tavistock. By this date the line to the
King's Road station was not used for
through traffic, but only to the nearby
goods depot which remained open
until 7 March 1971. From 7 September
1964, trains were diverted via the GW
route to St Budeaux, where they
branched right and joined Southern
metals to Tavistock. *Photo: C.Trethewey/
Colour Rail. Date: October 1964.*

16
Barnstaple Junction
180 SS 555325

Ivatt Class 2 2–6–2MTs, Nos 41206 and
41291, are seen at Barnstaple Junction
with the RCTS/PRC Exmoor Ranger
special, which had arrived from Halwill via
Torrington. The train was much
photographed by lineside enthusiasts from
a number of vantage points on the this
scenic route. *Photo: Bernard Mills.
Date: 27 March 1965.*

Now the area forms a major car park for the college of further education. The pedestrian bridge carrying a footpath between Providence Place and Paradise Road survives in good condition and is the only tangible link between these contrasting views. The line to Stonehouse Pool last saw traffic in 1966, but was closed, like the goods yard at King's Road, on 7 March 1971. A section of the embankment upon which the line was carried can still be found sandwiched between King's Road and Rectory Road. Passenger traffic from the Ocean Quay had ceased in 1911. *Date: 29 April 1993.*

The houses and the tree in Stoke on the other side of the GW main line are still recognisable, as is the brick-built structure on the extreme right. The trackbed of the former Southern main line from this point to where it passed under Molesworth Road has been made into a landscaped area with a public footpath winding along its length and is much used by local residents and their dogs. *Date: 29 April 1993.*

Seen from the former platform on the down side, Sprinter No 153327 leaves Barnstaple with the 12.30 service for Exmouth and passes the redundant wooden goods shed, whose future must be in doubt, as the canopy adjacent to it was in the process of being demolished. The next stop for the Sprinter, if requested to do so, will be Chapelton, otherwise Umberleigh is scheduled to be the first, which is obligatory for this working. *Date: 25 March 1993.*

17
Barnstaple Junction-River Taw curve
180 SS 554327

From Barnstaple Junction the line became single just after it passed under the A39 and curved sharply right to a point sandwiched between a joinery works and the main road bridge over the River Taw, from where it crossed on its own iron structure. This view taken from the cab of a DMU, on the last day of working to Ilfracombe, shows how sharply the track curved to meet the river bridge a few hundred yards round the bend. *Photo: Bernard Mills. Date: 3 October 1970.*

18
Barnstaple Town station
180 SS 558331

A marvellous aspect of the station is obtained from the cab of DMU as it leaves Barnstaple Town. There is so much to attract the eye in this atmospheric shot: the station's box, together with the signals and level crossing it controlled all go to make this a scene to remember how railways used to be. Sadly, this was to be the last chance to obtain such a shot, for after this day there would be no more trains run on this section, save for those used during the dismantling of the line. *Photo: Bernard Mills. Date: 3 October 1970.*

19
Halwill Junction (1)
190 SS/SX 454000

Drummond T9 4-4-0 No 30338, with wide splashers, leaves Halwill Junction having arrived with a train from Bude is about to cross the road at the south end of the station. For many years the T9s became almost synonymous with the North Cornwall line and could often be seen performing such duties until their withdrawal from both the Bude and Padstow branches. No 30338, then from 72A Exmouth Junction shed, was withdrawn from traffic in April 1961 and scrapped at the Eastleigh works in the following June. *Photo: D.H.Beecroft/Colour Rail. Date: August 1960.*

The trackbed has been made into a landscaped walkway and forms an extension to the 'Tarka Trail', which runs from Barnstaple along the the banks of both the Taw and Torridge estuaries to Torrington and from there, to Meeth. Note building on the right, which is more easily identified in the first photograph, as is the roof of Shapland & Petter's joinery works. *Date: 25 March 1993.*

The signal box and station building are the only survivors of the railway age and are dwarfed by a modern housing development built on the river bank. Despite the former trackbed in the immediate foreground being used as a car park, much of it has been made into a very pleasant riverside walk beside the Taw. Note the buildings on the extreme right, which have also remained unchanged. *Date: 25 March 1993.*

The housing development in the background, which now covers the station site, is somewhat appropriately named 'Stationfields', as the sign indicates. Apart from a portion of the Junction Inn, just visible on the extreme right, there is no evidence that this is the same place where the T9 once crossed over this road, which has subsequently been widened after removal of the level crossing, which, with the station, survived until the late 1980s. *Date: 29 October 1992.*

20
Halwill Junction (2)
190 SS 454001

A view taken from the up platform looking north shows Ivatt 2–6–2Ts Nos 41206 and 41291 standing at the station awaiting departure to Torrington with the RCTS 'Exmoor Ranger' railtour. The platform for Torrington is located beyond the two people on the right of the picture and accessed via the footpath connecting them.

The Padstow line branched left adjacent to the bracket signals in the distance, whilst those for Bude and Torrington diverged some 25 chains beyond.
Photo: Roy Hobbs. Date: 27 March 1965.

21
Padstow station
200 SW 921750

With the upper quadrant LSWR starter signal off, unrebuilt West Country class 4–6–2 No 34036 *Westward Ho*, proudly sporting the appropriate headboard, is about to depart at 09.33 with the four-coach Padstow portion of the up 'ACE'. The Bulleid was rebuilt the following year in 1960 and had another seven years in traffic, before being withdrawn in July 1967, whilst shedded at Nine Elms (70A). It was scrapped at Cashmore's, Newport, between February and March 1968. *Photo: A.E.Cope/Colour Rail. Date: July 1959.*

22
Wadebridge station
200 SW 993721

Just south-east of the station, the photographer standing near steps to a row of terraced cottages has a good view of Wadebridge station; but the subject of his interest was the Plymouth Railway Circle's brake van special, run to celebrate 130 years of steam. It is about to leave Wadebridge for the Wenford Bridge branch with ex-GWR 1366 class 0–6–0PT No 1369 in charge, whilst a second locomotive of the class stands at the entrance to the goods shed on the extreme left. *Photo: Bernard Mills. Date: 19 September 1964.*

There is not much left here to make the comparison, but remnants of the former Torrington platform still survive beyond the builder's wooden hut on the right. Soon this area will also be built on with a further two or three bungalows constructed here. Although not obvious from this view, the line formation to the site of the former junctions, despite being overgrown with young trees and bushes, is passable, making a pleasant walk for some distance northwards.
Date: 29 October 1992.

On the day of the 'Hobby Horse' festival the car park that now covers the station site was full, but by the time this late afternoon shot was taken, plenty of spaces are available. The station building and Metropole Hotel in the background stand securely as ever, although the latter has been relieved of the ivy that once climbed its walls. Date: 1 May 1993.

The goods shed has been restored and converted into an activities centre and the door where the 0–6–0 once stood has been glazed in. It is now known as the 'Betty Fisher Centre', in memory of the late wife of the town's mayor. Behind the former goods shed, the station building also survives and is now the John Betjeman Centre. Everything else has changed here and much building development has taken place over the recent years.

No 1369 survives today and resides at Buckfastleigh in the care of the South Devon Railway Association. At the time of writing, it had been stripped and was undergoing major repairs.
Date: 2 May 1993.

87
Tavistock North station
191/201 SX 481746

West Country class No 34002 *Salisbury* passes through Tavistock with a down fitted freight for Plymouth.

The station was originally destined to be sited near the old Launceston road, but this met with opposition from the local population, who petitioned the Duke of Bedford, a director of the PDSWJR. The Duke agreed to a change, since the contractors stated there would be no further expense involved, but in the event it cost him another £2,000 for land requirements. The station was eventually sited on the side of a hill north of the town, but close to its centre. The southerly approach was made across a substantial granite viaduct spanning a U-shaped valley and Bannawell Street. The station master's house and booking office were on the down side, but waiting rooms were also provided opposite. Both platforms had canopies and it was the only PDSWJR station thus equipped. Modest sidings and a goods shed were located beyond the signal box at the north end of the station. Tavistock North (the 'North' prefix was added after nationalisation) closed to freight on 28 February 1966 and remained open to passengers until 6 May 1968.
Photo: R. J. Sellick/National Railway Museum. Date: 27 October 1956.

23 (Opposite)
Wadebridge
200 SW 99619

Seen from the occupation overbridge on the south-east edge of the town, Beattie 2–4–0WT No 30585, built in 1874, hurries along with a short train of clay wagons for the Wenford Bridge branch, Cornwall's first locomotive line, opened in 1834. The two tracks were worked as single lines from Wadebridge: the one on the right was the LSWR/SR's North Cornwall line, whilst that on the left was a joint line to Boscarne Junction shared by both Southern and Western Region trains, each going to their respective stations of Bodmin North and Bodmin General. Wenford Bridge branch workings diverged at Dunmere Junction a few miles south of here.
Photo: R.C.Riley. Date: 13 July 1961.

The trackbed here now forms part of the 'Camel Trail' which extends not only from Padstow to Bodmin, but also along the length of the Wenford Bridge branch, last used by BR in 1982, to a point near the clay works. Many hundreds of walkers and cyclists use this leisure facility each day, particularly in the holiday season.

Two of the three much-loved Beattie well tanks that worked the Wenford Bridge branch are preserved. One of them, No 30585, resides at the Buckinghamshire Railway Centre, Quainton Road; although it has been out of traffic for some years, priority is being given to restoring it to working order. The other, No 30587, is part of the National Collection, but currently is on loan to the South Devon Railway for static display at Buckfastleigh. *Date: 2 May 1993.*

The station site was built upon some years ago and this is the view from the same aspect today, although the station master's house, booking hall, a portion of the down platform and canopy survives behind the houses, but council offices have been built on the site of the former goods yard. The elegant footbridge was rescued by the Plym Valley Railway and is currently being restored. The up side canopy was removed and has been re-erected to form a major part of the Launceston Steam Railway's station.

If the Tamar Valley line is to be extended back to Tavistock, a new site for a station has been earmarked adjacent to school playing fields on the south-west side of the town. The trackbed south of the town, although overgrown in places is largely intact, as is Shillamill Tunnel which is used as a farm track. The 12-span granite Shillamill Viaduct still stands, but is not accessible to the public.
Date: 21 April 1993.

The former station house is now called 'Beeching's Folly' and is owned by the widow of the station master. Access to the platforms was gained through the doors under the small awning.
Date: 21 April 1993.

Taken from the site of the up platform, this shot shows the station buildings and the down side canopy fenced off and partly hidden from view by trees. *Date: 21 April 1993.*

88 (Opposite)
Bere Alston station
201 SX 440674

Situated at the north side of the village, once an important miners' settlement, Bere Alston station became the junction on 2 March 1908 for the Callington branch, which owed its origins to the 3ft 6in gauge East Cornwall Mineral Railway. The main line from Tavistock to here wove a tortuous and undulating path on high ground between the rivers Tavy and Tamar. This north-facing view from the footbridge shows the curving layout of the station and the up island platform on the left, the outer face of which was used by branch trains. The junction for the Callington branch was located just off the south end of the station. On 28 February 1966 goods ceased to be handled in the yard, from which large quantities of fruit and flowers were once despatched. *Photo: R. C. Riley. Date: 28 July 1961.*

Today Bere Alston is the reversing point of what is now the Gunnislake branch – or the Tamar Valley line – which still enjoys reasonable custom due to the poor accessibility of Plymouth by road. The station retains all its buildings and cast-iron canopy, although those on the up side are not in public use and are utilised by the Civil Engineers' department. At the time of this visit the former signal box was undergoing repairs. The remaining track through the station terminates at buffers about a hundred yards round the bend. With the right of way granted by token and no signalling on the line, the guard of a train has to operate the ground frame at the end of the station for access to the Gunnislake branch. *Date: 8 September 1992.*

COMMENT: *With the footbridge having been removed, I had to simulate the same position with the camera mounted on poles, but I slightly misjudged it by about two feet or so, which accounts for the small difference in perspective. Time did not allow another try!*

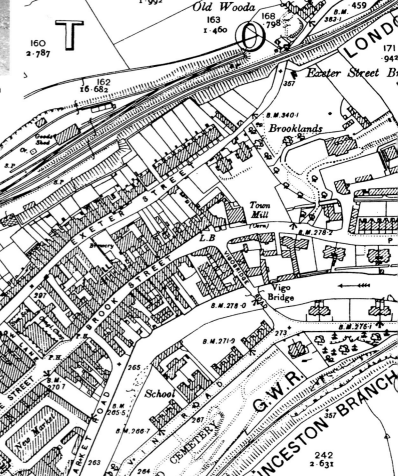

Map 30: Tavistock North (1905)
Note GWR's Launceston branch.

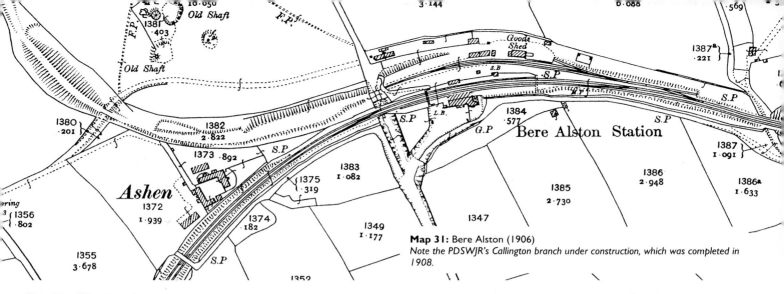

Map 31: Bere Alston (1906)
Note the PDSWJR's Callington branch under construction, which was completed in 1908.

89
Bere Ferrers station
201 SX 452636

Despite serving only a small village, the station was disproportionately large and rather grand. The main building on the down side was provided with a canopy, but the up side had only a small stone-built shelter. The goods yard, which closed on 8 October 1962, had a small but adequate shed.

A two-car DMU stops at Bere Ferrers with the 13.15 Plymouth to Gunnislake service. The line was singled soon after this photograph was taken. The sidings in the goods yard in the background beyond the train had already been lifted by this date. *Photo: Ronald A. Lumber. Date: 14 August 1969.*

Although Bere Ferrers is still in use, the station house has been sold off. The owner, Chris Grove, a keen railway enthusiast, has carried out an extensive programme of restoration over the years. One project was to rebuild the salvaged signal box from Pinhoe, which has been installed on the platform. Although not connected to the line, the goods yard has been resurrected and has had sidings laid. Amongst the rolling stock is a Gresley coach which is being refurbished along with two others and will be fitted out to offer bed and breakfast accommodation. A small Hunslet 0–4–0 diesel shunter is also in residence and able to run up and down the short sidings. Note the name of the station on the signal box, which was its original spelling.

Here Class 150 Sprinter No 150241 stops at the station with the 19.05 Gunnislake–Plymouth service. *Date: 21 April 1993.*

Battle of Britain class No 34069 *Hawkinge*, running tender-first with the 18.48 Tavistock North–Plymouth, is about to cross over the River Tavy viaduct, which took two years to build and cost £50,000. The bowstring girders are 120ft span and the 8ft diameter columns are sunk to a depth of 80ft. Apart from having a single track, the viaduct remains exactly the same today. *Photo: S. C. Nash. Date: 9 May 1961.*

The Tamar Valley line

Today the Tamar Valley line is actively promoted by Regional Railways as a tourist attraction. An information leaflet has been produced explaining its many delights, including notable engineering features like the Calstock and Tavy viaducts; it emphasises the scenic beauty of the Bere Peninsula and the Tamar, which the line follows closely. The spectacular views to be had from a train are highlighted, including of the Naval Dockyard at Devonport and Brunel's Royal Albert Bridge at Saltash. Many places of historic interest are mentioned, like Cotehele House, a National Trust property formerly the home of the Earl of Mount Edgcumbe and also Morwellham Quay, once the centre of world copper mining. The line is a delight which must not be lost and hopefully has a future in these uncertain times.

The old goods shed is being converted into a residence by the owner and a helper. Note the siding on the right. *Date: 21 April 1993.*

Tragedy at Bere Ferrers

Bere Ferrers had the dubious distinction of being the location of the worst railway tragedy suffered on the line. On 24 September 1917 a troop train left Plymouth bound for Salisbury Plain with members of the New Zealand Expeditionary Force, who had been in this country for only a matter of hours. On being told that food would be available at the first stop, when the train was halted at Bere Ferrers many of the men who had been instructed to collect it jumped out of the train on the wrong side and straight into the path of the 11.00 Waterloo–Plymouth express passing at speed. Ten were killed and many were injured.

Tamerton Foliot station
201 SX 450608

Situated over a mile from the village in Warleigh Wood near the confluence of the rivers Tamar and Tavy on a spit of land separating the impressive Tavy Viaduct and Tamerton Bridge, the station opened in January 1898. The main building on the down side was unusual in that it was of a different design and construction to others on the PDSWJR. The station had the distinction of having a lady station master, but it was closed on 10 September 1962; goods traffic had ceased to be handled in October 1956.

Having reduced speed and crossed the River Tavy on the viaduct, West Country Bulleid Pacific No 34035 Shaftesbury sweeps through Tamerton Foliot with an express for Plymouth. *Photo: R. J. Sellick/ National Railway Museum. Date: 27 May 1957.*

Sprinter No 150241, working the 17.20 Gunnislake–Plymouth service, passes the remains of the station. The remaining track has been slewed between the disused platforms and the former station house fenced off from the line. It has lain derelict for a number of years, but there has been an attempt at restoration and the roof has recently received attention. There was talk in 1986/7 of reopening the station here to provide facilities for walkers to visit Warleigh Wood, access to which was then only recently granted. Like many such schemes, lack of money has prevented it from becoming a reality. *Date: 29 April 1993.*

91
St Budeaux (Victoria Road) station
210 SX 446581

After crossing both the Tavy Viaduct and Tamerton Bridge, the line skirted the east bank of the Tamar before passing under Isambard Kingdom Brunel's famous Royal Albert Bridge opposite Saltash and swung almost due east – again to pass under the main GWR Plymouth–Penzance line – before reaching St Budeaux (Victoria Road) station. Situated in a cutting near a large residential area not far from Devonport dockyard, the station enjoyed good custom. It was provided with the usual facilities and waiting rooms protected by an ornate canopy on the down side, but had only a modest shelter on the opposite platform. However the station master's house was at road level together with the booking office, and they were originally connected to the down side platform's waiting rooms by a covered walkway.

A small boy gives a cheery wave to the driver of Battle of Britain class Light Pacific No 34055 *Fighter Pilot* which passes through St Budeaux with a three-coach portion of an express for Waterloo. *Photo: R. J. Sellick/National Railway Museum. Date: 2 July 1957.*

Class 150 Sprinter No 150241 restarts from St Budeaux with the 16.25 Plymouth–Gunnislake service. The station has been deprived of all of its buildings and only a small shelter has been provided on the up platform, which remains in use. *Date: 29 April 1993.*

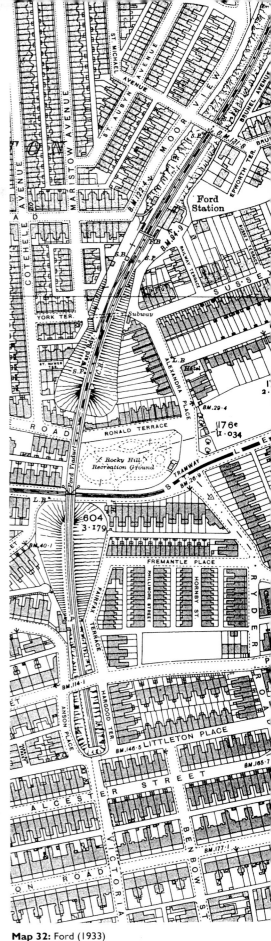

Map 32: Ford (1933)
The map shows the location of the station and viaduct, but not pictured in this volume.

Weston Mill Halt; Camel's Head Halt; Ford (Devon) station

Being the area's largest centre of population towards the turn of the century – and because of its proximity to the dockyard – the Devonport area was blessed with no fewer than twelve stations or halts, not only on the GW line, but also on the PDSWJR/LSWR which had three others between St Budeaux (Victoria Road) and Albert Road Halt – a distance of no more than two miles. Weston Mill Halt and Camel's Head Halt opened on 1 November 1906, but the former closed from September 1921, whilst the latter was shut from 4 May 1942. The platforms were of wooden construction; however, those at Camel's Head Halt were later replaced with concrete – a product of the Exmouth Junction works. Ford station, which was well appointed with the usual facilities and situated in a cutting near the viaduct, opened on 2 June 1890 and was closed from 7 September 1964. Regrettably, no photographs of publishable quality were found in time to enable facsimiles to be taken of these locations. It would, however, have proved impossible at Ford since the station was demolished during the 1970s and the cutting in which it stood filled in the early 1980s.

92
Albert Road Halt, Devonport
201 SX 456554

Set in a deep cutting between the Ford and Devonport Park tunnels, the halt opened on 2 June 1890, but closed from 13 January 1947. It was through Ford Tunnel that the PDSWJR passed beneath the one through which the GWR line ran under Devonport.

Photographs of the halt are extremely rare, and although this one is of poor quality it shows the layout to good effect, with the corrugated iron shelter on the down side being the only protection afforded from the elements. Seen emerging from Devonport Park Tunnel with a train for the Callington branch is what appears to be an ex-LSWR O2 class 0–4–4T. *Photo: Denys Rokeby/R. M. Casserley collection. Date: July 1939.*

There is no sign of the halt in the cutting, which is now almost totally overgrown. Only the most agile or young can climb down the embankments to the site of the former halt. The two tunnel portals are open here, but each has been sealed off at the other end. Careful study will reveal a tree with a bent trunk between the houses in the background as being the same, but it has grown only slightly over the last 54 years and certainly has not got any straighter! *Date: 29 April 1993.*

93
Devonport (King's Road) station (1)
201 SX 45949

The station, formerly called Devonport & Stonehouse, opened on 18 May 1876 as the terminus of the LSWR when it entered the city over the GWR's route from Lydford via Tavistock and Marsh Mills. The grandeur of the station buildings befitted a terminus in a part of the city which was considered of greater importance in passenger terms, as most commercial life revolved around the Dockyard in the late nineteenth century. It remained thus until 2 June 1890 when the PDSWJR's new Lydford–Devonport line and the LSWR entered the city from the west, so the up and down lines were reversed. Originally the station had an overall roof, but this was demolished in the 1950s, together with the remains of a gable at the west end, after having suffered bomb damage during the last war.

Rebuilt West Country class No 34104 *Bere Alston*, with the 14.25 Plymouth Friary–Waterloo train, cautiously negotiates the sharp curve at the western end of the station and in a few chains will enter Devonport Park Tunnel. *Photo: R. C. Riley. Date: 30 August 1961.*

All traces of the station have been erased: the Plymouth College of Further Education building now occupies the site. The only railway artefacts remaining are a retaining wall on the north side of the complex and the bridge over nearby Paradise Road, but these are obscured in this view which gives little or no clue to being the same location – which it is! *Date: 29 April 1993.*

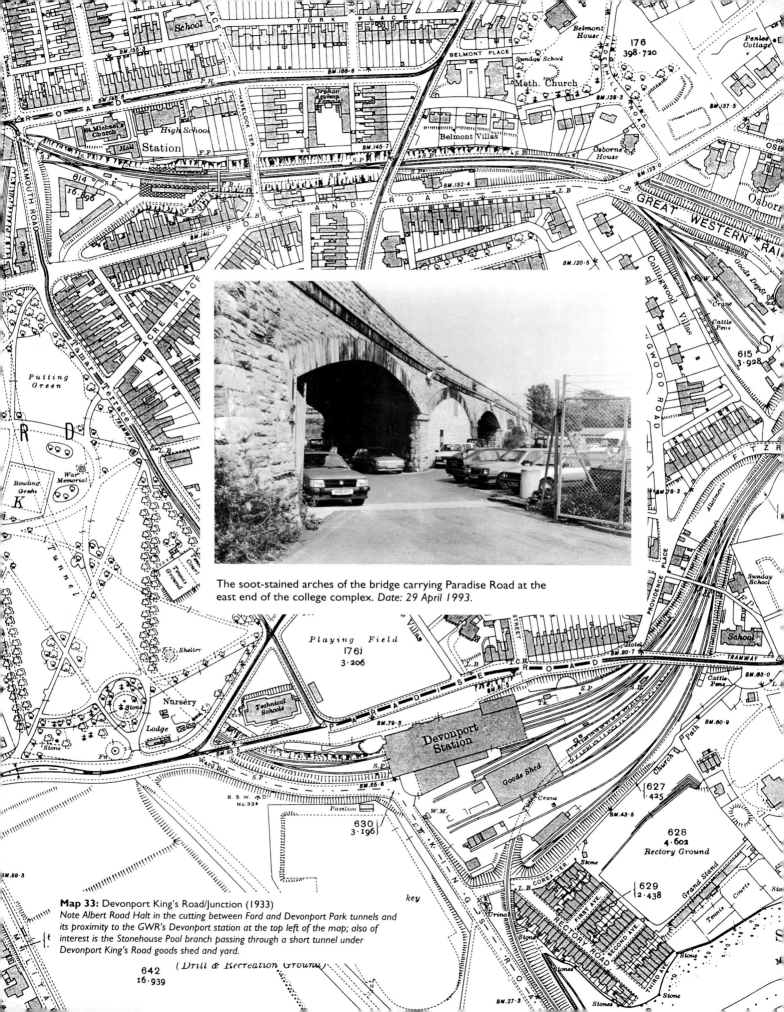

The soot-stained arches of the bridge carrying Paradise Road at the east end of the college complex. *Date: 29 April 1993.*

Map 33: Devonport King's Road/Junction (1933)
Note Albert Road Halt in the cutting between Ford and Devonport Park tunnels and its proximity to the GWR's Devonport station at the top left of the map; also of interest is the Stonehouse Pool branch passing through a short tunnel under Devonport King's Road goods shed and yard.

94
Devonport (King's Road) station (2)
201 SX 462549

A view looking west from the opposite end of the station shows the two centre roads ending at buffers, but crossovers provided onto the running lines. The station shows no sign of life, which was a far cry from the halcyon days at the turn of the century, and it looks ominously deserted as Battle of Britain class Pacific No 34056 *Croydon* restarts with the 08.41 Exeter Central–Plymouth Friary train. The station closed to passengers on 7 September 1964 when SR traffic was diverted via the GW route to St Budeaux and the junction linking the two systems there, which was installed during World War II. *Photo: R. C. Riley. Date: 3 May 1961.*

With the college's main building dominating the foreground, there is still no obvious sign of the railway ever having run through here although, just behind the camera, Paradise Road bridge gives a positive clue to its heritage as the arches still bear soot stains from locomotives' chimneys. *Date: 29 April 1993.*

95
Plymouth (North Road) station
201 SX 479555

The joint station was destined to be built of stone, but the LSWR's impatience with the GWR's delay in starting it led to its construction in wood. It finally opened on 28 March 1877 and was enlarged in 1908. A rebuilding programme started in 1938, but was halted during World War II and did not recommence until 1956. It was completed in 1962 with a tall office block attached and colour light signalling. When Friary closed on 15 September 1958, the station lost its 'North Road' qualification.

A Southern goods working, with Battle of Britain class 4–6–2 No 34074 *64 Squadron* in charge, trundles through the rebuilt station, which is nearing completion. *Photo: R. C. Riley. Date: 30 August 1961.*

The track layout was rationalised in April 1974 and very much simplified, as this shot illustrates. Apart from that, there has been little change to Plymouth station. Even some of the motive power remains the same and here an 08 class shunter busies itself with vans, which will comprise the 14.45 Plymouth–Leeds parcels service. Long range InterCity Class 47/8 No 47805 *Bristol Bath Road* has recently arrived with the 09.18 from Manchester and heads off light engine to the Laira depot, leaving its stock in the station, which will form the 15.48 service to Derby. Later, the locomotive will work the 21.00 Plymouth–Glasgow sleeper as far as Birmingham. *Date: 29 April 1993.*

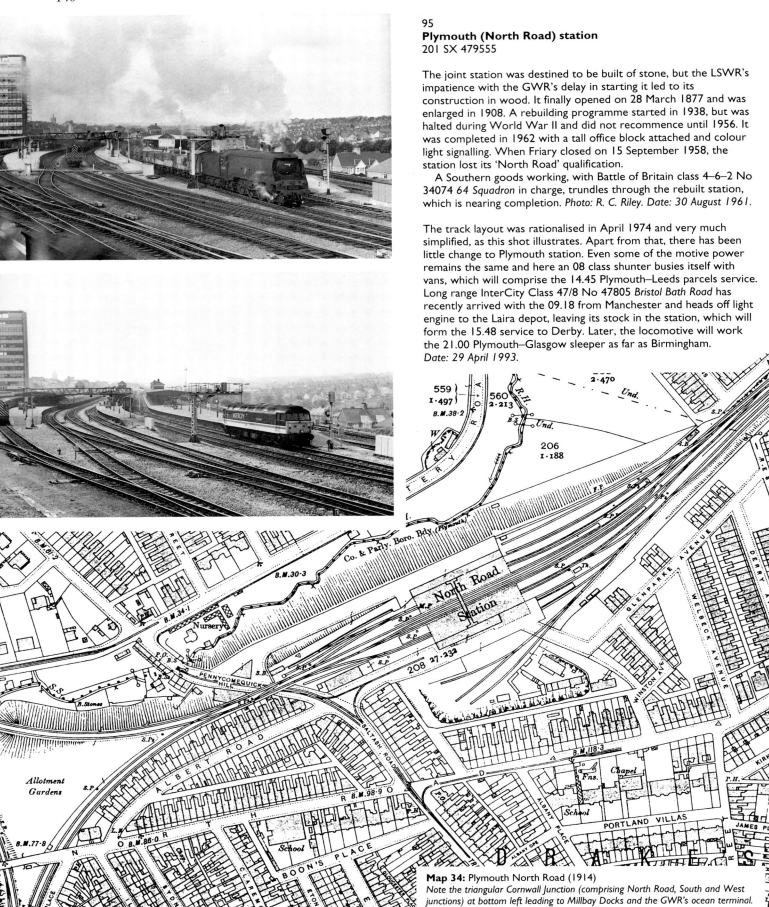

Map 34: Plymouth North Road (1914)
Note the triangular Cornwall Junction (comprising North Road, South and West junctions) at bottom left leading to Millbay Docks and the GWR's ocean terminal.

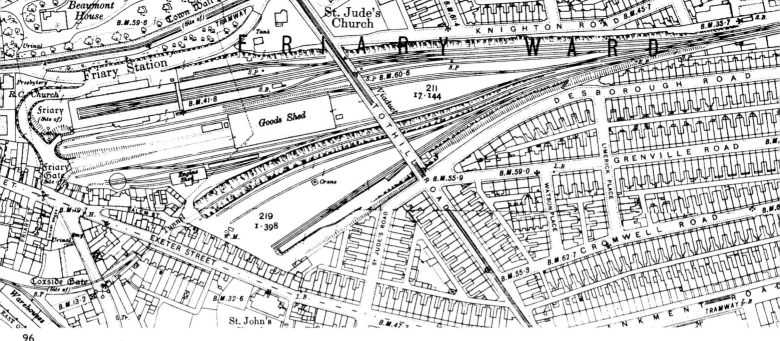

Plymouth Friary station
201 SX 488546

Map 35: Plymouth Friary (1914)

Going? A general view of Friary taken a month before closure shows GWR 4300 class Mogul No 7333 standing in the bay waiting with the 14.35 service to Exeter, which stopped at all stations; it returned on the Plymouth portion of the 15.00 service from Waterloo. Some services were operated with WR crews and locomotives for route familiarisation. Partly hidden by the signal box, a Bulleid Pacific waits at the up platform with a four-coach train which constitutes the 14.25 service to Waterloo.

The new LSWR terminus had opened on 1 July 1891 and placed the LSWR in the eastern part of the city. Having left Plymouth North Road, LSWR/SR trains traversed GWR metals via Lipson Junction, Mount Gould Junction, then along the west bank of the River Plym before regaining their own system at Friary Junction. From there the line swung almost due west and then ran up a short but stiff gradient to enter the terminus – thus LSWR trains had turned through more than 180° since leaving North Road! In traffic terms the station probably reached its zenith during World War II, for not only did main line trains use it, but also those on the Turnchapel and Yealmpton branches. It closed for passengers on 15 September 1958 to be converted into Plymouth's main goods station under modernisation plans and a new freight concentration building was erected. On closure of the Tavistock Junction marshalling yard on 4 January 1971, Friary also became the main goods marshalling facility for a time until moving back to the former. The station buildings were demolished in 1976. *Photo: E. Wilmshurst. Date: 20 August 1958.*

Going. Having remained derelict for a number of years, the tracks were taken up in the early 1990s and truncated abutting the east side of Tothill Road bridge, from where these shots were taken. Only remnants of the platforms are left in this view and they provide hard standing for building materials to be used in a new development which had recently started: the freight concentration depot was demolished and the land sold off. The building on the extreme left is a branch of Court's furniture superstore. *Date: 25 March 1992.*

Gone. Taken just over a year later, the last vestiges of the platform have been removed to make way for a new road and the housing development is nearing completion. *Date: 29 April 1993.*

COMMENT: *The slight difference between the two facsimiles is because the March 1992 shot was taken to match another original which was not used. In the event, it proved to have been taken only a matter two or three feet from the correct position, so it was good enough to illustrate the changes that have taken place in the last year or so!*

Plymouth Friary shed
201 SX 494547

For some years after Friary station closed to passengers, the associated shed was still used to service and house Southern engines. Standing outside the shed on the day of closure, the last two engines, rebuilt West Country class No 34036 *Westward Ho* and N class 2–6–0 No 31406, are about to leave for Laira. *Photo: S. C. Nash. Date: 5 May 1963.*

Today the site of the shed has been given over to a large fertiliser depot. There is no way this shot could be lined up totally accurately, but careful study of the pictures will reveal houses and the former main running lines on the extreme left of both, which are the same. Who would know any differently? *Date: 29 April 1993.*

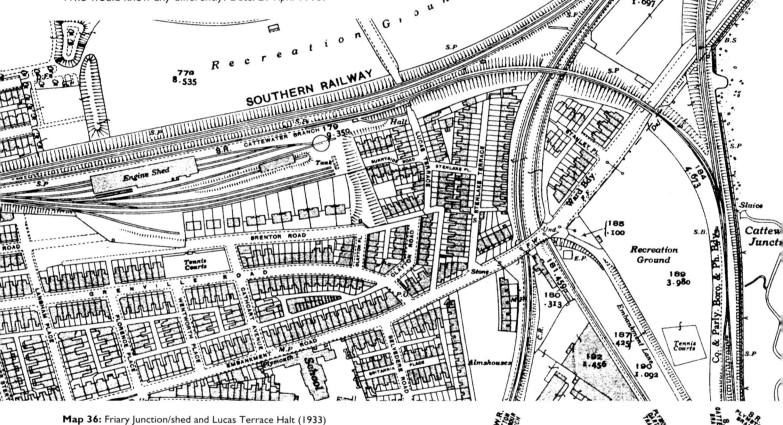

Map 36: Friary Junction/shed and Lucas Terrace Halt (1933)
Note Lucas Terrace Halt just to the east of the shed's turntable. LSWR/SR metals were gained at Friary Junction.

98
Turnchapel branch – Lucas Terrace Halt
201 SX 498548

Opened in October 1905, some years after the branch, the halt was situated just to the east of Friary shed and the junction with the LSWR main line. Originally constructed with a wooden platform and a corrugated iron shelter, it was later rebuilt in concrete.

On Turnchapel branch duties, O2 class 0–4–4T No E200, built in 1891, stands with an LSWR gate-set at Lucas Terrace Halt, then in its original form. Note Friary shed in the background bristling with a number of tall venting chimneys. The main line on the extreme right can be seen rising up towards Friary station in the background. Between 3 November 1941 and 7 October 1947, the halt was also used by GWR trains for Yealmpton. *Photo: H. C. Casserley. Date: 5 August 1928.*

The replacement concrete platform remains in reasonable condition, despite being disused for over forty years, and the track is still in place. Today this and a section of the short LSWR Cattewater branch (opened 1879–80 to Victoria Wharf) is used once-daily for Esso bitumen trains. These have to be reversed at the ex-Friary yard, but since the tank wagons cannot be propelled down the branch, a locomotive has to run round its train there. An 08 shunter is used on these duties due to the limited clearance of a bridge under which it has to pass *en route*. Note the two tracks of the former LSWR main line which remain on the right to service the branch. *Date: 29 April 1993.*

Turnchapel branch

The LSWR branch opened on 1 January 1897 and ran from the Friary terminus to a small station at Turnchapel, then it extended a further half-mile to wharves on the River Plym, which were taken over by the Admiralty during World War I and proved a good source of revenue for the line. The LSWR station at Plymstock, which later was jointly run with the GWR when an Act of 1894 gave it rights over the section to Yealmpton, became the junction for the Turnchapel branch and there was only one intermediate station, Oreston. Lucas Terrace Halt, situated on a triangle between Friary and Plymstock, was built later. At one time there were no fewer than sixty trains a day passing through Plymstock, but passenger services steadily declined due to road competition, despite the expansion of Plymouth. The branch closed from 10 September 1951, although services had been temporarily suspended in the January, due to the fuel crisis, but resumed again in July. After cessation of passenger services, a few special tours were run over the branch during the years the line remained open for goods; it closed from 2 October 1961.

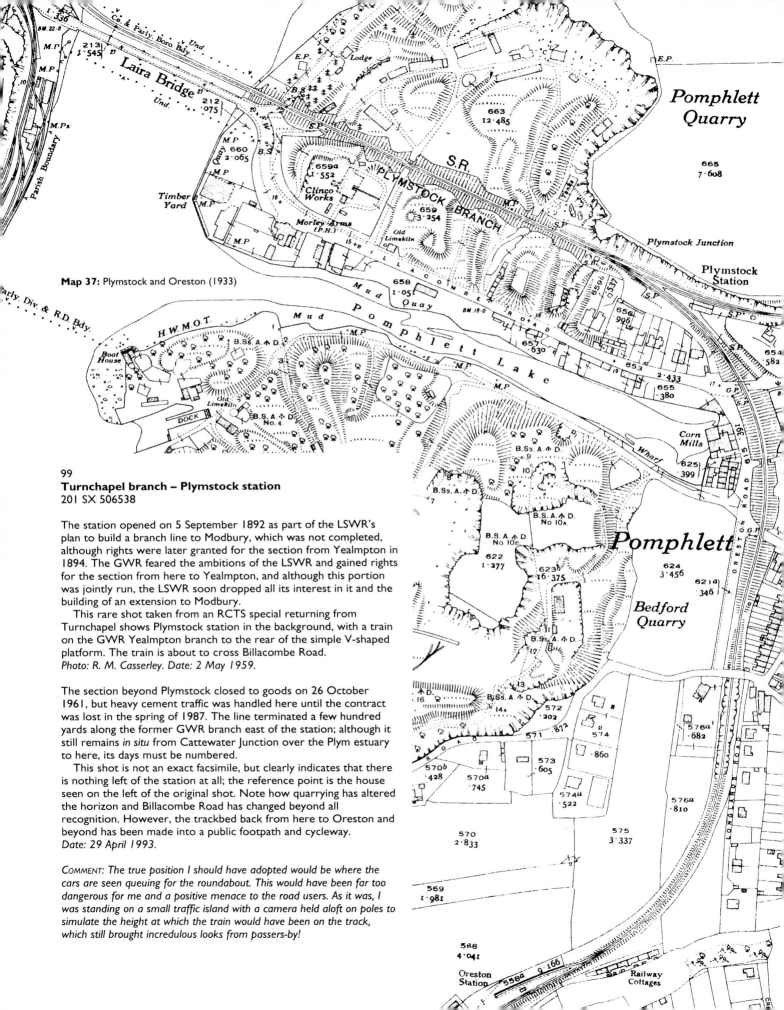

Map 37: Plymstock and Oreston (1933)

99
Turnchapel branch – Plymstock station
201 SX 506538

The station opened on 5 September 1892 as part of the LSWR's plan to build a branch line to Modbury, which was not completed, although rights were later granted for the section from Yealmpton in 1894. The GWR feared the ambitions of the LSWR and gained rights for the section from here to Yealmpton, and although this portion was jointly run, the LSWR soon dropped all its interest in it and the building of an extension to Modbury.

This rare shot taken from an RCTS special returning from Turnchapel shows Plymstock station in the background, with a train on the GWR Yealmpton branch to the rear of the simple V-shaped platform. The train is about to cross Billacombe Road.
Photo: R. M. Casserley. Date: 2 May 1959.

The section beyond Plymstock closed to goods on 26 October 1961, but heavy cement traffic was handled here until the contract was lost in the spring of 1987. The line terminated a few hundred yards along the former GWR branch east of the station; although it still remains *in situ* from Cattewater Junction over the Plym estuary to here, its days must be numbered.

This shot is not an exact facsimile, but clearly indicates that there is nothing left of the station at all; the reference point is the house seen on the left of the original shot. Note how quarrying has altered the horizon and Billacombe Road has changed beyond all recognition. However, the trackbed back from here to Oreston and beyond has been made into a public footpath and cycleway.
Date: 29 April 1993.

COMMENT: *The true position I should have adopted would be where the cars are seen queuing for the roundabout. This would have been far too dangerous for me and a positive menace to the road users. As it was, I was standing on a small traffic island with a camera held aloft on poles to simulate the height at which the train would have been on the track, which still brought incredulous looks from passers-by!*

Turnchapel branch – Oreston station
201 SX 504534

Stark simplicity. Oreston station was basic in the extreme; however, it did have a small goods siding to the rear of the platform, which remained in use until 2 October 1961. The station had opened on the same date as the branch. *Photo: R. M. Casserley. Date: c1959.*

Today the only evidence of the station is the one remaining concrete lamp post and the platform edging which can be spotted when walking over the trackbed, raised to its level to form a car park for use in conjunction with an adjacent football pitch. Note the chimneys of the house on the extreme right, which provide another clue. *Date: 29 April 1993.*

101
Turnchapel branch – Turnchapel swingbridge
201 SX 497530

The line crossed over a creek at Turnchapel on a swingbridge. Here Class O2 0-4-4T No 30182 approaches Turnchapel from Oreston with an RCTS special, the 'Brunel Centenarian', run over the branch as part of the Royal Albert Bridge centenary celebrations.
Photo: Peter W. Gray. Date: 2 May 1959.

Only the columns survive today. There is no sign of the trackbed on the far side of the creek and the ground has been levelled to form a boatyard and hardstanding for yachts. Although the day was hazy compared to the one in 1959, partly obscuring Plymstock in the background, it is plain to see how much housing development has taken place over the years. *Date: 29 April 1993.*

COMMENT: *Despite this and the next photograph looking fairly innocuous, taking them proved to be really quite traumatic for me. Both locations were inside a derelict compound previously used by the MOD and South West Gas. Having spotted a hole in the fence through which I could crawl, I stooped as low as my bad back would allow, but suddenly recoiled when my head struck a strand of barbed wire. In no time at all, I was covered in blood pouring from a head wound. Not knowing how bad the injury was, I flagged down a car which happened to be passing in this remote part of Turnchapel and asked the shocked-looking driver whether he knew where the nearest casualty department was; but he was a stranger to the area. Gloom. However, just then a second car drew up, the occupants of which had noticed something wrong. I just could not believe my luck and in what must be a million to one chance, it was a doctor friend of mine and his wife who had travelled down from Somerset and, because of heavy traffic on the other road, were taking the back way to the marina where they kept their yacht. I was saved. Joy!*

Map 38: Turnchapel (1933)
Note the short tunnel leading to Turnchapel Wharves.

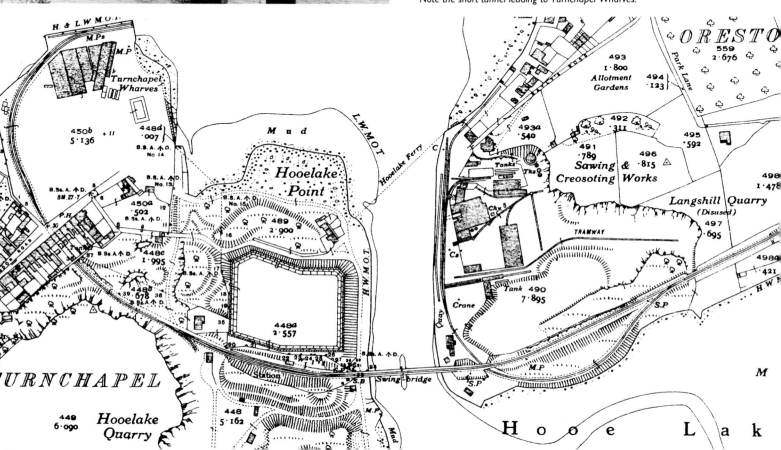

102
Turnchapel branch – Turnchapel station
201 SX 496530

The station was sited in an old quarry and as at Oreston, the LSWR did not spend much money in providing comprehensive facilities at Turnchapel, which again was of a simple design providing only a basic shelter on the one platform. Besides having a loop, the line swung north for a few hundred yards before passing under a minor stone bridge, which led to wharves on the River Plym. In addition, a spur ahead of the station led to underground chambers, which were used by the Admiralty for storage.

Class O2 No 30182 arrives at Turnchapel with the RCTS 'Brunel Centenarian'. Soon practically all the occupants will disembark to take photographs of the train; a number have since been published. This example shows the O2 arriving at the platform, the simplicity of which can be judged here. *Photo: Peter W. Gray. Date: 2 May 1959.*

In a shot which was extremely difficult to line up, it is still possible to see the hill at Plymstock. The fence line on the left has been broken because over the interim years a reservoir for providing an emergency supply of water for a gas storage depot was built, but is now empty. The station site lies under several feet of soil and rubble probably extracted during the reservoir's construction.
Date: 29 April 1993.

Only this portion of the platform at Turnchapel shows through the spoil and undergrowth. *Date: 29 April 1993.*

North Devon (Tarka) line:

After a long gestation period with dealings fraught with difficulty and acrimony, which also involved lengthy arguments over the gauge, the North Devon Railway, a company which had taken its name from a still-born forerunner of 1845, previously promoting it under the Taw Vale Extension, opened the line to Barnstaple on 1 August 1854 as an extension of the Exeter & Crediton broad gauge. Having been a major shareholder in the company, from 1 February 1862 the LSWR took over the lease of the Exeter & Crediton (later the Bideford Extension from 1 August 1862 and the North Devon from 1 January 1863 – which were amalgamated with the LSWR on 1 January 1865). As a result, mixed gauge came into use on 2 March 1863 before the broad gauge was finally made redundant on 30 April 1877. Of the 27½miles in total, the two-mile section of the line from Coleford Junction to Copplestone and 6½ miles from Umberleigh to Barnstaple were eventually doubled: just under a third of its length (although powers were gained for the remainder) and the route could be described as a secondary main line.

Over the years it became extremely busy seasonally, with both passenger and freight traffic. In the summer months express trains, which included the 'Atlantic Coast Express' and the short-lived 'Devon Belle', ran from Waterloo to North Devon; but despite being popular, the Bristol Channel coastal resorts always came a poor second to those on the south coast served by the GWR.

Today the route from Exeter to Barnstaple is marketed as the 'Tarka Line' and operated as a single track from Cowley Bridge Junction, with passing loops at Crediton and Eggesford. The line had been actively promoted under the 'Tarka Project', which lasted from September 1988 until 10 June 1993, but is only a shadow of what it used to be and its future has been questioned, with constant rumours of closure.

103
Copplestone station
191 SS 767031

The station, situated north of the village, marked the highest point on the North Devon line to Barnstaple. From here the line became single until double track was regained at Umberleigh and crews had to collect or deposit a tablet before proceeding. Built to a standard design, the station house and booking office with waiting rooms was on the down side with a shelter provided on the up platform, access to which was via a crossing at the station's north end. The small goods yard had two sidings with cattle loading dock and a wooden shed with an internal two-ton crane; these were closed on 6 September 1965, as was the 10-lever signal box on 17 October 1971 when the line to here was singled.

West Country class No 34002 *Salisbury* enters the station with the up 'ACE' and the fireman prepares to hand the single line tablet to the signalman who is waiting on the platform to receive it. Note the crossover from the yard to the up line and the extent of the double track beyond the station. *Photo: Ronald A. Lumber.*
Date: 5 May 1964.

The station house is now privately owned and has been fenced off from the platform, and a garage has been built on the site of the former goods yard. The remnants of the up platform lie crumbling on the other side of the single track. In the 1993 winter timetable, only one train a day (Monday–Saturday) in each direction can be stopped on request at Copplestone; this is increased in summer to two down and three up. *Date: 19 February 1993.*

104
Morchard Road station
191 SS 750051

N class 2–6–0 No 31840 is seen approaching Morchard Road with an up train. The country station, nestling close to the road junction of the A377 and B3320, was very similar in layout to Copplestone, as was the standard North Devon Railway main building on the down side. The yard was not so extensive and only two short sidings were provided, one of which was a cattle loading dock, near the small wooden goods shed. Besides the crossing loop, there was a long siding to the south end of the station on the down side adjacent to a slaughterhouse, which it served; this extended beyond the attractive three-arched stone-built bridge carrying the road to

Morchard Bishop over the line. The 1873 vintage 12-lever signal box, mostly obscured by the train, closed on 6 March 1964. The goods yard had closed a few months before on 30 December 1963.
Photo: R. J. Sellick/National Railway Museum. Date: 20 June 1959.

This is the comparison: no up line – no train! The up platform has been demolished and only a few bricks remain in the undergrowth. Morchard Road's station building is now, like Copplestone and all those on the North Devon line, privately owned. The retaining wall of the cattle loading dock survives just off the end of the platform, upon which can be seen the type of shelter now installed at all stations on the line. The station is a request stop for four trains in each direction a day in winter; the 1993 summer timetable states four down and three up can be stopped here. *Date: 25 March 1993.*

Lapford station (1)
191 SS 727080

The station was unconventional in its design, for the up and down platforms were staggered and separated by the main A377 road which skewed over the line. The down platform, seen here, was built by the LSWR and came into use on 1 October 1873 (together with the signal box) and was sited east of the road bridge, since there was no room for it opposite the existing one, which had been built earlier. The rear of the platform was fenced off from the up line and only a small shelter was provided. Access to it was gained via a sleeper crossing over the up line and a path led between the two; there were also wooden steps leading down from the A377 road bridge.

In charge of the 12.15 Ilfracombe–Waterloo service, the now-preserved West Country class No 34023 *Blackmore Vale* leaves Lapford and passes the down platform. Note the design of the three-arch stone bridge in the background, which was a typical example of those constructed on the line. This one carried the road to the village over the railway. *Photo: Peter W. Gray.*
Date: 5 August 1963.

Class 150 Sprinter No 150232 with the 12.30 Barnstaple–Exmouth service speeds past the site of the down platform, which was demolished around 1970, when the loop was converted into a siding. The running line was then slewed to give a straight passage between the two bridges.

No 34023 was the first air-smoothed Bulleid to work in preservation; it is currently based on the Bluebell Railway.
Date: 17 February 1993.

106
Lapford station (2)
191 SS 727080

Warship No D804 *Avenger* passes Lapford with the 15.00 Ilfracombe–Paddington. A legacy of Lapford's LSWR heritage, the station building, like Chapelton's, was built to a different design from others on the line. The splay of sidings connected to the down loop line were well used at one time, for Lapford became synonymous with the adjacent Ambrosia creamery built in 1927 and opened in 1928. Over the years it provided much business for the line, but closed in 1970. Note how the station letters have been spelt out on the bank on the left, probably the handiwork of a dedicated member of staff.

From Lapford to Barnstaple the line was always in the company of a river: having crossed twice and flirted with it briefly a half-mile south-east of here, the line skirted the River Yeo for just over another mile, crossing it three more times, before reaching the confluence with the River Taw, the course of which it will follow in its valley all the way to the North Devon market town.
Photo: Ronald A. Lumber. Date: 15 July 1967.

Class 150 Sprinter No 150249 passes Lapford with the 16.18 Barnstaple–Exeter Central service. Lapford is still very much the same today, although two of the sidings have been removed, as has the signal box. Today, the former Ambrosia factory is split into small factory units, but the major portion is used by Kemira Fertilisers as a storage depot. The sidings were used until April 1993 for the occasional fertiliser train which usually arrived in the early hours of a Monday morning before normal passenger services started, which would give the locomotive time to clear the section on its return to Exeter. All deliveries are now made by road.
Date: 24 April 1993.

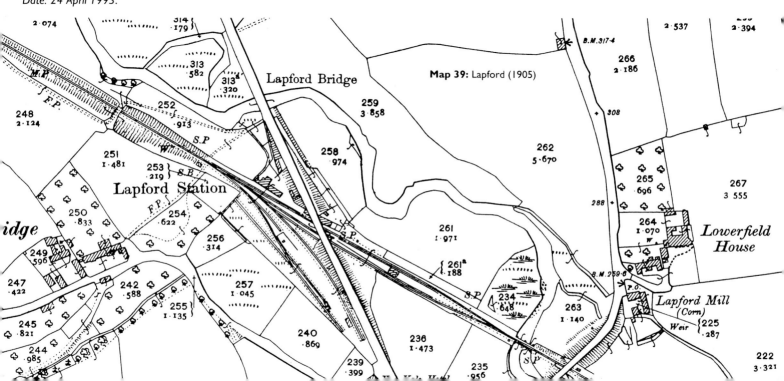

Map 39: Lapford (1905)

107
Eggesford station
191 SS 682114

Although the station was remote from any sizeable population, at one time many of the local inhabitants either worked on the railway, or were associated with it in some way. The station was built on a curve adjacent to a road junction and was flanked by the River Taw on its immediate left. The main building of North Devon design was situated on the up platform and the moderately-sized goods yard, equipped with two cranes and a shed, was also on the up side. In addition, a long siding with a loop, serving a cattle loading dock and slaughterhouse, extended to the rear of the Fox and Hounds Hotel, a notable establishment just a few hundred yards north of the station. The goods yard closed on 4 January 1965.

This view of the station was taken a little over a year before disastrous floods on 21 November 1967 swept away much of the down platform and undermined the signal box. This rendered the down loop unusable until the river bank was restored and a new box was built, which opened in 1969. The down platform was not restored to its full length or width and only a short section was extended beyond the part of it which remained. *Photo: Andrew Muckley/Ian Allan library. Date: July 1966.*

The station building has hardly altered at all, but is now in private ownership. On approaching Eggesford in either direction, the guard of a train has to go forward to open the lifting barriers of the crossing immediately at the south end of the station, but they close automatically once the train has passed. Eggesford is the only passing loop on the line and the points are operated by the trains hydro-pneumatically. Since there is no signal box here, authority to proceed in either direction is given over the telephone by the signalman at Crediton and a token is exchanged from a machine in a cabin at end of each platform, one of which can be seen in the background on the the down side. *Date: 17 February 1993.*

108
King's Nympton
(South Molton Road) station
180 SS 661171

Originally called South Molton
Road, the station served the
market town about nine miles
north north-east of here and
had no competition until the
Devon & Somerset Railway
opened in 1873; however, it
retained its old name until 1
March 1951. The station had a
short passing loop which gave
rise to problems when lengthy
trains crossed: up trains would
have to reverse into a long
siding from the loop to allow
the passage of the one heading
in the other direction. The small
goods yard and wooden shed
were located on the up side at
the south end of the station;
these closed on 4 December
1967. The signal box closed on
26 July 1970, when the line was
singled and the down platform
taken out of use.

The now-preserved Battle of
Britain class No 34070 *Manston*
leaves King's Nympton on the
09.00 Waterloo to Barnstaple
Junction service. The layout of
the station can be seen well,
although the train in the
foreground obscures the points
for the loop, which are between
the first and second coaches.
Photo: Peter W. Gray.
Date: 23 August 1963.

Class 150 Sprinter No 150247
approaches the A377 road
bridge having left King's
Nympton with the 12.45
Exmouth–Barnstaple service.
The rationalisation that has
taken place here is quite evident:
there are no sidings or crossing
loop, but the goods shed
survives and another use has
been found for it.
Date: 24 April 1993.

109
Portsmouth Arms station
180 SS 631193

West Country class Pacific No 34028 *Eddystone* draws into Portsmouth Arms with a train for Ilfracombe, and the fireman is about to pick up a single line token from the signalman standing on the down platform near the 10-lever box. The station was located near the public house named after the 4th Earl of Portsmouth, who was responsible for building the turnpike road (now A377), alongside which it sits. The station's main building was on the down side abutting the road, whilst a short stone-built shelter was on the up platform together with a small goods shed seen just beyond it. The short siding was accessed from the down loop; this was withdrawn from use on 3 July 1961 and the signal box, built in 1873,

closed on 3 April 1966. *Photo: R. J. Sellick/National Railway Museum. Date: 14 September 1952.*

The up platform is overgrown, although its main fabric remains intact, but its surface is largely covered in small trees and scrub which have seeded themselves on the crumbling surface. Portsmouth Arms lost its platform buildings some years ago and only a shelter has been provided for the very few passengers who use the station today, which, in the 1993 winter timetable, was only a request stop for three trains a day in each direction and was not scheduled for Class 150 Sprinter unit No 150239 as it passes by with the 14.20 Barnstaple–Exeter Central. The former station master's house survives and is in private hands, as is Light Pacific No 34028, which has been preserved and is currently undergoing restoration in a siding at Sellindge, Kent. *Date: 24 March 1993.*

110
Umberleigh station
180 SS 610239

A view taken from the attractive three-arch stone bridge near the station shows N class 2–6–0 No 31843 standing at Umberleigh with a six-coach down train. Of interest is the tall upper quadrant down starter signal placed between the tracks to aid visibility, since the station was built on a sweeping curve. The width between the platforms stems from its broad gauge days, which ended on 30 April 1877 when it was finally taken out of use. Two sidings and cattle pens were built on the down side just south of the station; it was from this point the line became double track to Barnstaple. In addition, a small loading dock and a goods shed were situated off the north end of the down platform, as can be seen here. On the other side of the bridge was a further siding accessed by points on both up and down lines. Goods yard facilities were withdrawn on 4 January 1965 and the signal box closed on 21 May 1971, when the line was singled. *Photo: R. J. Sellick/National Railway Museum. Date: 20 June 1959.*

The station building has not changed except for a few minor details: the gentlemen's lavatory has been converted to another use – not so convenient for passengers – and the drainpipes have been painted blue, no doubt reflecting the language of those in need! The up platform is extant and remains in reasonable condition, but without a function. All trains in each direction call at Umberleigh; it and Eggesford are the only scheduled stops. Here Class 150 Sprinter unit No 150230 prepares to leave with the 14.20 Barnstaple–Exeter Central service. *Date: 17 February 1993.*

111
Chapelton station
180 SS 581261

Having wound its way through the Taw valley from the confluence with the Yeo near Lapford and crossing the river no fewer than ten times, the line from Chapelton, which was built on a curve, ran more or less straight for the next 4½ miles to Barnstaple. The station opened in 1875 with the LSWR-designed building on the north end of the up side; a shelter and a wooden 23-lever signal box were constructed on the down platform, behind which two sidings formed the goods yard. From its opening in 1930 the adjacent sawmills of Chappel & Walton kept the yard's 10-ton crane busy loading pit props and other products, including fence posts. However, the goods yard closed on 4 January 1965 and the signal box a year later on 26 January.

A 3DMU enters Chapelton on the 16.13 Barnstaple–Exeter Central, but by this date the sidings had been lifted, the points to which were between the platform and the car.
Photo: Ronald A. Lumber. Date: 14 October 1970.

The privately owned station house is in immaculate condition and has been painted to complement railway colours. Chapelton's sign has been beautifully restored, although the up platform upon which it sits no longer forms part of the station. Note the subtle extensions to the building, including the balcony, no doubt giving an excellent view of the passing DMUs, like No 150240, which has just left at 16.01 with the 15.03 Exeter Central–Barnstaple. Departing at 16.18 from Barnstaple, it will return here at 16.25 with a few students from the local college, who will be met by a mini-bus to take them to their country homes. *Date: 17 February 1993.*

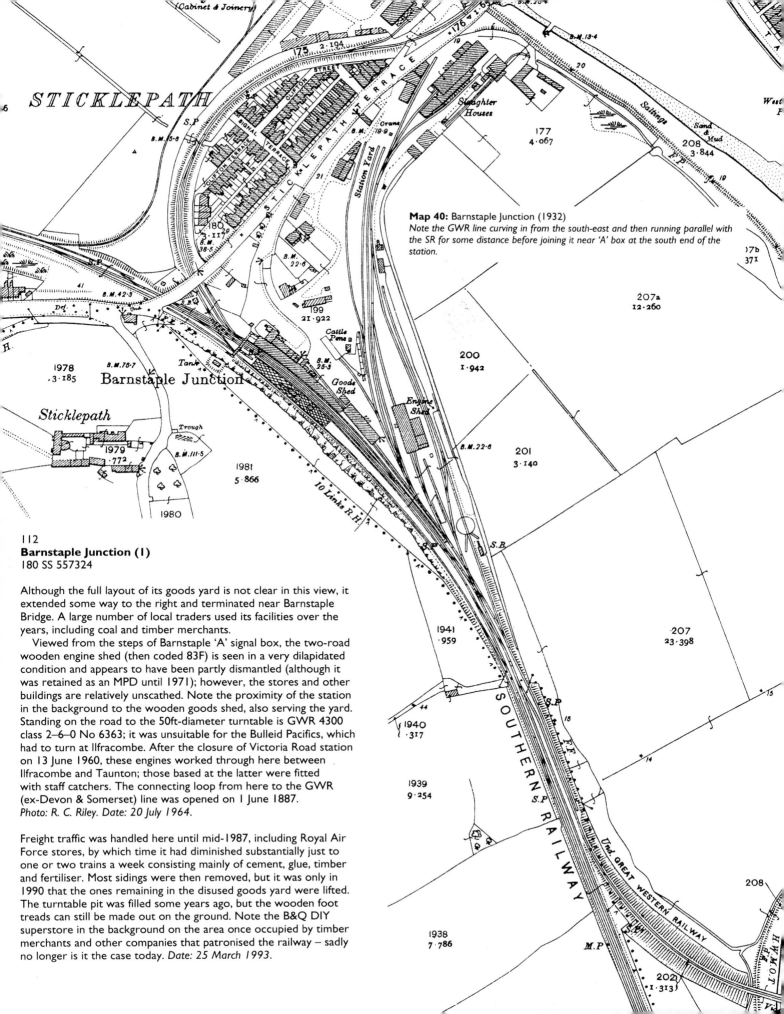

STICKLEPATH

Barnstaple Junction

Sticklepath

Map 40: Barnstaple Junction (1932)
Note the GWR line curving in from the south-east and then running parallel with the SR for some distance before joining it near 'A' box at the south end of the station.

SOUTHERN RAILWAY

Und GREAT WESTERN RAILWAY

112
Barnstaple Junction (1)
180 SS 557324

Although the full layout of its goods yard is not clear in this view, it extended some way to the right and terminated near Barnstaple Bridge. A large number of local traders used its facilities over the years, including coal and timber merchants.

Viewed from the steps of Barnstaple 'A' signal box, the two-road wooden engine shed (then coded 83F) is seen in a very dilapidated condition and appears to have been partly dismantled (although it was retained as an MPD until 1971); however, the stores and other buildings are relatively unscathed. Note the proximity of the station in the background to the wooden goods shed, also serving the yard. Standing on the road to the 50ft-diameter turntable is GWR 4300 class 2–6–0 No 6363; it was unsuitable for the Bulleid Pacifics, which had to turn at Ilfracombe. After the closure of Victoria Road station on 13 June 1960, these engines worked through here between Ilfracombe and Taunton; those based at the latter were fitted with staff catchers. The connecting loop from here to the GWR (ex-Devon & Somerset) line was opened on 1 June 1887.
Photo: R. C. Riley. Date: 20 July 1964.

Freight traffic was handled here until mid-1987, including Royal Air Force stores, by which time it had diminished substantially just to one or two trains a week consisting mainly of cement, glue, timber and fertiliser. Most sidings were then removed, but it was only in 1990 that the ones remaining in the disused goods yard were lifted. The turntable pit was filled some years ago, but the wooden foot treads can still be made out on the ground. Note the B&Q DIY superstore in the background on the area once occupied by timber merchants and other companies that patronised the railway – sadly no longer is it the case today. *Date: 25 March 1993.*

113
Barnstaple Junction (2)
180 SS 554326

Barnstaple Junction was known as 'Barnstaple' until the Ilfracombe branch and its 'Quay' station on the east bank of the River Taw opened on 20 July 1874. An island platform 400ft in length was constructed in readiness for the opening of the Ilfracombe branch and had come into use the previous May.

A view of the station taken from the A39 road bridge shows 2–6–2T No 41297 on station pilot duty, whilst West Country Pacific No 34106 *Lydford* stands on the down road of the line to Torrington, having just been detached from its train. On summer Saturdays Barnstaple Junction saw many trains depart to and arrive from all over the country and was particularly busy. Note the fine station building designed by Sir William Tite and the covered footbridge, over which can be seen the goods shed and the skeletal remains of the engine shed. *Photo: R. E. Toop. Date: 11 May 1963.*

A somewhat different panorama from the bridge today: the station has been stripped like the carcass of a chicken and only the bare bones are left. During a rationalisation scheme, which became effective from 26 April 1971, platform 1 was made a terminal and platform 3 taken out of use the following month on 21 May. The footbridge survived until the late 1970s and the buildings on the island platform until around 1980. In July 1990 a new run-round loop was constructed south of the station and the down road removed alongside platform 2, including a short portion of the Torrington branch, which had been used until then. The remaining line was then truncated at the end of the former up platform. Still standing is the wooden goods shed, but its fate was cast with demolition scheduled for September 1993. Work had already started on dismantling much of the station canopy, which had become unsafe, and the Red Star parcels office behind. In 1989 the Travel Centre (opened on 10 November 1981) was reduced to a booking office; although tickets were still issued here in 1993, the station is due to become unstaffed in the near future. *Date: 25 March 1993.*

114
Barnstaple Junction (3)
180 SS 555325

GWR 4300 class 2–6–0 swings round the junction from the Ilfracombe branch with the 10.12 train to Cardiff. The branch line to Torrington is on the left. Of interest are the check rails on the sharp curves of the junction. 'B' ('West' until 2 October 1949) signal box situated between the two bridges replaced a much taller structure in the mid-1920s. The single line section to Barnstaple Town station was worked by electric token. *Photo: E. Wilmshurst. Date: 15 August 1964.*

This point literally marks the end of the North Devon line, as the buffers and sand trap indicate. It also marks where the 'Tarka Trail' starts, access to which is gained from the station forecourt and via a path behind the two surviving bridges, which carry the A39. Since the remaining portion of the Torrington branch was removed (last used in 1990 as a run-round loop), a path has been constructed from the road bridge across the trackbed to the operational platform. Bicycles can be hired from near here for those wishing to cycle along the trail via Bideford and Torrington to Meeth; a facility which has become extremely popular. *Date: 25 March 1993.*

Barnstaple & Ilfracombe Railway

Ilfracombe was destined to remain unconnected to the rail system until a subsidiary of the LSWR received Royal Assent when an Act was finally passed on 4 July 1870. The line between the two towns was built with difficulty: the economy was severely depressed, which had resulted in many labourers emigrating, so problems were experienced in obtaining sufficient navvies to build it. The engineering works on the 14mile 74chain route were substantial, for not only had the River Taw to be crossed on a lengthy iron bridge, but many cuttings and embankments had to be constructed and a tunnel dug near Ilfracombe – where the first sod was cut on 27 September 1871. The line was opened almost three years later on 20 July 1874; it had the most severe gradients to be found on any main railway route in the country: down trains faced a climb of three miles at 1:40 to the summit reached at Mortehoe and then descended at an alarming 1:36 for a further 2¼ miles before entering the North Devon seaside town of Ilfracombe. With the exception of a short section either side of the Taw bridge and including Barnstaple Town station, the line was doubled between 1889–91.

The branch to Ilfracombe finally closed on 5 October 1970, although the last train ran two days before on 3 October. Despite two preservation attempts the line was lifted in 1975.

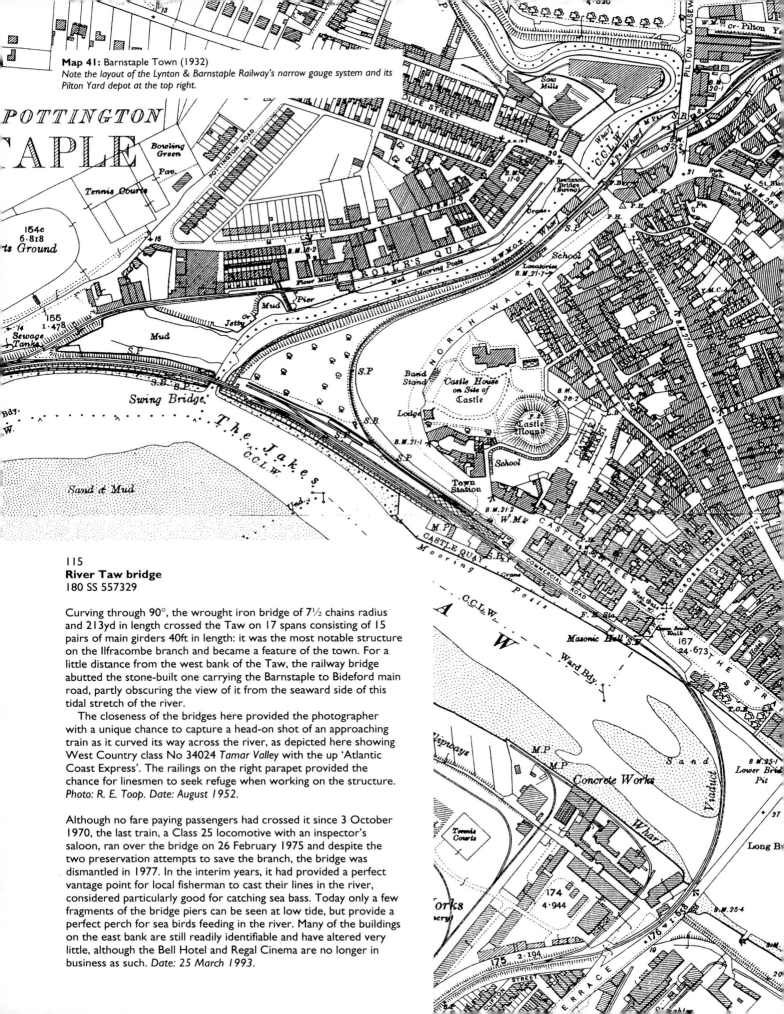

Map 41: Barnstaple Town (1932)
Note the layout of the Lynton & Barnstaple Railway's narrow gauge system and its Pilton Yard depot at the top right.

115
River Taw bridge
180 SS 557329

Curving through 90°, the wrought iron bridge of 7½ chains radius and 213yd in length crossed the Taw on 17 spans consisting of 15 pairs of main girders 40ft in length: it was the most notable structure on the Ilfracombe branch and became a feature of the town. For a little distance from the west bank of the Taw, the railway bridge abutted the stone-built one carrying the Barnstaple to Bideford main road, partly obscuring the view of it from the seaward side of this tidal stretch of the river.

The closeness of the bridges here provided the photographer with a unique chance to capture a head-on shot of an approaching train as it curved its way across the river, as depicted here showing West Country class No 34024 *Tamar Valley* with the up 'Atlantic Coast Express'. The railings on the right parapet provided the chance for linesmen to seek refuge when working on the structure. *Photo: R. E. Toop. Date: August 1952.*

Although no fare paying passengers had crossed it since 3 October 1970, the last train, a Class 25 locomotive with an inspector's saloon, ran over the bridge on 26 February 1975 and despite the two preservation attempts to save the branch, the bridge was dismantled in 1977. In the interim years, it had provided a perfect vantage point for local fisherman to cast their lines in the river, considered particularly good for catching sea bass. Today only a few fragments of the bridge piers can be seen at low tide, but provide a perfect perch for sea birds feeding in the river. Many of the buildings on the east bank are still readily identifiable and have altered very little, although the Bell Hotel and Regal Cinema are no longer in business as such. *Date: 25 March 1993.*

116
Barnstaple Town station
180 SS 558331

The original 'Quay' station was built near the bridge, but was too cramped for incorporating the 1ft 11in gauge Lynton & Barnstaple Railway and a new one, Barnstaple Town, was constructed 11 chains north. Both it and the L&BR opened on 16 May 1898. Until the narrow gauge line closed on 30 September 1935, the station was shared with the L&BR, whose terminus was on its east face; this required the station building to be sited at the south end of the 500ft platform. Limited standard gauge sidings were provided here, but double track was regained soon after the line had crossed the 110ft swing bridge over the River Yeo a few chains north of the station.

Looking north towards Ilfracombe from the crossing at the end of the station gives a good impression of the snaking curvature of the platform, at the end of which a DMU is seen departing for Ilfracombe. On 17 December 1967 the line was singled between Barnstaple and Ilfracombe as an economy measure.
Photo: Andrew Muckley/Ian Allan library. Date: August 1964.

The main station building and signal box survive and are surrounded by a recent housing development. The box has been restored and is used as a museum and headquarters of the Lynton & Barnstaple Railway Association, whose motto is *Perchance it is not dead, but sleepeth.* The group is committed to reopening some of the former narrow gauge line from Barnstaple. Much of the standard gauge trackbed now provides a very pleasant riverside walk, which extends for some distance beyond the station site to where a Civic Centre has been built.
Date: 24 March 1993.

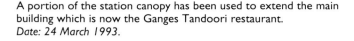

A portion of the station canopy has been used to extend the main building which is now the Ganges Tandoori restaurant.
Date: 24 March 1993.

The Lynton & Barnstaple Railway

Despite the fact that the fabled 1ft 11½in narrow gauge line was operated by the LSWR and latterly the Southern Railway until its demise in 1935, regrettably there was no room to include it in this 'then and now' volume. The history of the railway has been extremely well documented and there have been a number of noteworthy publications devoted to the line over recent years. Some of these give a good insight into what survives today and the preservation programme to restore part of it, including a portion which is in use as an operating narrow gauge steam railway.

117
Wrafton station
180 SS 491352

The station served not only the village, but the adjacent Royal Air Force station, Chivenor, and was sandwiched between the two. During World War II it was particularly busy and used by personnel travelling to and from the air station, which was operated by Coastal Command and had an important rôle to play in the Battle of the Atlantic.

This view shows the two platforms and the modest station building situated on the west end of the up side near the level crossing, over which the back road to the airfield was gained. The small signal box sat opposite on the down side, in front of which on the extreme left can be seen the buffers of one of the two sidings at the station. One of these was sometimes used by the RAF, but in the 1950s two six-berth camping coaches were sited here: if it was

not the trains that kept one awake, it might have been the aircraft! The sidings were taken out of use on 15 February 1965. On 17 December 1967, the signal box was reduced to a ground frame, but was severely damaged by fire a few months after closure of the line. *Photo: Andrew Muckley/Ian Allan library. Date: September 1964.*

Quite remarkably, most of the station's artefacts remain in place, including the platforms' concrete light standards and the SR-type down starter signal, although its arm has been swung over. The station's nameboards also survive, but are in poor condition. The trackbed has been filled in almost to platform level and makes a lawn for the former station master's house, which is now a private residence. Note that a porch has been added to the front door and the 'gents' now has a flat roof. The tracks remain on the former level crossing and can just be seen either side of a car in the background. The trackbed has been made into a cycleway from the outskirts of Barnstaple to Braunton, but skirts the station site and is regained the other side of the former level crossing. *Date: 24 March 1993.*

COMMENT: No sooner had I arrived here, when I was treated to the most spectacular and thrilling air display by a Hawk aircraft, of the type currently based at Chivenor, which is now the home of a tactical weapons unit. Quite funny really, as I had not the slightest idea they were expecting me! On a more serious note, despite having had something in the order of £20 million spent on it recently, the airfield is 'under review' and may well close in the near future. It would be a bitter blow to the area's economy if it were not to survive.

The rails are still embedded in the road of the former level crossing. In the background, behind the down starter signal, is the hangar of the air sea rescue unit at Chivenor airfield. *Date: 24 March 1993.*

118
Braunton station
180 SS 484366

Conveniently sited in the middle of the village near its main crossroads, the station was ideally placed for holiday traffic to Saunton Sands and Croyde. The main building was situated on the down platform, which was somewhat shorter than the up side. A goods shed, cattle loading dock and five associated sidings were also on the up side at the southern end of the complex; two further sidings were sited opposite on the down side. Banking engines used the latter and were kept particularly busy, especially on summer Saturdays. On 7 September 1964 the goods yard was closed.

About to begin the assault: Light Pacific No 34096 *Trevone* enters Braunton with a train for Ilfracombe and shortly after leaving, will be faced with a stiff climb commencing at 1:74 increasing to 1:40 before the summit is reached at Mortehoe.
Photo: R. J. Sellick/National Railway Museum. Date: 27 September 1958.

Who would ever guess that a railway ran through here? The station master's house is now a newsagent's shop. During the conversion the booking hall and parcels office has been demolished, but the signal box was removed and has been preserved. Much of the station area and goods yard is now a car park, but the goods shed is extant with a modern extension added to it and functions as a youth centre. Beyond the telephone booths is the Braunton Countryside Centre and a tourist information office. The trackbed back south of the station has been consumed by a modern housing development, whilst north of the road it forms a pleasant garden sponsored by the Rotary Club in 1984 and a public amenity. Further north much of the line formation has also been turned into gardens; for some way beyond it is not at all well defined until the village boundaries are reached — and even then, it is only the occasional bridge which gives a positive clue to a railway past. *Date: 24 March 1993.*

119
Mortehoe bank – Heddon Mill
180 SS 499404

The struggle is on: having passed Heddon Mill Crossing and the small signal box, GWR 4300 class 2–6–0 No 6346, banked by Ivatt 2–6–2T No 41298, on the 08.50 Taunton–Ilfracombe, work hard up the 1:40 gradient at the halfway point on the climb to Mortehoe & Woolacombe station, 600ft above sea level. To make matters even more difficult, the course of the line swung wildly through the Caen valley closely following the main Barnstaple to Ilfracombe road (A39), before veering away from it about a mile north of this point.
Photo: Peter W. Gray. Date: 27 August 1963.

Very little explanation is needed to sum this up: the line simply does not exist here. For some distance from Heddon Mill crossing, where the railway cottage still survives, the line formation has been obliterated, including at this point where a new road has been created as an entrance to a caravan park. The farm building has changed little though, but the increase in traffic on the widened A39 is obvious.

The Ivatt Class 2 2–6–2T has been preserved and resides at the Buckinghamshire Railway Centre, Quainton Road.
Date: 24 March 1993.

120
Mortehoe & Woolacombe station
180 SS 484440

Mortehoe station was actually built two miles from the seaside village and the resort of Woolacombe, which it also served. Set at 600ft above sea level, it could be a bleak place in winter when swept by Atlantic gales. The cement-rendered station building was on the down side, whilst the up platform was provided with a shelter. The station was renamed Mortehoe & Woolacombe in 1950. By the time this photograph was taken, which shows 4300 class No 6346 leaving the station on the 08.50 Taunton–Ilfracombe, the sidings on the up side of the line had been removed and the rest were lifted in 1966, goods services having been withdrawn on 7 September 1964. Of interest are the crossovers which were used by banking engines either returning to Braunton or to Ilfracombe. *Photo: Peter W. Gray. Date: 27 July 1963.*

For years the station had a derelict air about it, but apart from the main building, which is a private residence, the site was converted and made into a children's adventure centre known as 'Once Upon a Time'. A new building has been constructed on the 'up' platform and an enclosed canopy links the two. The Fortescue Arms has had a facelift in recent years and looks much more of a salubrious establishment than it did some thirty years ago. A new store built next door gets its custom in summer from several caravan parks in the immediate vicinity. The bridge which carried the B3343 has been demolished and the road widened; it once marked the summit and the point where the line plummeted at 1:36 within a mile from here. The deep cutting on the north side of the bridge has been filled in, but the trackbed beyond it is quite distinct and is walkable. *Date: 24 March 1993.*

121 (Opposite)
Ilfracombe station
180 SS 514464

Even the most brilliant of Victorian engineers could not have solved the problem of placing the station closer to the town centre than it was eventually sited, for it was loftily perched on a hill some 225ft above sea level overlooking Ilfracombe. The approach from the south was a precipitous 1:36, easing to 1:71 at the end of the platforms; but even at the buffer stops, the line was still descending at 1:353!

The station underwent several changes over the years and the island platform was extended to cope with longer holiday trains. Originally the engine shed was sited on the west side of the platform, but a new one was constructed in July 1928 on a site south of the station, together with a 64ft 10in turntable, which was eventually replaced by one of 70ft to cope with the Bulleid Pacifics. Spoil and rock removed from the hillside were utilised to level out the ground on the west side for further carriage sidings. The goods shed and associated yard were on the east side of the platform; these were closed on 7 September 1964.

When starting from the station, locomotives were faced with the immediate challenge of a climb of 2¼ miles at 1:36, which was always a stirring sight for the observer. On this occasion, the photographer had tucked himself into the nearby pine woods to get a dramatic view of the omnipresent West Country class No 34106 *Lydford*, with steam sanders on, getting to grips with the five-coach portion of the 'Atlantic Coast Express' as it stormed up the gradient after leaving Ilfracombe station, just seen in the background. *Photo: George Heiron. Date: May 1963.*

A modern factory unit has been built on the station site itself, but the trackbed immediately to its south is used as a public footpath and cycleway for about two miles. The twin tunnels a half-mile distant from here are still in good condition, although the down side has been blocked in, only allowing enough room for bats to get in and out of a small slot. *Date: 24 April 1993.*

The children's adventure centre as seen from an embankment at the southern end of the complex. Among the attractions are four BR Mark 1 coaches which have been converted for activities use. A miniature train ride is also available on the site of the former up platform. *Date: 24 March 1993.*

A panorama taken a few yards from the previous shot shows more clearly the layout of the station. The 50-lever signal box is seen over the roof of the engine shed in the foreground, in front of which was the 70ft turntable cut into the hillside. *Photo: John Scrace.*
Date: 8 September 1963.

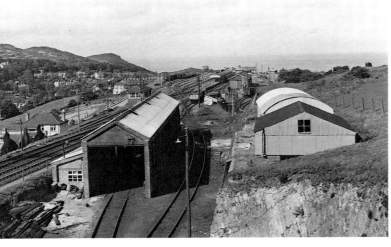

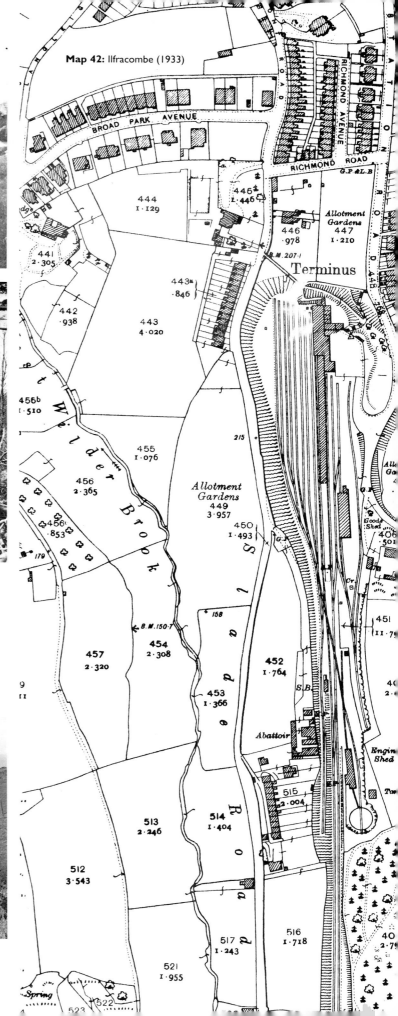

Map 42: Ilfracombe (1933)

122

Fremington station and quay
180 SS 513332

The station, inconveniently placed for the village on the east bank of a creek on the Taw estuary, was not so important as the adjacent quay. Many goods were imported or exported from here, including coal, timber and china clay. Some 50,000 tons of coal were handled annually, much of it for railway use. When the Southern Railway modernised the quay between the wars, it became the second busiest in Devon after Plymouth.

This east-looking view towards Barnstaple of Fremington station shows a notable feature in the form of the tall and rather elegant signal box, with a small brick-built shelter attached. The modest station buildings of wooden construction were on the down side. A

steam crane stands on the quayside in the sidings, which appeared to be rather empty; however, a North British Class 22 diesel is busy shunting wagons at the far end of the yard, which closed to goods on 6 September 1965. The quay functioned until 30 March 1970 and much clay was still being exported from here. *Photo: Andrew Muckley/ Ian Allan library. Date: September 1964.*

Sad to relate that this is all that remains of the station: it is now just a few untidy piles of rubble, but the end of the up platform can still be recognised. To the left the quay remains in good condition, but without a purpose. A derelict railway cottage at the site entrance has been occupied by New Age travellers, whose motley range of vehicles are dotted about in the yard, which is squalid and littered with rubbish and junk. The path in the foreground forms part of the 'Tarka Trail'. *Date: 25 March 1993.*

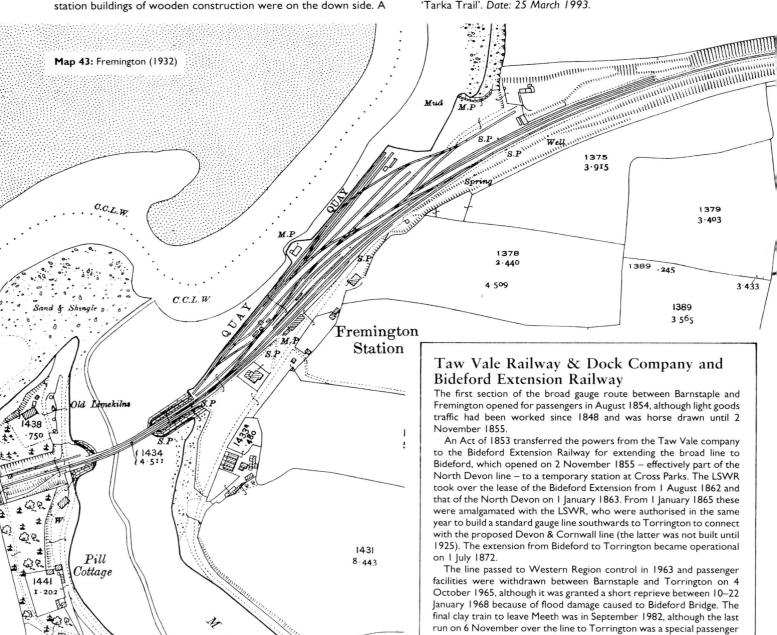

Map 43: Fremington (1932)

Taw Vale Railway & Dock Company and Bideford Extension Railway

The first section of the broad gauge route between Barnstaple and Fremington opened for passengers in August 1854, although light goods traffic had been worked since 1848 and was horse drawn until 2 November 1855.

An Act of 1853 transferred the powers from the Taw Vale company to the Bideford Extension Railway for extending the broad line to Bideford, which opened on 2 November 1855 – effectively part of the North Devon line – to a temporary station at Cross Parks. The LSWR took over the lease of the Bideford Extension from 1 August 1862 and that of the North Devon on 1 January 1863. From 1 January 1865 these were amalgamated with the LSWR, who were authorised in the same year to build a standard gauge line southwards to Torrington to connect with the proposed Devon & Cornwall line (the latter was not built until 1925). The extension from Bideford to Torrington became operational on 1 July 1872.

The line passed to Western Region control in 1963 and passenger facilities were withdrawn between Barnstaple and Torrington on 4 October 1965, although it was granted a short reprieve between 10–22 January 1968 because of flood damage caused to Bideford Bridge. The final clay train to leave Meeth was in September 1982, although the last run on 6 November over the line to Torrington was a special passenger working comprising 15 coaches hauled by a Class 31 diesel.

123
Instow station (1)
180 SS 473301

Instow station, at the mouth of the River Torridge and on its east bank, was built on a sweeping curve and had two platforms with a passing loop. The buildings on the up side were built of wood, with a slate roof and a rounded canopy protecting the front. A concrete shelter was provided on the down platform. Goods facilities were modest; these were withdrawn on 30 April 1962.

Having come from Halwill Junction via Torrington and Bideford, ex-LMS 2–6–2T No 41249, running bunker first, approaches Instow with a train for Barnstaple. *Photo: E. Wilmshurst.*
Date: 15 August 1964.

French schoolgirls pause to take a rest at Instow whilst cycling on the 'Tarka Trail' and look on in astonishment as a well-known local 'character' cycles by in his top hat. The former station building has sprouted a garage at the far end and has been fenced off from the remaining portion; it is now part of a boatyard and yacht club. On the opposite side the down platform is intact, but the preserved station sign still slants at an angle and has not been straightened! *Date: 25 March 1993.*

The preserved signal box, section of relaid track and reconstructed level crossing gates at Instow.
Date: 25 March 1993.

The Bideford and Instow Railway Group
This group was formed on 1 January 1992 following the merger of the Bideford Railway Station Group and the Instow Signal Box Group. It has taken on the responsibility of the two former railway stations and continues to work closely with Devon County Council, who own the sites along the 'Tarka Trail'. The partnership is unique and its success is plain for all to see at either place in the high standard of restoration, ensuring the area's railway history is not forgotten.

124
Instow station (2)
180 SS 473300

A railcar leaves Instow for Barnstaple, giving a better view of the station building and its attractive canopy. The signal box in the background also controlled the level crossing at the Barnstaple end of the station: note the SR-type upper quadrant starter signal, the post of which is comprised of redundant rail sections.
Photo: Andrew Muckley/Ian Allan library. Date: August 1964.

In the early 1980s the Instow Signal Box Group had succeeded in saving the signal box from demolition and campaigned for it to be the first one to be listed. When the line was lifted in 1984, Devon County Council purchased the land for use as a cycleway and footpath. After renovation, the box was rededicated in 1989 and handed to the Group, who restored the inside to its former glory and opened it on alternate summer Sundays. In conjunction with the DCC, the Group also enhanced the station area, relaid a section of track alongside the box and installed replica level crossing gates. The results of their efforts can be seen beyond the schoolgirls, who are still enjoying a respite from their cycling efforts along the trail; just behind them, the post for the up starter signal still stands and the down platform's surface is in very good condition, as can be judged here. The Tarka Country Park, of which the trail is a part and incorporates the South West Peninsula Coastal Path, was opened on 22 April 1987 by the Rt Hon William Waldegrave, Environment Minister; the event is commemorated by a Countryside Commission plaque sited here. *Date: 25 March 1993.*

125
Bideford station
180 SS 457264

The station was actually sited in East-the-Water, across the river bridge from the main part of the town. Here 72E Barnstaple Junction M7 0-4-4T No 30255 waits at Bideford with a down train for Torrington. Both platforms had squat stone buildings, each with an attractive canopy supported by iron columns. The parcels office was situated on the down side, opposite which was a wooden signal box sited on the up platform. Bideford was a crossing loop and a few short sidings were situated on the south side of the station, though the main goods yard, adjacent to the river, was on the Barnstaple side of the station, access being controlled by a ground frame. These closed for goods traffic on 6 September 1965, a month before the cessation of passenger services.

No 30255 was withdrawn from service a year after this photograph was taken and broken-up at the Eastleigh works in October 1960. *Photo: R. J. Sellick/National Railway Museum. Date: 26 September 1959.*

Due to the good offices of the Bideford Railway Station Group, which was formed in 1989 to recreate the railway atmosphere at the old station, it was gradually restored to the condition it is seen in here. Working in conjunction with Devon County Council, the debris and vegetation were cleared; a concrete railway shed was then moved from Yelland and placed here. The signal box was totally rebuilt and erected on its original site; in addition, a section of double track was relaid, together with points at the southern end of the station. A coach now resides on the former down line, adding to the atmosphere.

In 1991, Devon County Council acquired the former railway building and have made it the headquarters of their Countryside Management Service and Heritage Coast. The BRSG has use of the building for their club and committee meetings. They hope to rebuild the canopy and restore it to its position on the building: this, and an ongoing programme of improvements, will ensure they are kept busy for many years to come. *Date: 25 March 1993.*

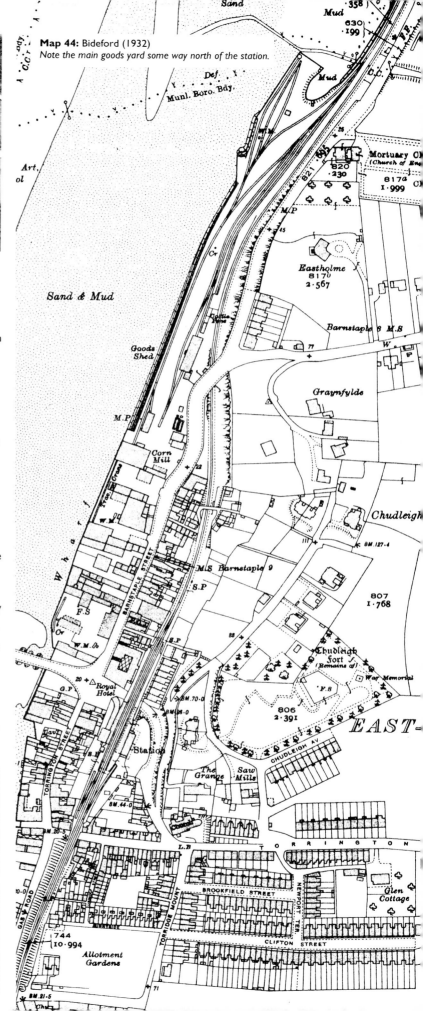

Map 44: Bideford (1932)
Note the main goods yard some way north of the station.

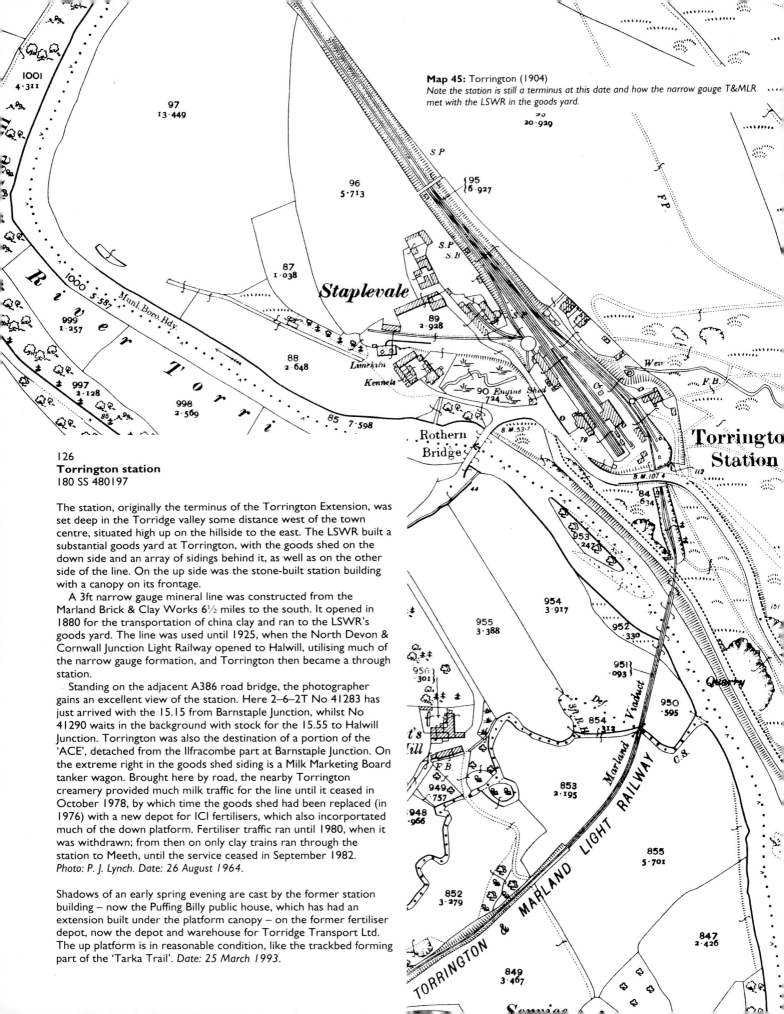

Staplevale

Rothern
Bridge

Torringto
Station

126
Torrington station
180 SS 480197

The station, originally the terminus of the Torrington Extension, was set deep in the Torridge valley some distance west of the town centre, situated high up on the hillside to the east. The LSWR built a substantial goods yard at Torrington, with the goods shed on the down side and an array of sidings behind it, as well as on the other side of the line. On the up side was the stone-built station building with a canopy on its frontage.

A 3ft narrow gauge mineral line was constructed from the Marland Brick & Clay Works 6½ miles to the south. It opened in 1880 for the transportation of china clay and ran to the LSWR's goods yard. The line was used until 1925, when the North Devon & Cornwall Junction Light Railway opened to Halwill, utilising much of the narrow gauge formation, and Torrington then became a through station.

Standing on the adjacent A386 road bridge, the photographer gains an excellent view of the station. Here 2–6–2T No 41283 has just arrived with the 15.15 from Barnstaple Junction, whilst No 41290 waits in the background with stock for the 15.55 to Halwill Junction. Torrington was also the destination of a portion of the 'ACE', detached from the Ilfracombe part at Barnstaple Junction. On the extreme right in the goods shed siding is a Milk Marketing Board tanker wagon. Brought here by road, the nearby Torrington creamery provided much milk traffic for the line until it ceased in October 1978, by which time the goods shed had been replaced (in 1976) with a new depot for ICI fertilisers, which also incorporated much of the down platform. Fertiliser traffic ran until 1980, when it was withdrawn; from then on only clay trains ran through the station to Meeth, until the service ceased in September 1982.
Photo: P. J. Lynch. Date: 26 August 1964.

Shadows of an early spring evening are cast by the former station building – now the Puffing Billy public house, which has had an extension built under the platform canopy – on the former fertiliser depot, now the depot and warehouse for Torridge Transport Ltd. The up platform is in reasonable condition, like the trackbed forming part of the 'Tarka Trail'. *Date: 25 March 1993.*

TORRINGTON & MARLAND LIGHT RAILWAY

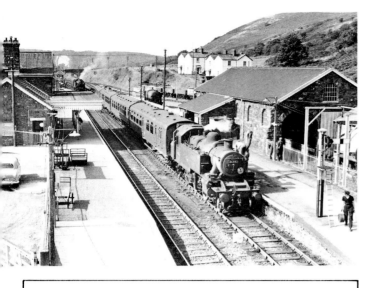

North Devon & Cornwall Junction Light Railway

Although authorised in 1865, the LSWR showed no inclination to extend the line from Torrington to meet the Devon & Cornwall's line at Halwill. It was only due to the prodigious light railway builder Colonel H. F. Stephens that the line was finally constructed, and was the last to be built by him. The first sod was cut on 30 June 1922, before the major grouping of 1923. Opening on 27 July 1925, the line was worked from the outset by the Southern Railway under terms agreed with the LSWR. Passing through sparsely populated countryside, the *raison d'être* for its existence was to connect with the mineral and china clay workings in the area, particularly at Marland near Petrockstow and Meeth. As far as passenger traffic was concerned business was extremely light, and it has been said the line ran from nowhere in particular to nowhere at all! In 1959 Hatherleigh station, the largest on the line serving the small market town with a modest population, could drum up only one passenger a week on average. Railwaymen were so accustomed to their own company, that any passenger was greeted with amazement! It was no surprise when closure to passengers was announced, which came on 1 March 1965. The last section of line was lifted in 1984, two years after clay traffic from Meeth ceased.

127
Torrington – River Torridge viaduct
180 SS 482195

Rather like the creature in the film featuring Doctor Doolittle, the push-me-pull-you, ex-LMS Ivatt 2–6–2Ts Nos 41206 and 41291 coupled bunker to bunker approach the viaduct over the Torridge at Torrington with the RCTS/PRC 'Exmoor Ranger' on their return from Halwill Junction. The train's round trip that day was: Exeter St David's, Okehampton, Halwill Junction, Torrington, Barnstaple Junction, Barnstaple Victoria Road, back to Barnstaple Junction and on to Ilfracombe; returning via Barnstaple Junction on ex-GWR metals to Dulverton, Taunton and Exeter St David's! The line between Meeth and Halwill was kept intact for three weeks after closure to enable this special to run; the track was lifted shortly afterwards.

It was at this point that the NDCJLR passed alongside the former narrow gauge line, which had its own wooden viaduct across the river, but this was demolished shortly after the standard gauge line was opened. *Photo: Peter W. Gray. Date: 27 March 1965.*

The viaduct's future is assured as part of the 'Tarka Trail', which extends beyond this point to Meeth. Despite what is suggested by this rather gloomy photograph taken on a dull day against the light, the walk or cycle ride through the deeply wooded valley at this point is spectacularly beautiful and is to be recommended, particularly in spring when bluebells and other wild flowers abound. *Date: 6 April 1993.*

128
Watergate Halt
180 SS 468176

One of the products of the Exmouth Junction concrete works on this line: the first halt reached after Torrington was Watergate, set remotely along the wooded valley near a crossroads on the B3227 road between Torrington and the village of Langtree. What the reasons were for siting this simple halt here, like some others on the line, could be brought into question and defy the imagination; however, it is thought that forestry workers occasionally used its facilities, which were basic in the extreme. *Photo: Andrew Muckley/ Ian Allan library. Date: July 1964.*

Although rhododendron bushes have encroached through the fencing, the platform remains completely intact and only its gravel surface has allowed grass to grow on it. The good condition of the 'Tarka Trail' passing the redundant halt is self evident. *Date: 6 April 1993.*

COMMENT: *It is worth pointing out that during the research for this book many photographs were obtained depicting workings on this line, but often the trains obscured the stations or halts from the camera's view. Others were either impossible to replicate or not worthy of publication, due to their poor quality. I felt it more important to show the structures and layout of the stations on the line – even though some may be deemed rather dull when compared to a shot showing a steam locomotive, which were generally Ivatt 2–6–2Ts in the latter years of passenger operation.*

129
Yarde Halt
180 SS 490144

The line wove its way on through the wooded valley from Watergate to the hamlets of West and East Yarde, which were served by this halt. The community's prosperity revolved around the china clay workings in the area and those using the halt provided some custom for the line, particularly at the beginning and end of a working day, with clay workers travelling from their nearby homes to their places of employment in the clay mines and pits. It has been suggested that as many as fifty people caught the early morning train from here, which is hard to imagine, judging from the limited amount of space available on the platform! A local man remembers when, on leave from national service, he travelled from Germany to here by train, which, according to him, only involved two changes in this country! *Photo: Andrew Muckley/Ian Allan library. Date: July 1964.*

The last rays of the evening sun cast the photographer's shadow over the derelict trackbed and halt. A successful attempt has been made to expose the platform's noticeboard posts, but the work by a local man to clear the rest of it was halted by the local council, which forbade him to continue. The station sign posts survive under the bushes which remain. The course of the 'Tarka Trail' bypasses the platform and a new path has been cut to the left of it to emerge on the minor road, seen behind the gate, on the other side of which a new car park has been built for the benefit of those using the trail; many choose this as a rendezvous point, if a one-way journey is envisaged. *Date: 25 March 1993.*

130
Dunsbear Halt
180 SS 503133

Set in the middle of nowhere, the halt could not have seen more than a handful of passengers in its entire existence, other than those miners wishing to alight for the nearby clay workings of Little Marland just to the south of it! At least the narrow stone-faced platform was provided with a reasonable shelter and a bench. This photograph, taken from the minor road with an ungated crossing,

typifies the halts built on the line. *Photo: Andrew Muckley/ Ian Allan library. Date: July 1964.*

The platform surface is slowly crumbling but is still quite distinct, despite being largely overgrown. The 'Tarka Trail' tends to peter out here, and is relatively little used when compared with the section between Torrington and Yarde. Nearby, the WBB Devon Clays Ltd North Devon works survive and still provide some local employment, although all traffic now goes by road.
Date: 6 April 1993.

131
Petrockstow station
191 SS 516106

Situated about a half-mile north of the village, the station was one of three passing loops on the line between Torrington and Halwill Junction; it also had a modest goods siding. All the buildings were on the up side of the station and not even a shelter was provided on the down platform, which was accessed by a sleeper crossing near the ungated road crossing. There were no signal boxes on the line and all such functions were carried out from ground frames, one of which can be seen here at the far end of the station near the loading gauge. Goods facilities were withdrawn on 7 September 1964. The

neat and tidy appearance of this staffed station is self evident; after all, there was little else for platform staff to do between trains, which invariably carried very few or no passengers!
Photo: Peter W. Gray. Date: 31 May 1964.

Taken a half-hour after sunset, this comparison shows that the platforms are still much in evidence, although a recently erected fence has isolated them from the now widened road. The former goods yard is used by the Devon County Council as a depot and the station forecourt as a car park for the 'Tarka Trail'. Note how the pine tree in the middle of the picture has grown over the years.
Date: 25 March 1993.

132
Meeth Halt
191 SS 547078

Having passed the clay works between Petrockstow and Meeth, the line continued to meander south-eastwards for a further mile or so before the halt was reached, situated on the west side of the A386 Great Torrington to Okehampton main road. Identical in design to Dunsbear, except that this one was built on a curve, the platform had a fairly substantial shelter built at the road end of the halt. Again, there was no gated level crossing over the road, so locomotive crews had to be cautious when negotiating it. *Photo: Andrew Muckley/ Ian Allan library. Date: July 1964.*

The halt is slowly being enveloped in undergrowth and scrub. Surprisingly, the shelter has not been demolished, despite lying derelict and disused for 28 years, but it has lost much of its roof and it is only a matter of time before it succumbs completely to the elements. After the closure of passenger services in 1965, the remaining portion of the line to the clay works was left to a point just over a half-mile north of here, before that too was removed in 1984. The trackbed towards Hatherleigh is overgrown in places, but is quite distinct in others. Many of the structures survive, but the bridge over the A386 south of this location has been demolished, allowing more headroom for the heavy lorries from the ECC ball clay works at Meeth. *Date: 6 April 1993.*

133
Hatherleigh station
191 SS 533054

The station, nestling the east bank of the River Lew close to its confluence with the Torridge, ostensibly served the small market town a mile to the south-east. Not the most conveniently sited, it proved far quicker for people to travel by road to Okehampton, seven miles away: the equivalent journey by train was a distance of no less than twenty! It is generally accepted that the line should have run directly to Okehampton rather than to Halwill Junction in this otherwise sparsely populated Devon countryside, but it was not to be.

This photograph shows a general view of the station, which was the second passing loop and the major one on the line. An attractive building was constructed on the up platform but, as at Petrockstow, passengers were not provided with any facilities on the down side. The small goods siding, which closed on 7 September 1964 and over which a loading gauge straddles, can be seen in the background. Situated between it and the end of the up platform, a 7-lever ground frame controlled both the siding and the signals. *Photo: Andrew Muckley/Ian Allan library. Date: July 1964.*

Some years after the closure of this section of the line the station building was converted into a holiday cottage; now it is a private residence which is occupied by its owner and has been extended forward under what used to be the platform canopy. The building in the immediate foreground is a garage, which extends across the trackbed at this end. The area between the platforms has been made into a sunken lawn. Apart from the down platform just visible to the side of the garage, the only other artefact to be seen in this study taken from the overgrown trackbed is the SR-designed down starter signal post on the extreme right. *Date: 6 April 1993.*

134
Hole station
190 SS 468035

The nearest sizeable population to Hole station was the village of Black Torrington 1¼ miles to the north – and that was hardly large! Hole was most remotely situated down a lane just south of the A3072 road. It was the third station to have a passing loop and was identical in design to Petrockstow and Hatherleigh, with two platforms but only one building, which was on the up side (to Barnstaple Junction!). During the last war (c1942), Italian POWs were responsible for constructing a large warehouse and depot for the War Agricultural Committee adjacent to the station, which was served by a siding. This provided some freight custom for the station, which up until then had virtually nothing. A feature of the NDCJLR was the 'mixed' trains: often a truck or freight wagon would be tacked on to the end of a single coach. Note the siding at the rear of the building, which leads to the large ex-Warag warehouse, just out of view in this shot.

Approaching Hole from Halwill Junction, some three-and-a-half miles away, Ivatts 2–6–2Ts Nos 41206 and 41291 are about to pass the station with the RCTS/PRC 'Exmoor Ranger' railtour.
Photo: Peter W. Gray. Date: 27 March 1965.

Much of the station survives, but is largely overgrown in what is now a Devon Trust for Nature conservation area; its remoteness is ideal, and to that end beehives have been placed on the end of the former down platform. The trackbed is unpassable here; however, towards Halwill it becomes more distinct than this area suggests and some of it has been incorporated to become farm tracks, as in the case of the Hatherleigh direction. From the early 1950s the warehouse was disused; the Runnymore Timber company took it over in the 1980s, but have since vacated it and it now lies empty. *Date: 6 April 1993.*

COMMENT: *In days of yore, it might have been acceptable for me to indulge in some undergrowth hacking and removal of small trees to allow a better portrayal of the subject. Now, however, the young silver birch tree obscuring the view of the station was quite safe from my attentions, particularly since this is a nature conservation area!*

The main building is largely intact and it appears that some attempt has been made to maintain it, for the windows and doors have been painted in chocolate and cream. *Date: 6 April 1993.*

135
Halwill Junction - Torrington branch platform
190 SS 443002

Almost as if by default, the platform serving the Torrington branch was set apart from the others at the station and only a path linked the two. Halwill Junction was remarkable insofar as it was remote from a centre of population, except for the village which grew up around it. The station spawned several businesses including an abattoir, the shadow of which can be seen on the extreme right of this view, which shows 2–6–2T No 41308 waiting with the 18.30 to Torrington. Apart from a few station staff standing on the down platform in the background, Halwill looks typically quiet and only

sprang to life when trains for the Bude branch and North Cornwall line met or divided here. *Photo: S. C. Nash. Date: 10 June 1960.*

Late on an autumn afternoon the sun's rays shine through the clouds on what remains of the Torrington branch platform at Halwill. At this date the majority of it was still there, but its fate was not in doubt and it was due for demolition once the building of new bungalows had commenced. Soon this area will be transformed from a messy building site into a neat housing development: then there will be no trace of the railway left at all, apart from the trackbed at each end of the village. *Date: 29 October 1992.*

BUDE BRANCH

Bude branch

Powers were obtained in 1865 by the Okehampton Railway (later renamed Devon & Cornwall) to construct a line to Bude, but these lapsed. Some years later a further attempt was made, and in 1873 it was authorised to build only as far as Holsworthy. In 1876 work started on the 17¾-mile single line from a junction at Meldon, which strode across the high ground of West Devon and had a ruling gradient of 1:78, before dropping to sea level at Bude. The line opened on 20 January 1879 and Holsworthy became a railhead for the LSWR, who had leased it from the Devon & Cornwall Railway. A local company obtained its Act in 1893, but had failed to make progress, so the 10½-mile extension to Bude was built by the LSWR between 1895–6; in the interim a luxury coach service was instituted by them until the line was opened on 10 August 1898.

Until the early 1960s, like the North Cornwall line, the branch had become the stomping ground for well over thirty years of the Drummond T9 4–4–0s, which were well suited to working the heavily graded and twisting line. Then, in 1963, the 28¼-mile Bude branch passed into Western Region control and came under scrutiny following publication of the Beeching report. After some rationalisation and economies had been implemented, including dieselisation, the line was closed on 3 October 1966.

136
Meldon Junction
191 SX 554926

After leaving the main line at Meldon Junction, seen in the background and dominated by Yes Tor rising 2,028ft above sea level, the Bude branch turned north through 90° on a 15-chain curve built on a massive embankment striding across the valley to Maddaford Moor, passing over the main Okehampton to Launceston road (A30) in the process. A view taken from the gardens of railway cottages shows Drummond T9 4–4–0 No 30313 crossing the A30 road bridge with the four-coach 17.51 Okehampton–Padstow train. The T9 was destined only to remain in service for a further two months, before being withdrawn in July 1961 and scrapped at Eastleigh works in the September. *Photo: S. C. Nash. Date: 12 May 1961.*

A gloomy view taken on a dismal late afternoon in November. Yes Tor provides the immediate clue, since most of the embankment from the former junction is now overgrown with scrub, although the line formation itself is quite distinct but has been severed by the new A30 dual carriageway of the Okehampton bypass, which has supplanted the old road and the bridge demolished in the 1980s.

Many individual trees can still be readily identified and have grown relatively little in the intervening years. *Date: 12 November 1992.*

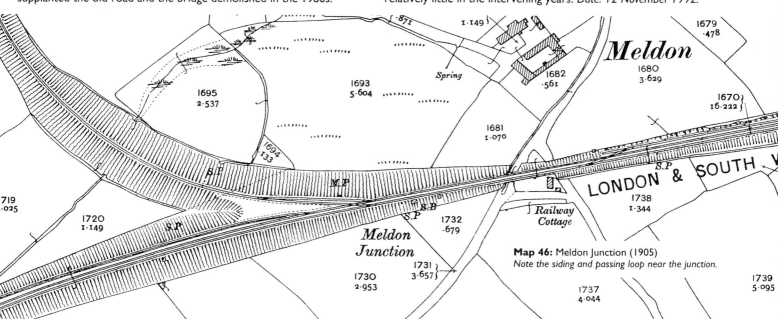

Map 46: Meldon Junction (1905)
Note the siding and passing loop near the junction.

137
Thorndon Cross – Maddaford Moor Halt
191 SX 533940

Like the T9 featured previously, also only two months before withdrawal, N class 2–6–0 No 31855, on the 17.51 Okehampton–Wadebridge train, drifts down the 1:264 gradient and approaches the B3218 road bridge, a few chains on the other side of which is Maddaford Moor Halt, not seen in this view.

Opened on 27 July 1926, Maddaford Moor Halt was constructed by the SR with the intention that it should serve a proposed health resort at Thorndon Cross, but little became of the enterprise.

However, the halt served the local community and the nearby railway cottages; it remained in use until the closure of the branch in October 1966. Prior to the platform being built, a passing loop existed at Maddaford Moor from about 1900 until it was taken out of use in April 1919. *Photo: Ronald A. Lumber. Date: 11 July 1964.*

A large plantation now covers the banks of the short cutting, but the line formation is used as a farm and forest track. There is little sign of Maddaford Moor Halt and much of the trackbed is now overgrown on the north side of the road bridge, which is on a nasty bend and has been the scene of several accidents.
Date: 28 February 1993.

138
Ashbury station
191 SX 484963

After the Maddaford Moor crossing loop closed in 1919, Ashbury was the only passing place on the line between Meldon and Halwill. Set in sparsely populated rolling countryside, the station served the village of North Lew, nearly two-and-a-half miles to the north. The main building was on the down side, behind which a small goods yard and a disproportionately large shed were situated. The up platform, access to which was gained via a sleeper crossing near the small 1879-vintage 10-lever wooden signal box, was provided with a simple shelter.

Running bunker-first, BR Class 4MT 2–6–4T No 80042 approaches Ashbury with the 15.35 Bude to Okehampton local. The fireman is about to exchange a token with the signalman, who will hand him another for the single section to Meldon Junction, whence double track will be gained. Note the layout of the station and the oil lamps which adorn the platforms. There are still trucks in the goods yard, but facilities were withdrawn a month later on 7 September. *Photo: Peter W. Gray. Date: 4 August 1964.*

When viewed from the adjacent road bridge today, trees practically obscure the station building, which is now a private residence. The trackbed has been made into a sunken lawn and the platforms have been grassed over. The goods shed still stands in the former yard and the letterbox built into the side of the station building is still there, although neither can be seen from this vantage point. East of the bridge the line formation is overgrown, but much of it between Maddaford Moor and here remains quite clear and is visible on the sections that closely follow the B3218 road. *Date: 29 October 1992.*

139
Madworthy
190 SX 452982

On leaving Ashbury the line fell at 1:80, increasing to 1:78 as it gently wove its way across Broadberry Down with its spectacular views before reaching Madworthy, where the line turned north and rose mostly at 1:78 on a straight section to reach Halwill Junction a mile away.

Having left Halwill Junction, seen in the distance, N class 2–6–0 No 31846, with the first of two evening freight workings, which includes a number of cattle trucks, sweeps round the sharp curve at Madworthy before beginning the arduous nine-mile climb to Meldon Junction. From there the fireman will have an easy task all the way to Exeter, the gradient to which is mostly downhill. Sadly, No 31846 was withdrawn a month after this photograph was taken; it was broken-up at Cohen's, Morriston, Swansea, in December that year. *Photo: Peter W. Gray. Date: 4 August 1964.*

Despite being bitterly cold and with snow falling on nearby Dartmoor, the visibility on this winter's day was perfect, as is more often the case than during the height of summer, when it is frequently less clear. The glorious nature of the countryside can be appreciated well in this shot showing the village of Halwill Junction, which has expanded considerably when compared to nearly thirty years before. The line formation is quite unmistakable, but is less visible in summer when foliage covers the trees and scrub which rampage unchecked over the embankments. Most of the hedgerows seemed to have survived in this rural part of the county, which is predominantly sheep country. *Date: 28 February 1993.*

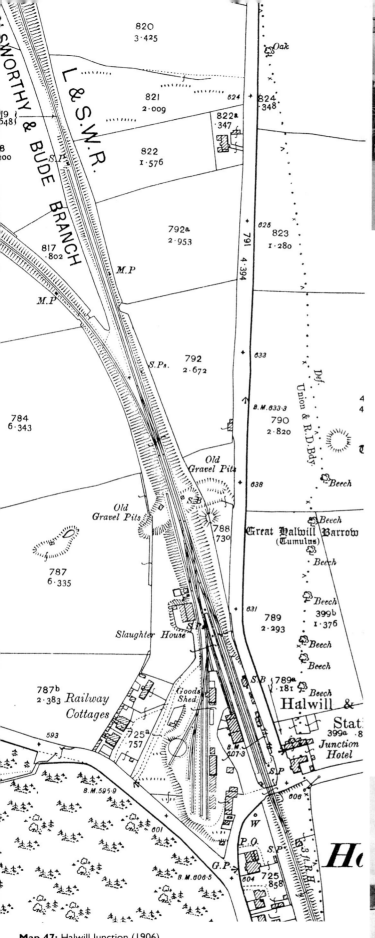

Map 47: Halwill Junction (1906)
Note that the map does not include the NDCJLR branch from Torrington, which was yet to be built. During World War II further sidings were added south of the Junction Hotel.

140
Halwill Junction (1)
190 SS 444002

When the Devon & Cornwall station opened on 20 January 1879 it was named Halwill & Beaworthy, also serving the latter village a mile or so east. A few months after the opening of the North Cornwall line to Launceston on 21 July 1886, the name was changed in March 1887 to Halwill Junction, which it signified on the signal box, although the nameboards remained the same. When the Torrington line opened in 1925, the station sign indicated it as 'Halwill for Beaworthy', underneath proclaiming it was the junction for the Bude, North Cornwall and Torrington lines. With the exception of the Torrington platform, just signifying 'Halwill Junction', the station carried these nameboards until closure of the line in 1966. A sizeable community grew around the railway and the village still retains its name today, long after the line closed.

N class 2–6–0 No 31841 arrives at Halwill with an up afternoon train from Padstow to Waterloo. In the distance the Bude portion waits to be backed on to the train. The signalman waits to hand the token to the fireman for the single line section to Ashbury, where it will be exchanged for another to Meldon Junction on the main line. The signal box was fitted with a four-tablet machine, which was necessary for the single line sections on the branches in either direction controlled from here. Of interest in this shot are the water churns on the down platform, which were probably destined for a crossing keeper's cottage or a signal box on one of the branches that did not have mains water.

Halwill was very much a place of quietude between trains, but it would suddenly spring to life when branch trains and their connecting services met; then there would be a short burst of activity before reverting to another long period of calm.
Photo: Ronald A. Lumber. Date: 23 August 1960.

The site is now a modern housing development consisting mainly of individually designed bungalows, and ironically the road leading to it is called 'Beeching Close' – no doubt spurred from 'Axe Road'! The only reminder of former days from this aspect is the small hillock that formed the cutting sides, seen above the locomotive in the first view. *Date: 29 October 1992.*

141
Halwill Junction (2)
190 SS 443003

If Meldon Junction was the shoulder of the LSWR's 'withered arm', then surely Halwill Junction was its elbow, for here the Padstow and Bude branches diverged (perhaps the former, being the longer 'bone', was the ulna, and the latter, the radius!). Later, due to the efforts of the prodigious light railway builder, Colonel H. F. Stephens, the North Devon & Cornwall Junction Light Railway, built from Torrington to Halwill and opened in 1925 under the auspices of the Southern Railway, was like an extension which had curiously grafted itself to the 'withered arm', but had little function.

A splendid north-looking view of the junction taken at 10.22 on a bright summer's morning from high on the embankment shows to best advantage the three separate lines: the Padstow branch veers sharply away to the left, whilst the Bude and Torrington branches continue into the distance before they too diverge – north-west and north-east respectively. In the foreground ex-LMS Class 2 2–6–2T No 41283 arrives with the 08.52 train from Torrington, behind which BR Class 4 2–6–4T No 80039 with the 09.30 from Bude waits to attach its train to the rear of the up 'Atlantic Coast Express'. This would be the last year of through trains to Waterloo and the final

one for the 'ACE'. On the extreme left are cattle trucks, shunted into the siding adjacent to the abattoir. Of note are the LSWR lattice bracket signals at the junction of the Padstow branch and beyond, whilst the Torrington branch starter in the foreground is a Southern design fabricated from rail sections. *Photo: Peter W. Gray. Date: 22 August 1964.*

Were it not for the tree line of the Halwill Moor plantation on the horizon, it would be impossible to judge whether this was the same spot where Peter Gray once stood. The trackbed is completely overgrown with young trees but is still walkable, as there is a path cut through the middle which extends towards the site of the former junction and provides a local amenity for dog walking and other activities. *Date: 29 October 1992.*

COMMENT: *Getting to the spot was no mean feat, since the steep embankment from the trackbed was covered in brambles and gorse bushes; but I was able to wade through these with relative impunity, which speaks volumes for my rather tatty but virtually thornproof Barbour jacket. However, it has its limitations, for it did not prevent me from falling down a fox earth I had failed to notice in the thick tangle and into which I promptly plunged to a depth of several feet!*

142
Halwill Junction (3)
190 SS 443003

A few minutes later Peter Gray turns in the opposite direction, looking south, and has an excellent panorama of Halwill Junction during one of its busier periods before tranquillity returns: the time is 10.29 and, having left the station minutes before with the 08.30 Padstow–Waterloo 'ACE', N class No 31846 can just be seen a mile away in the distance rounding the curve at Madworthy. At the station Ivatt 2–6–2T No 41283 has come to a halt at the platform and waits, having arrived with the 08.52 from Torrington, whilst BR Standard Class 4MTs 2–6–4T Nos 80039 and 80041 stand in the down bay. Shortly after crossing with No 31846 at Ashbury, No 80038 is due to arrive at Halwill with the 10.12 from Okehampton and, with the train having been divided, will take on the coaches for Bude, whilst No 80041 will be attached to the Padstow portion, leaving No 80039 in the station to await other duties. The abattoir on the right and the layout of the moderate goods yard, which closed two weeks later on 7 September, are seen clearly from this high position. *Photo: Peter W. Gray. Date: 22 August 1964.*

Clouds pass across the sun long enough to take this comparison view from the same position. The changes are plainly obvious, as new houses abound in the 'Stationfields' development. The bungalows in Beeching Close in the foreground are already occupied, but further development is under way, and by the spring of 1993 this scene will be further transformed, as more dwellings will have been constructed adjacent to where 2–6–2T No 41283 once stood.

The large building on the extreme left is the Junction Inn, which has many photographs on its walls to signify Halwill's heritage. Beyond it is the area where, in September 1943, a marshalling yard capable of holding 250 ammunition wagons was constructed. This was in preparation for the D-Day landings and the influx of American troops into the area. Satellite yards were also constructed at Whitstone & Bridgerule and Tower Hill (on the North Cornwall line); they and the one at Launceston handled some 35,000 tons of ammunition during the 1943–4 period. After the war, the marshalling yard at Halwill was used for wagon storage, but these sidings were gradually lifted between 1958 and 1963.
Date: 29 October 1992.

From Halwill Junction, 600ft above sea level, and after leaving the North Cornwall line, the branch ran parallel for 15 chains with the Torrington branch before turning westwards on a 40-chain curve, descending at 1:88 to run through the large Cookworthy Moor plantations on either side of the track. These had been established in 1919 by the Forestry Commission and provided a source of revenue for the railway with pit props being transported from Halwill.

Dunsland Cross was reached some three-and-a-quarter miles from Halwill in splendid isolation and sited nowhere in particular; the question must be asked why the station was built here. For many years the station sign signalled that this was the alighting place for Shebbear College, a boys' public school. The station had a crossing loop, but timings meant that trains rarely crossed here, unless late running was involved. The main building, of standard design for smaller stations on the branch, was on the down side and the dumpy 10-lever signal box opposite controlled the crossing loop and small yard, which at one time handled sea sand used by farmers as dressing. In the 1930s Bibby's erected an animal feed store here, which was sited next to a handsome goods shed. The yard closed on 7 December 1964.

About a year before closure of the line, 2–6–2T No 41283 leaves the crumbling station of Dunsland Cross with a Great Western Society special, which was organised by the South West branch of the society to commemorate the centenary of the GWR reaching Launceston. *Photo: Peter W. Gray. Date: 5 September 1965.*

(i)
A view from the other side of the panel fencing shows the station house to full advantage, and how the line formation has been made into a lawn abutting the down platform. The up platform no longer exists, but the loading dock near the goods shed is still extant. *Date: 29 October 1992.*

The station building is only just visible from the same aspect today. Much of it and the former goods shed has become holiday accommodation. A few years ago the present owner established here Lyne Acres, a major archery centre, which included building an indoor 50 metre range. The impressive building was constructed just west of the old goods yard and cannot be seen in this north-looking view. *Date: 6 April 1993.*

(ii)
The former goods shed looks a picture and has been very tastefully converted into self-catering holiday accommodation for those visiting the archery centre. Just beyond it can be seen Bibby's old animal feed store. *Date: 6 April 1993.*

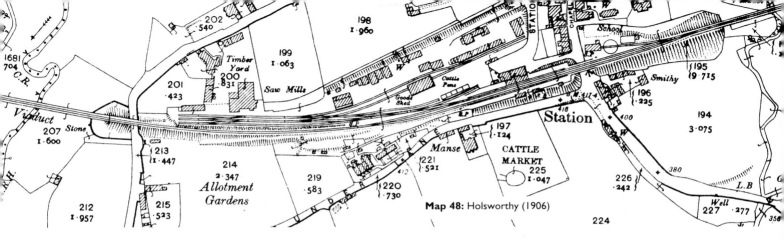

202
540

198
1·960

1681
704
O.C.R.

199
1·063

Timber
Yard
200
·831

201
·423

Saw Mills

195
9·715

Smithy

196
·225

School

194
3·075

Station

Viaduct
207
1·600

Stone

213
1·447

Good
Shed

Cattle
Pens

416

197
·124

Manse

CATTLE
MARKET
225
1·047

226
·242

100

380

L.B

214
2·347
Allotment
Gardens

219
·583

221
·521

220
·730

Map 48: Holsworthy (1906)

224

Well
227 ·277

212
1·957

215
·523

144
Holsworthy station
190 SX 343035

The important West Devon market town and livestock centre of
Holsworthy was the original terminus of the Devon & Cornwall
Railway when the line opened. As its popularity grew, the demand
for home-killed meat ensured plenty of trade was generated from
the town for the railway. In the years leading to closure of the
branch, demand had diminished substantially due to heavy
competition from road transport; however, fertiliser and coal
continued to be handled until the yard was closed on 7 September
1964.

Built in local stone, the original single platform for the terminus
(which was built with a run-round loop) was on the right, whilst the
down side was of brick, being constructed later ready for the
extension to Bude, opened in August 1898; the 20-lever signal box
also dates from that time.

Entering Holsworthy with the Great Western Society's
Launceston centenary special, is Class 2 2–6–2T No 41283. By this
date the Y-shaped yard, seen beyond the platform, had closed and
the sidings were already overgrown with weeds. The large goods
shed can just be made out behind the station building.
Photo: Peter W. Gray. Date: 5 September 1965.

After closure of the line, the station site was used for commercial
purposes and various businesses operated from here and the former
goods yard, including a road haulage company. At the time of this
visit the station building, now slate-hung, was boarded up and the
site lay derelict. The platform edges can be made out quite clearly,
but the area between them has been filled in; at the far end a loading
dock had been constructed at some stage. On a chilly winter's day
the site was not looking its best. In these economically uncertain
times, what future lies in store for the old station is in doubt, but
hopefully some other purpose will be found for it in due course.
Much of the twisting line formation between here and Dunsland
Cross survives in good condition, especially where it is exposed on
embankments, but most of the cuttings are overgrown with small
trees. *Date: 28 February 1993.*

COMMENT: *It is not often I persuade a member of my family to accompany
me on expeditions to derelict stations in winter, and judging by my wife's
well-wrapped appearance as she waits patiently by the car, it is no
wonder!*

The most notable structures on the line were the five-arch
Woolston and nine-arch Derriton viaducts, the first to be
constructed with concrete blocks; Holsworthy East Viaduct, just
east of the station on the south side of the town, was built in local
stone, being the first which provided access to the original terminus.
Like that of Derriton, with its nine 50ft arches striding 95ft above
the River Deer on the west side of the town, the eight-arch
structure of Holsworthy East still stands today, but is not in such
good condition and many of the coping stones have been hurled
from its parapets to the valley below. This view on a rainy day was
taken from the A3072 road. Note the tower of Holsworthy church
peeping through the middle arch. *Date: 6 April 1993.*

145
Whitstone & Bridgerule station
190 SX 269015

Although undulating slightly, the line fell on a ruling gradient of 1:82 for the next five miles to Whitstone & Bridgerule, a few chains west of the River Tamar but still just in Devon and three-quarters of a mile from the Cornish border by rail, but only a quarter-mile south by road. The station was sited just off what is now the B3254 road between the two villages which names it served. Passenger traffic was sparse, but freight, mainly coal and agricultural products, managed to hold up reasonably well. The small yard closed on 7 September 1964, along with the others on the branch.

In this view, looking east from an occupation bridge at the end of the station, Exmouth Junction shed (83D) BR Class 3 2–6–2T No

82040 arrives bunker-first with the 14.42 Halwill–Bude and passes the section of platform which was removed in 1943 to make way for the ammunition sidings in the yard just beyond; it was restored to its full length in 1947 when they were removed. Unaffected was the small 13-lever signal box, the roof of which can be spotted between the station canopy and the building. No 82040 was withdrawn from service the following May and scrapped at Bird's, Long Marston, in November. *Photo: Peter W. Gray. Date: 2 January 1965.*

The station building is now a private home, but has managed to retain its canopy. Infilling between the platforms has enabled some sort of lawn to be created, although it would not win any prizes in the best-kept garden category – at least it appears to be an ideal play area for the family children! *Date: 28 February 1993.*

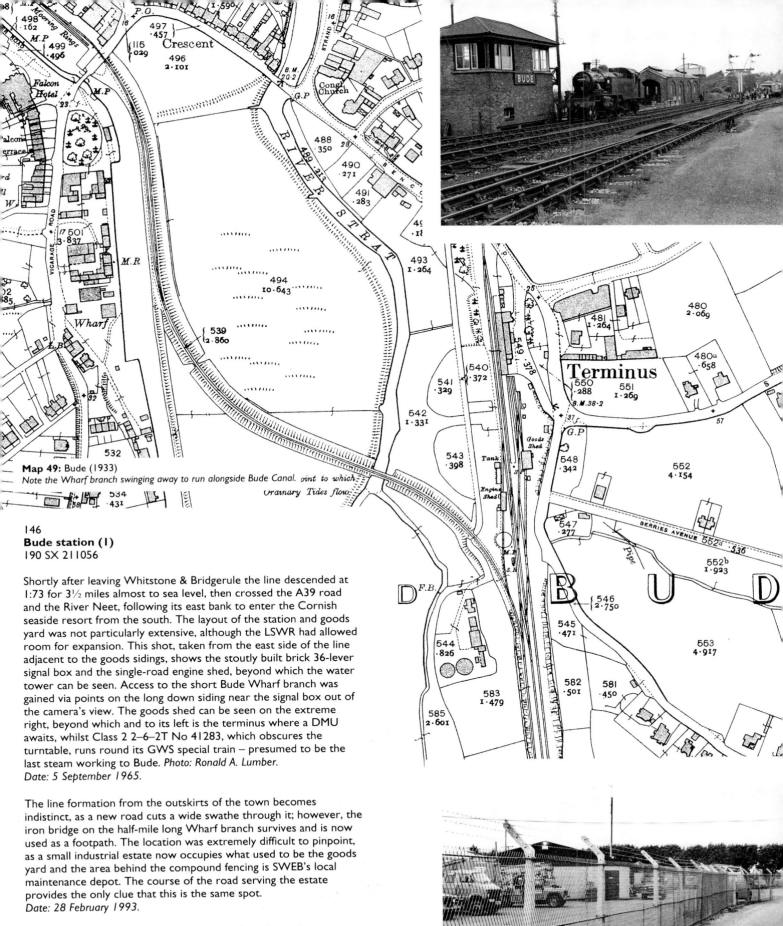

— Map 49: Bude (1933)
— Note the Wharf branch swinging away to run alongside Bude Canal. *oint to which*
Urainary Tides flow

146
Bude station (1)
190 SX 211056

Shortly after leaving Whitstone & Bridgerule the line descended at
1:73 for 3½ miles almost to sea level, then crossed the A39 road
and the River Neet, following its east bank to enter the Cornish
seaside resort from the south. The layout of the station and goods
yard was not particularly extensive, although the LSWR had allowed
room for expansion. This shot, taken from the east side of the line
adjacent to the goods sidings, shows the stoutly built brick 36-lever
signal box and the single-road engine shed, beyond which the water
tower can be seen. Access to the short Bude Wharf branch was
gained via points on the long down siding near the signal box out of
the camera's view. The goods shed can be seen on the extreme
right, beyond which and to its left is the terminus where a DMU
awaits, whilst Class 2 2–6–2T No 41283, which obscures the
turntable, runs round its GWS special train – presumed to be the
last steam working to Bude. *Photo: Ronald A. Lumber.*
Date: 5 September 1965.

The line formation from the outskirts of the town becomes
indistinct, as a new road cuts a wide swathe through it; however, the
iron bridge on the half-mile long Wharf branch survives and is now
used as a footpath. The location was extremely difficult to pinpoint,
as a small industrial estate now occupies what used to be the goods
yard and the area behind the compound fencing is SWEB's local
maintenance depot. The course of the road serving the estate
provides the only clue that this is the same spot.
Date: 28 February 1993.

COMMENT: *The biting wind and clouds rolling in from the north-east
suggested that snow was imminent – a few minutes later, I was proved
right!*

147
Bude station (2)
190 SX 210057

The 570ft island platform was initially thought to be longer than necessary for normal passenger services, but it came into its own when excursions comprising eight or nine coaches ran to Bude, 228¼ miles from Waterloo. However, in the 1930s holiday traffic required the length of trains to be increased further and work started in 1939 to alter the layout, which involved the starting signals being moved further away from the platform: this enabled trains of up to 15 coaches to be divided and loaded simultaneously from either face.

Here, Class 2 2–6–2T No 82023 is backed into the bay to couple up to its train for Halwill. Behind it is the goods shed, which closed for business on 7 September 1964. *Photo: R. C. Riley. Date: 16 June 1962.*

Like so many stations which met their demise in the Beeching era, often there is nothing left to signify a railway was ever there. However, careful study will reveal that the only clue is the house seen on the extreme left of the original photograph, which can *just* be identified here. After surviving for nearly two decades following closure, becoming ever more derelict, the station was finally demolished and the entire area built on a few years ago; these houses now form Ceres Court, a modern development which includes sheltered accommodation. *Date: 28 February 1993.*

COMMENT: *Such was the transformation here that I had to ask a local person if he knew where the station once stood, which fortunately he did!*

148
Bude station (3)
190 SX 210058

BR Class 4 4–6–0 No 75025 runs round its train, which had formed the 12.10 from Okehampton. Although not ideal, a better view is to be had of the main building protected by an attractive canopy. The station was provided with all the trappings necessary for the amount of traffic expected in the summer months. This included a refreshment room, waiting rooms and large lavatories – all of which were well patronised in season! On this winter's day it looks like the locomotive's crew and guard will be the only ones travelling to Okehampton, with not a passenger in sight. *Photo: Peter W. Gray. Date: 2 January 1965.*

On entering Bulleid Way, the only clue to a railway past, one would not have any other hint that this was where Peter Gray stood to photograph the station and train. The one exception is the same house which was seen in the first study, visible directly over Bulleid set No 857. When surveying this scene, it is almost impossible to think that a portion of the fabled 'Atlantic Coast Express' once ran to Bude and also stood here – it certainly stretches the imagination somewhat! *Date: 28 February 1993.*

COMMENT: *This shot was taken just after the watery sun had disappeared over the horizon out to sea and the first flakes of snow had started to fall, a portent of which are the dark clouds scurrying in from the north-east, blown by biting gale-force winds. Boy, was I glad to get back to the car, to my wife and a nice cup of hot coffee!*

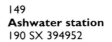

North Cornwall Railway

The Launceston, Bodmin & Wadebridge Junction Railway was incorporated in 1864 to form a link with the Bodmin & Wadebridge Railway, which had been in splendid isolation since it began operations in 1834. However, the LBWJR's powers lapsed and it was not until 18 August 1882 that the North Cornwall Railway, promoted by the LSWR, gained powers to construct a line from Halwill Junction to Launceston and Padstow. It enabled the LSWR to link with the little Bodmin & Wadebridge Railway, whose line it had purchased without parliamentary authority and operated since 1847, when their own metals had only reached westwards as far as Dorchester!

Shortage of funds and the difficult North Cornwall terrain meant progress was slow: the Halwill to Launceston section opened on 21 July 1886, and it was a further six years before the line was extended to Tresmeer, which was reached on 28 July 1892. The section from Tresmeer to Camelford opened on 14 August 1893, followed by the extension to Delabole on 18 October that year. Over eighteen months elapsed before the line was completed to Wadebridge, opening on 1 June 1895. It was almost another four years before Padstow was reached from Wadebridge by a line built along the Camel estuary, which opened on 27 March 1899.

Previously, the coming of the railway to North Cornwall had not been universally welcomed and was seen as a mixed blessing by many. However, it brought prosperity to some, and to Delabole in particular, to the slate quarry – then the largest in the world. In gratitude, its owners gave three-quarters of a mile of trackbed to the LSWR; passengers could peer out of a train window and look down into the chasmic hole to see ant-like men at work far below. Freight handled included not only slate, but also meat from the livestock centre of Launceston and fish from Padstow, which continued until 1964. The North Cornwall line closed to passengers on 3 October 1966, but the Wadebridge to Padstow section remained open until 30 January 1967, linked by the ex-GWR's line from Bodmin Road; Wadebridge Quay, however, survived until 1973. The final train to run from Wadebridge was a DMU special on Sunday 3 December 1978.

149
Ashwater station
190 SX 394952

Soon after leaving Halwill Junction and diverging from the Bude branch, the line turned sharply south-west and within two-and-a-half miles picked up the course of the River Carey, which it followed closely to the hamlet of Ashmill nestling in a narrow and most attractive setting, where the station, the first on the North Cornwall line, was situated. Serving Ashwater, a larger village a half-mile to the west, the station was built in a dark, grim-looking stone, but its arched gable windows and steeply pitched main roof gave it a certain charm, which was repeated with variations on the rest of the line.

Seen from the old road bridge looking south-west, this marvellous photograph typifies the tranquil atmosphere that used to prevail on some of Britain's rural lines: on a fine sunny day Ashwater looks its best, and the station could not be neater. Whilst the main buildings were on the up side, a small shelter kept close company with the small signal box, which controlled the goods yard opposite: it looks totally deserted and was to close officially on 7 September, a few days after this shot was taken. *Photo: Peter W. Gray.*
Date: 22 August 1964.

The bridge was bypassed a few years ago when the road was straightened and an embankment constructed to carry it. The Armco barriers can be seen through the thicket that has grown up on the remaining portion of the trackbed sandwiched between the two. The former station's roof can just be made out through the small trees.

Ashwater station building is now a private residence owned by a couple who are keen railway enthusiasts aware of its heritage; they ensure that this is not lost, and much of it is in original condition. The former goods yard is owned by a coal merchant.
Date: 6 April 1993.

(i)
Taken on a particularly dull and drizzly late afternoon, this is how the former station looks today when viewed from the end of the garden, which marks the point where the platforms once ended; they are indistinct now, but the occasional edging stone can be made out through the 'lawn'. *Date: 6 April 1993.*

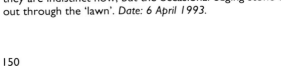

(ii)
The concrete station sign survives on the up side. The vehicles are in the coal yard. *Date: 6 April 1993.*

150
Tower Hill station
190 SX 369903

Still nestling the east bank of the River Carey in its deep valley, the line entered Tower Hill, almost four miles distant from Ashwater. The station, like the one before, largely served a scattered rural community. A row of railway cottages to a design repeated at other places on the line was constructed to the west of the line and to the rear of the main building, which was built close to a standard design; these were situated almost in total isolation with hardly another house in sight. Tower Hill had a small goods yard, but was not used a great deal over the years and closed on 6 January 1964.

Like all the stations on the line, Tower Hill was a crossing loop and here the guard of the 09.56 Okehampton–Padstow, with T9 No 30719 in charge, checks his watch to see if the 09.33 Padstow–Waterloo portion of the 'ACE' is running to time, as his train waits for it to pass. *Photo: R. C. Riley. Date: 15 July 1960.*

This sorry scene is all that remains of Tower Hill: the building was inexplicably demolished some years ago and only a few fragments of the platforms remain, which can be made out to the left of the stable. Most of the station site has been given over to a horse paddock, which extends southwards past the old goods yard. The former railway cottages have been made into delightful homes. Where the Carey valley opens from this point, much of the line formation has been lost to fields; further south it becomes distinct once again. *Date: 6 April 1993.*

One item found was the 218¾-mile post (from Waterloo). *Date: 6 April 1993.*

151
Launceston station
201 SX 330850

With the gradient gently falling at 1:165 and the valley opening out, three-quarters of a mile after leaving Tower Hill the line crossed the River Carey and followed its west bank to pass under Boldford Bridge, only to cross the river again, and a road, on a three-arch bridge at Heale, the lowest point on the line until Wadebridge was reached. Rising at 1:94 another mile further on, the line passed over the River Tamar and into Cornwall, swinging westwards to enter Launceston from the east, crossing the GWR line from Lydford in the process.

The LSWR station, originally its terminus, was placed at the north side of the town in the Kensey valley and adjacent to that of the GWR, which had arrived 21 years previously on 1 July 1865. The LSWR's timetable, offering no fewer than five trains from Launceston to London each day, ensured that its rival soon became the poor relation. This rivalry continued until nationalisation, although the necessities of war required a spur to be built connecting the two. From 30 June 1952 Western trains were required to use the former LSWR station, with their own terminus being relegated to goods status; this ceased on 28 February 1966.

Here N class 2–6–0 No 31859 enters the curving station with a Waterloo–Padstow working, whilst the signalman from the double-framed box saunters to the end of the platform before crossing the line to hand the token to the driver for the single section to Egloskerry. The N class was withdrawn two months later and broken-up at Bird's, Morriston, Swansea, in the following December. Note the two goods sheds beyond the water tower.
Photo: Ronald A. Lumber. Date: 11 July 1964.

The area once occupied by both goods yards was developed into the Newport Industrial Estate some years ago. In the background is the building belonging to Truscott's of Launceston, the local Peugeot dealers. For years after closure in 1966 the station lay derelict and neglected, soon becoming overgrown. However, with the establishment of the narrow gauge Launceston Steam Railway, the site was purchased and cleared to create a car park for the new station constructed on the west side of the main A388 road bridge. The only artefact here is a GWR starting signal at the entrance to the car park, although one stone pier of the old LSWR footbridge remains, from which this comparison was taken. Note the housing development which has taken place on the hillside in the background. *Date: 30 April 1993.*

Map 50: Launceston (1932)
Note the proximity of the GWR terminus to the LSWR/SR station.

Launceston Steam Railway's station incorporates the up platform's canopy from Tavistock North. The compact nature of the site is evident in this aspect, taken from the embankment near the A388 road bridge. *Date: 30 April 1993.*

Launceston Steam Railway

In 1972, Martin Bowman and a colleague visited Launceston looking for a site on which to establish a narrow gauge railway. They approached the council with a view to constructing a line to follow the course of the LSWR through the Kensey valley. The local authorities supported the enterprise from the outset. After 11 years of negotiations, which included the piecemeal purchase of parcels of land from British Rail and a stretch previously sold to a property developer, the first train ran on the 2ft-gauge line on Boxing Day in 1983.

Today, the line extends for some two-and-a-half miles, with a further extension planned to reach Egloskerry. The rails came from a variety of sources, including the Royal Naval Ordnance Depot, Ernesettle, the Penrhyn Railway and the North Wales narrow gauge lines; even sections from the old Lynton & Barnstaple have been utilised. The rolling stock includes Hunslet Engine Co No 317 *Lilian* (1883) and No 679 *Covertcoat* (1898), No 409 *Velinheli* (1886) and No 1760 *Sybil*, built in 1906 by W.G.Bagnall & Co; diesels are represented by Simplex No 5646 built by Motor Rail in 1933. A variety of carriages and trucks from a wide range of sources are also to be seen on this charming line. A museum, which houses a variety of railway memorabilia and other objects, including industrial engines and motorcycles, has been established along with workshops, much of it utilising the old buildings of the former Launceston Gas Company; the station houses a café and shop. Martin and Kay Bowman run an enterprise which is well worth a visit and is actively promoted by the English Tourist Board, bringing many visitors to Launceston, the gateway to Cornwall.

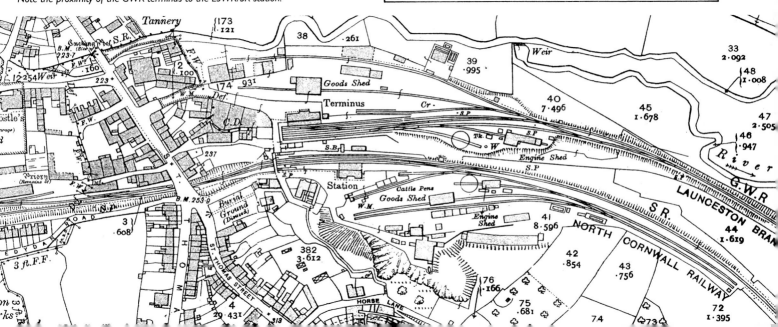

152
Egloskerry station
201 SX 270864

The line climbed fairly steeply up through the Kensey valley for four miles to the station at Egloskerry, situated conveniently a quarter-mile south-west of the village centre. Like all stations on the NCR, it was built to a fairly typical pattern: the main building, constructed in red brick, was situated on the up side, at the extreme east end of which was a signal box controlling the passing loop and a small yard, which closed on 9 May 1960. Access to the down platform, upon which stood a brick-built shelter, was via a boarded crossing at the western end. The siting of a hand-operated level crossing at this end of the station required the signalman to walk the length of the platform to open or close the gates on each occasion a train passed. In later years, a porter shared these duties.

Two months before withdrawal, N class Mogul No 31855 stands at Egloskerry with the 13.00 Padstow–Okehampton train, which included a couple of parcels vans. The neat appearance of the station typified the care staff took over their workplaces – little else to do between trains! *Photo: Ronald A. Lumber. Date: 11 July 1964.*

Today the station building is a private house, making a superb home for its owners, who offer comfortable bed and breakfast accommodation; the booking office has been converted into a sitting room for guests. The trackbed has been infilled to platform level, but has enabled a superb cultivated garden to be created, as this study indicates. Note that the station sign still survives, seen on the extreme left of the picture. The goods yard is occupied by rural workshops. Much of the line formation both east and west of here is now overgrown, but at other locations it has been erased altogether. *Date: 30 April 1993.*

153
Tresmeer station
190 SX 222886

Having weaved a tortuous path through numerous cuttings and embankments, which had to be built on the difficult terrain from Egloskerry – nearly bankrupting the railway company during its construction – and heading generally in a north-westerly direction, the line climbed for the last 1½ miles to Tresmeer at grades varying between 1:73 and 1:78. Reached on 28 July 1892, Tresmeer was the LSWR's temporary terminus on the NCR, until the line was extended to Camelford on 14 August 1893, two months before the opening of the extension to Delabole on 18 October. The station was actually sited in the curiously named hamlet of Splatt, about a mile north-west of the small village the station purported to serve – probably to maintain the right sophisticated image suited to the

LSWR! As at Halwill and other locations, an abattoir was established here to cater for the demand for home-killed meat. Taken from the adjacent road bridge looking south-west towards Otterham, this view shows the abattoir building in the goods yard beyond the station. The main building, as at Egloskerry, was of red brick. The goods yard closed on 7 September 1964. *Photo: Peter W. Gray. Date: 22 August 1964.*

The former station is still unmistakable: like others on the line, it has been made into a desirable home. The trackbed between the surviving platforms has been made into an attractive sunken garden and the station sign on the up platform is extant, remaining in good condition. The goods yard is used for commercial purposes and a transport company occupies much of the site. Note the pear-shaped cat at the bottom right of the picture, sitting comfortably enjoying the evening sun on the old up platform! *Date: 30 April 1993.*

154
Otterham station
190 SX 154893

This probably is the embodiment of all that the nation has lost with the demise of the rural railway, and a scene which can never be recaptured is depicted here for posterity: N class 2–6–0 No 31859 has just left Otterham with the 13.00 Padstow–Okehampton train, the beating echo of its exhaust the only sound to disturb the rural peace on a beautiful summer's day, whilst the station staff return to other duties, having ensured its departure on time. Having reached the summit 800ft above sea level, shortly before entering the station, the train will have an easy run to Tresmeer, the line descending mainly at 1:73 for the next few miles and, apart from a few small stretches, it is all downhill to Launceston.

Otterham station was remotely situated south-west from the village, nearly two miles by road. Opening on 1 October 1942, a large airfield was established at Davidstow Moor two miles to the south, 970ft above sea level and the highest in the United Kingdom. Bleak in winter, it was not a popular place for either the RAF or USAAF airman who found themselves stationed there during the three years (almost to the day) it remained operational. During its life it provided some passenger traffic for the railway, which again returned to blissful tranquillity in 1945 – at least in summer, without the numbing winter Atlantic gales sweeping in from the west making it a less desirable place to be! The small goods yard and fertiliser store closed on 7 September 1964, the same date as many others on the line. *Photo: Peter W. Gray. Date: 22 August 1964.*

Having recently exchanged hands, Otterham station is now the home of a young couple, who are in the process of renovating the building. The platforms have been grassed over, but the occasional edging stone can be spotted in the lawn. A trailer park was established on the northern end of the site many years ago, but the former fertiliser store has survived the passage of time. The road bridge was demolished during the widening of the A39, and to straighten what was once a dangerous crossroads. The line formation to its west, leading to the point where the line once reached its summit, has been filled in for some distance.
Date: 2 May 1993.

155
Camelford station
200 SX 101856

Snaking in a south-westerly direction from Otterham summit and across the gently undulating Waterpit Down on easy grades, picking up the course of the infant River Camel on the way, the line reached Camelford station, 240¾ miles from Waterloo. At its opening ceremony on 14 August 1893, it was estimated that an astonishing figure of some nine thousand people crowded the station to welcome the first train. Situated 1¼ miles north of the small town up a long hill, it was not the most conveniently sited station. A handsome stone building with a large canopy supported on decorative iron columns adorned the up platform, and small waiting rooms were built on the down side. The goods yard at the northern end was well appointed and had a reasonably large layout and a stone-built shed of modest proportions.

Watched by a young lady dressed in natty shorts sitting on the bench, N class 2–6–0 No 31836 on a down freight stands and blows off impatiently, whilst it waits at Camelford for the passing of an up passenger working. On the up platform, a barrow stacked with what could be boxes of day-old chicks waits to be loaded on to the up train – possibly the 'Perisher'. Leaving Padstow for Exeter at 15.13, it usually had two braked and heated vans for parcels traffic, some of perishable nature – hence the name accorded to it.
Photo: Ronald A. Lumber. Date: 29 August 1960.

Used for many years after closure by an agricultural merchant, today the station is the site of the Museum of Historic Cycling. It is devoted to the history of cycling from 1818 to modern times and over one hundred examples are displayed, together with other

memorabilia. It is fair to suggest that the concrete extension to the former station building might be considered to have a carbuncular appearance and not necessarily be in keeping with its character. Only these sections of the platforms in the immediate foreground remain visible, but the goods shed, previously obscured by the down platform's building, can now be seen, although it is in an extremely poor state of repair, roofless and in danger of collapse. The road bridge over the old railway has been demolished and the A39 realigned. *Date: May 1993.*

COMMENT: The saga of Mrs Bank-Smith. *Whilst visiting the Cornishman, a famous hostelry in Tintagel, I was told the wonderful tale of Mrs Bank-Smith, the much-treasured and loved doll of Karin Knight, the landlord's daughter. She and her mother had just caught the train from Camelford and were leaning out of the window waving goodbye, when disaster struck: Mrs Bank-Smith was accidentally dropped from the carriage and plummeted on to the lineside below. Wail of despair from Karin – prompt action by the guard: without further ado he stopped the train, jumped down on the line and ran back to retrieve Mrs Bank-Smith, who was found none the worse for the experience! Great relief all round. Today Mrs Bank-Smith lives in a box somewhere in an attic.*

On another occasion, when travelling by train at night to visit relatives at Halwill, grandmother Knight was not so lucky, for as the train approached the station, the guard called out the stop – but it was halted at signals near the junction. Thinking that it was Halwill, which was not the best-lit station, Mrs Knight stepped from the train into the abyss and promptly broke her leg! (As a postscript to these tales from railway days, the landlord was quite insistent he regularly saw both the Flying Scotsman and the King George V on the line. I knew Cornish beer was good - but not that good!)

Delabole

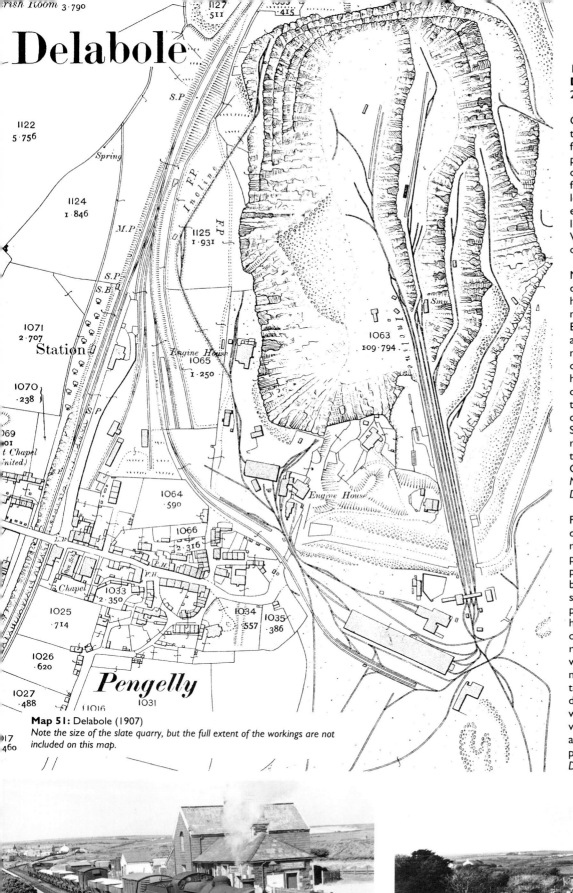

1127
511

1055
415

1122
5.75⁶

1124
1.846

Spring

S.P.

M.P.

1125
1.931

S.P.

S.B.

1071
2.707

Station

1070
.238

069

01

t Chapel
nited)

Engine House
1065
1.250

1063
109.794

Smy.

Engine House

Map 51: Delabole (1907)
Note the size of the slate quarry, but the full extent of the workings are not included on this map.

1064
.590

1066
2.316

Chapel
1033
2.350

1025
.714

1034
.557

1035
.386

1026
.620

1027
.488

1031

11016

Pengelly

17
460

156
Delabole station
200 SX 071837

Conveniently placed in the centre of the village and adjacent to the world-famous slate quarry, the station was proportionally the same as the others on the line, but what better material to face the main building with than the locally mined product? For just over eighteen months Delabole was the line's full stop, until the section to Wadebridge was completed, opening on 1 June 1895.

Once more the ubiquitous N class No 31836 is seen: again it is on freight duties and passes Delabole station heading towards Wadebridge with a mixed train of vans and ballast wagons. Both the guard and driver will be busy and a touch of brake will be required nearly all the way down the gradients of up to 1:73 almost to the town at the head of the Camel estuary. Note the quarry sidings curving round behind the station building. General goods ceased to be handled here on 7 September 1964, but the quarry sidings remained open for a short time after the line closed to passengers on 3 October 1966. *Photo: R. J. Sellick/ National Railway Museum. Date: 19 June 1959.*

For years the station building lay derelict and was boarded up, but it is now the home of a young couple who purchased it recently. However, a property developer-cum-builder bought most of the remaining station site and was granted planning permission to construct a number of houses and bungalows on it. The owners of the old station house refused to sell their property, which was going to have to be demolished to make way for the new: soon it will be totally surrounded by the housing development, which was well under way in the spring of 1993. The last vestiges of the down platform cling to a precarious existence, but will probably not last long.
Date: 1 May 1993.

Port Isaac Road station
200 SX 039789

Continuing its winding and downward plunge, the line entered the station set in rolling country some three miles south-east of the fishing village.

Situated on a curve, the station was built in stone to the standard NCR design, but its face was not hung with slate. The goods yard and shed were situated on the up side, together with a loading bay. Just south-east of the station, a 330yd tunnel was dug to pass under the tiny village of Trelill; it was the only one constructed on the line – surprising, considering the nature of the terrain through which it ran.

A 'Greyhound' at work: T9 4–4–0 No 30717 enters Port Isaac Road with an up train. The crew's attention seems have been caught by the photographer, and the fireman holds the single-line tablet aloft for the benefit of the camera, whilst further down the platform the signalman slings the one he has exchanged it for over his shoulder.
Photo: R. J. Sellick/National Railway Museum. Date: 19 June 1959.

Left unchecked for years and this is what happens: the bush has burgeoned almost to the size of a tree, obscuring the station house from view! After years of use as an office for the adjacent fertiliser store, the building is now a family home and in the process of renovation. The new owners have moved here to set up their business restoring Lotus cars and will adapt the former goods shed and fertiliser store as workshops.

Trelill Tunnel is dank and rather eerie; despite that, even after all these years it still manages to fill the nostrils with the magical redolence of the steam age.
Date: 1 May 1993.

A view of Port Isaac Road looking north-west shows that practically all of the station survives intact, and is without doubt the best-preserved example on the former line to remain in original condition. *Date: 1 May 1993.*

St Kew Highway station
200 SX 031751

The landscape had changed from the rolling and bleak countryside through which the line had woven unobtrusively in innumerable cuttings to reach St Kew Highway, where it changed to a more fertile pastureland. The station was conveniently sited for the village south of the main A39 road, which it abutted. It was similar to the others, but the station's goods facilities were limited to one short siding on the up side at the south end.

A sudden and welcome burst of activity at St Kew Highway: pausing to wait for the 12.58 Padstow–Okehampton up train to pass, which was to be hauled by No 31874, the now preserved LSWR-liveried Drummond T9 No 120 waits with an RCTS/PRC special to Padstow and Wenford Bridge. Starting from Exeter, the locomotive traversed the North Cornwall line and, judging by the number of people standing on the platforms, it was well patronised.
Photo: Ronald A. Lumber. Date: 27 April 1963.

Standing in the same position today, the scene has changed somewhat! A shed blocks the view to the former station house, now a private dwelling. The tree line on the extreme right provides a clue to the location, although these have thinned out over the years and it is difficult to identify them individually.

Today No 120 forms part of the National Collection and has been on loan to the Swanage Railway, but was scheduled during 1993 to be restored to main line running condition; No 31874 is also preserved and resides on the Mid-Hants Railway.
Date: 1 May 1993.

A totally different aspect is presented from the other side of the shed: although the trackbed has been filled in to platform level, forming a lawn and an ornamental fish pond, the former station buildings survive in original condition, apart from a small conservatory built on the front of the old booking hall. *Date: 1 May 1993.*

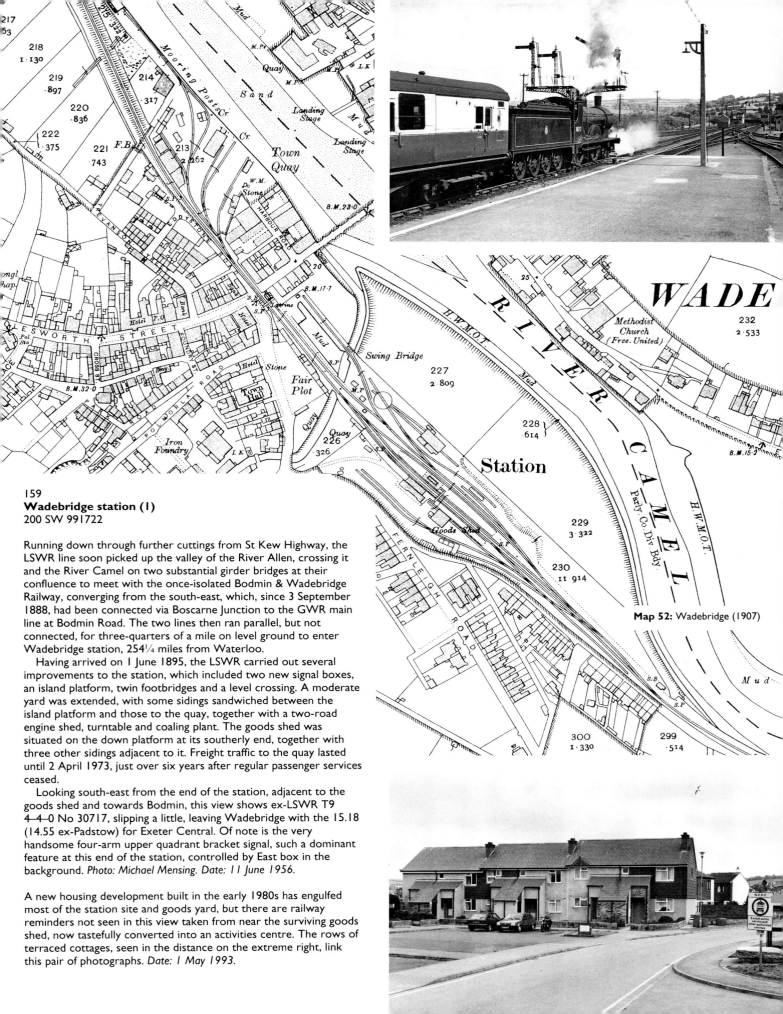

159
Wadebridge station (1)
200 SW 991722

Running down through further cuttings from St Kew Highway, the LSWR line soon picked up the valley of the River Allen, crossing it and the River Camel on two substantial girder bridges at their confluence to meet with the once-isolated Bodmin & Wadebridge Railway, converging from the south-east, which, since 3 September 1888, had been connected via Boscarne Junction to the GWR main line at Bodmin Road. The two lines then ran parallel, but not connected, for three-quarters of a mile on level ground to enter Wadebridge station, 254¼ miles from Waterloo.

Having arrived on 1 June 1895, the LSWR carried out several improvements to the station, which included two new signal boxes, an island platform, twin footbridges and a level crossing. A moderate yard was extended, with some sidings sandwiched between the island platform and those to the quay, together with a two-road engine shed, turntable and coaling plant. The goods shed was situated on the down platform at its southerly end, together with three other sidings adjacent to it. Freight traffic to the quay lasted until 2 April 1973, just over six years after regular passenger services ceased.

Looking south-east from the end of the station, adjacent to the goods shed and towards Bodmin, this view shows ex-LSWR T9 4-4-0 No 30717, slipping a little, leaving Wadebridge with the 15.18 (14.55 ex-Padstow) for Exeter Central. Of note is the very handsome four-arm upper quadrant bracket signal, such a dominant feature at this end of the station, controlled by East box in the background. *Photo: Michael Mensing. Date: 11 June 1956.*

A new housing development built in the early 1980s has engulfed most of the station site and goods yard, but there are railway reminders not seen in this view taken from near the surviving goods shed, now tastefully converted into an activities centre. The rows of terraced cottages, seen in the distance on the extreme right, link this pair of photographs. *Date: 1 May 1993.*

Map 52: Wadebridge (1907)

Wadebridge station (2)
200 SW 991723

On a Monday afternoon, a DMU is about to get under way from Wadebridge with the 12.05 from Bodmin Road to Padstow. The main station building is on the right, whilst a smaller structure containing waiting rooms was built on the island platform opposite, beyond which can be seen trucks standing in the coaling plant siding. Note the Exmouth Junction concrete product linking the two platforms. East box can just be seen in the distance beyond the smartly attired station master. *Photo: Andrew Muckley/Ian Allan library. Date: 7 September 1964.*

More of the housing development is seen – but the station building and canopy have survived. After years of neglect and decay, increasingly falling into an appalling state of dereliction, it was rescued at the eleventh hour and has been beautifully restored to become the John Betjeman Centre, where memorabilia of his life and work can be studied for all to enjoy. The building also doubles as a fine meeting room, which is in constant use. The canopy is in particularly good condition and in a better state now than it had probably been for many decades before.

The road through the housing development also doubles as part of the 'Camel Trail' which runs along the line formation from Padstow to Bodmin, together with the major portion of the former Wenford bridge branch. This is another example of good planning and provides much enjoyment for countless thousands of visitors as well as locals, particularly for cycling, for which it is ideally suited and intended. *Date: 1 May 1993.*

COMMENT: Standing on a pair of steps in the middle of the road was a fairly hazardous occupation, which most motorists seemed to tolerate well. Several pedestrians and cyclists stopped for extended chats when they discovered my purpose, and wanted to impart countless anecdotes from the railway days.

Wadebridge's restored station building and goods shed, now the John Betjeman Centre and the Betty Fisher Centre repectively. *Date: 1 May 1993.*

161
Wadebridge station (3)
200 SW 991723

A view from the Padstow end of the station shows a meeting of two former rivals: N class No 31847 waits with an SR working from Exeter to Padstow, from where ex-GWR 4500 class 2–6–2T No 4565 enters Wadebridge with a working to Bodmin Road. The passage of the line through the town was fairly cramped and had a severe speed restriction imposed, especially for the crossing over the A39 road passing through the middle of the town.

For the final 5½ miles to Padstow, the line hugged the south side of the Camel estuary, never more than a few yards from its bank. *Photo: Ronald A. Lumber. Date: 25 August 1960.*

This certainly shows the total transformation that has taken place over the years. At first glance there is nothing to correspond with the former scene, until one looks over the cab of the N class locomotive in the first photograph, noticing the town clock and the roof of an old timber-clad chapel, now used as an MOT service station and garage. These provide the continuity with yesteryear's view. *Date: 1 May 1993.*

162
Little Petherick Creek
200 SW 923741

The most notable structure on the extension to Padstow was the girder bridge built straddling Little Petherick Creek, some half-mile south-east of the seaside town. The steel bridge of three 150ft girder spans, supported on four braced columns piled deep into the estuary, was the most photogenic of locations, for the creek was at the foot of Dennis Hill upon which the photographer could have a breathtaking and uninterrupted view over the estuary towards the sea and back to Wadebridge, with the line winding along its bank.

Having climbed halfway up the hill, the photographer pauses to capture T9 4–4–0 No 30711, which has slowed to the mandatory 15mph, crossing the bridge with the 14.28 Wadebridge–Padstow train. *Photo: Peter F. Bowles/Ian Allan library. Date: 26 April 1954.*

The bridge is still in use today but does not echo to the thunder of iron wheels passing over its spans, only to the sound of voices and the gentle swish of bicycle tyres softly crunching on the compacted gravel surface of the 'Camel Trail'. *Date: 1 May 1993.*

COMMENT: *Due to the extent of undergrowth and gorse covering the hillside, I initially thought it impossible to climb up to stand in the same position. Eventually finding a way, almost crawling on hands and knees, I stumbled into the corner of a field and happened upon a writhing pile of stark-naked young couples engaged in a group activity the vicar would have been none too pleased about! Highly embarrassed, I blurted out an apology for the intrusion and went on my way without even a backward glance. Ah well, such are the hazards of railway photography . . . it quite spoilt the magical view for me!*

163
Padstow station
200 SW 921750

259¾ miles from Waterloo, the LSWR's furthest outpost was reached at Padstow, which had remained for 65 years cut off from a railway, to the annoyance of the townsfolk, since the Bodmin & Wadebridge Railway was so tantalisingly close. Arriving on 27 March 1899, the railway brought long-awaited prosperity to the town and businesses soon boomed: a fish store and market built near the station enabled locally caught *fruits de mer* to be transported far and wide. A year after the coming of the railway, the imposing Metropole Hotel overlooking the station and conveniently placed to it, opened its doors for the first time.

The station had one platform with a run-round loop; in addition, two carriage sidings were laid alongside, together with two more serving the fish store and market. A turntable was sited at the south end of the complex, from where this view of Padstow was taken, which depicts T9 No 30709 ready to leave with the 15.13 to Exeter. Note the fish store on the extreme right. *Photo: E. Wilmshurst. Date: 19 August 1958.*

A car park has been formed out of the station site, but the main building still stands. Part of it is used as a public lavatory, but the main portion by HM Customs & Excise; it is also the Visitors' Advice and Police Liaison Centre. The shed on the right is still used by the fisheries industry and a chandlery; it also houses the Padstow Shipwreck Museum. The Metropole in the background still dominates the scene. The car park was busy, for it was the day of the 'Hobby Horse' festival. *Date: 1 May 1993.*

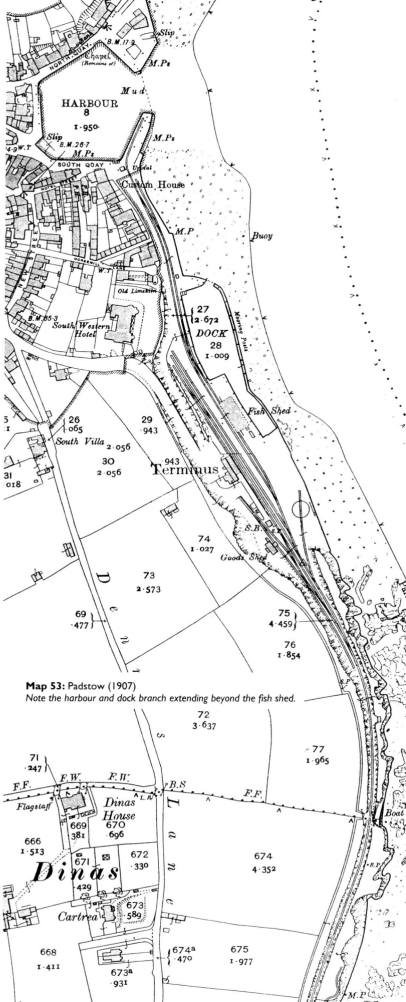

Map 53: Padstow (1907)
Note the harbour and dock branch extending beyond the fish shed.

CORNISH MINERAL LINES
Wadebridge–Bodmin;
Wenford Bridge Branch

Bodmin & Wadebridge Railway

The B&WR had the distinction of being Cornwall's first railway to be worked by locomotives. Its main line from Wadebridge to Wenford Bridge, just under twelve miles in length, opened to Dunmere on 4 July 1834, together with the short branch to Bodmin. On 30 September the line was extended to Wenford Bridge, the same day as the short freight-only branch to Ruthern Bridge (to close on 1 January 1934 after nearly one hundred years of operation). The railway was primarily constructed with the purpose of hauling sea sand dredged from the Camel estuary, and also for the export of minerals, including granite and clay (the latter was to ensure survival of the freight-only Wenford Bridge branch until the 1980s). Initially worked by two locomotives and some forty wagons, the £35,000 cost of the B&WR was borne by local people. In 1847 LSWR purchased the Bodmin & Wadebridge Railway, but it remained in isolation until 3 September 1888, when it was connected to the GWR's main line with a branch built from Bodmin Road (via Bodmin) to Boscarne, where a junction joined the two. The LSWR's line from Waterloo finally arrived at Wadebridge on 1 June 1895, thus facilitating easy interchange between the B&W and its parent system – which had owned it illegally until 1886! Rivalry between the two systems was guaranteed, and this lasted well after nationalisation: having passed to the Southern, the B&WR became the responsibility of the Western Region in 1950 before reverting to SR control in 1958, only to be transferred again to the WR in 1963.

The sharp radius curves and the light axle loading permitted on the B&WR proved to be the salvation for three of the diminutive Beattie 2–4–0 well tanks built in 1874 and 1875, for they worked the branch for nearly nine decades, outlasting others of the class by some seventy years. The final BR freight hauled by one of these locomotives was on 8 September 1962, after which date ex-GWR Class 1366 0–6–0PTs continued to work the line for a further two years until the end of steam in September 1964, when the last, No 1369, was withdrawn from service at Wadebridge, but is now preserved by the South Devon Railway Association. The branch was also the last section of BR in Cornwall to be worked by steam, after which Class 08 diesel shunters took over the clay traffic workings from Wenford Bridge (the quarter-mile section beyond the clay dries had closed from 13 February 1967). After the withdrawal of steam, diesel units were used on the Padstow–Wadebridge–Bodmin Road passenger workings.

From 15 June 1964, a reduced service was introduced and passengers to and from Bodmin North had to change at a new exchange platform constructed at Boscarne; a four-wheeled diesel railbus was employed for the shuttle service, although a three-coach school train was also used on the branch. All passenger workings ceased on 30 January 1967, and the route between Boscarne Junction and Wadebridge closed completely from 1 January 1979. Clay workings continued to be handled by 08 shunters between Wenford Bridge and Bodmin Road until 26 September 1983, with official closure from 18 November – just short of 150 years of operation. The track on the Wenford Bridge branch was lifted in the spring of 1985 and, together with the section to Bodmin North, the formation from Wadebridge is now part of the 'Camel Trail'.

164
Polbrock
200 SX 013695

From Wadebridge the line headed south-east to cross the River Camel at Pendavey, a mile distant and just beyond the point from which the North Cornwall line diverged, heading in a north-easterly direction. Closely following the river in its deep wooded valley, another mile further on the line passed under a road bridge near Polbrock, where this photograph was taken of Class O2 0–4–4T No 30200, seen sauntering along bunker-first with the 16.05 Bodmin North–Padstow two-coach train. The locomotive, then shedded at Wadebridge (72F), was to remain in service for a further two years before being withdrawn in August 1962; it was scrapped at Eastleigh the same month. *Photo: Peter W. Gray. Date: 10 September 1960.*

The road bridge now strides across the 'Camel Trail' formed from the trackbed, which provides an excellent surface for cycling through this delightful and picturesque river valley. The passing cyclist was just one of several hundred using the trail on this fine sunny May morning. Note the tree line on the horizon, giving the clue to the location. *Date: 2 May 1993.*

Grogley Halt
200 SX 015685

About a half-mile from the bridge at Polbrock, Grogley Halt was built near the tiny settlement of Brocton nestling in the Camel valley under the woodlands of Great Grogley Down. The platform was originally built of wood and a corrugated iron shelter provided for passenger comfort, but it became unsafe and was replaced in the 1950s by a concrete structure. However, a modified corrugated iron shelter with a flat roof was retained. A snapshot taken from a passing train shows the replacement structure and shelter. Note the 20mph speed limit imposed on this section of line. It is extremely questionable whether this tiny halt ever paid its way, as it only served a small and scattered population. *Photo: H. B. Priestley. Date: 12 August 1960.*

The concrete platform remains in excellent condition and, although it does not witness any passing trains, there is plenty of activity on the 'Camel Trail', with countless cyclists, walkers and horse riders passing every day. A car park has been provided behind the platform, as at several other locations along the trail, and the halt is sandwiched between it and the sparkling waters of the Camel, which provide excellent game fishing. *Date: 2 May 1993.*

166
Nanstallon Halt
200 SX 034675

The halt was built less than a half-mile from the village. A manned and gated level crossing was necessary to provide access to the small settlement north of the line. Reconstructed during its life, the halt is seen here in its final form, but still retains the GWR style of pagoda shelter typical of those on the line. Of interest is the squat LSWR signal box and bracket signal on the other side of the crossing. *Photo: Lens of Sutton. Date: c1960.*

With the exception of the edging slabs, the concrete platform alongside the trail has largely been fenced off and a garage constructed for an adjoining property, pronouncing above its doors 'Nanstallon Halt', which cannot be seen from this aspect looking towards the former level crossing. The trail was particularly busy on this bank holiday Sunday, as noted by the number of people pausing for a short rest here. *Date: 2 May 1993.*

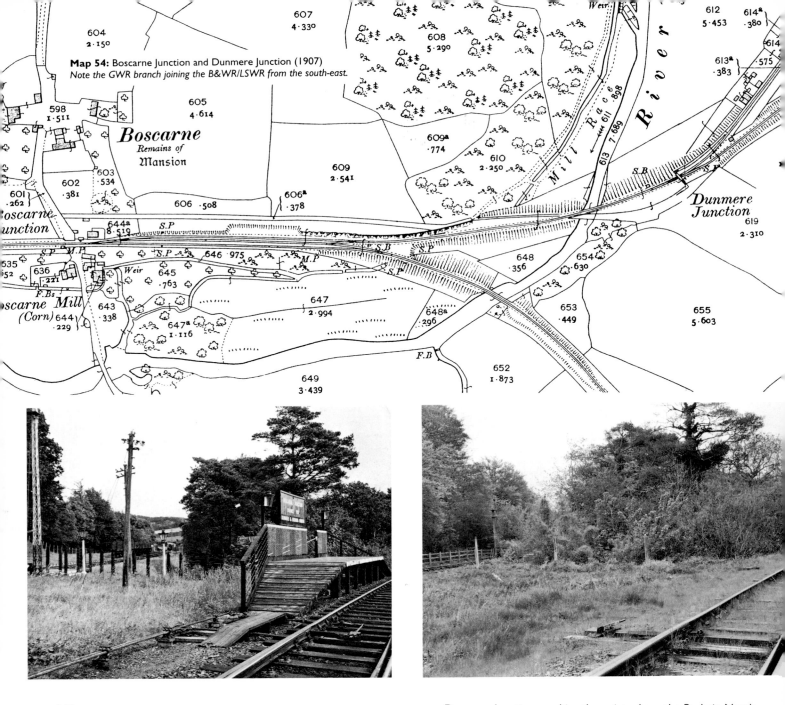

Map 54: Boscarne Junction and Dunmere Junction (1907)
Note the GWR branch joining the B&WR/LSWR from the south-east.

167
Boscarne Junction and exchange platform
200 SX 042674

With the reduction of services on 15 June 1964, a new platform was constructed at Boscarne Junction which enabled passengers travelling on the former GWR branch to transfer to the railbus service operated between here and Bodmin North, a little over a mile-and-a-quarter away (the distance from here to the freight terminus at Wenford Bridge was 6 miles 70 chains). Boscarne exchange platform was required for conventional trains using the former GWR line, but was unnecessary on the Bodmin North branch, for the railbus had centrally placed steps enabling passengers to alight or mount from track level.

A photograph taken shortly after its opening shows the platform was basic in the extreme and constructed from sleepers. A short path lit by three handsome lanterns, complementing the two on the platform, linked the two branches. Just a few chains round the bend

was Dunmere Junction, marking the point where the Bodmin North and Wenford Bridge branches diverged. Seen beyond the trucks in the siding and the bridge over the Camel is the ground frame hut which controlled the junction. *Photo: Andrew Muckley/Ian Allan library. Date: July 1964.*

The track in the immediate foreground is that of the Bodmin & Wenford Railway, which now operates the former GWR branch from Bodmin Road (Parkway) and runs steam and diesel services on the preserved section. The line here is currently under restoration, and although regular operations do not extend to Boscarne as yet, there are plans in the offing which may also see freight trains passing here once again. The remaining portion of track seen on the former Wenford Bridge branch is currently not connected to the one in use and remains isolated – albeit if temporarily. Note the three concrete lamp posts remaining alongside the former path between the two branch lines. *Date: 2 May 1993.*

Bodmin & Wenford Railway plc

After the closure of the Bodmin to Wenford Bridge line, a meeting was held in 1984 which resulted in a preservation group being formed to save the line. The Bodmin Railway Preservation Society formed a limited company to raise the £139,600 necessary for the purchase of the line from Bodmin Parkway to Boscarne Junction via Bodmin General (the former GWR terminus). They soon acquired six miles of track, but the Wenford Bridge line was abandoned because of passenger safety restrictions. The North Cornwall District Council purchased the land from British Rail and have assisted the Bodmin & Wenford Railway plc with various preservation schemes, including the restoration of Bodmin General station.

The first open day was in 1986, and at Easter the following year, the railway was able to offer its first passenger rides. On the day after the granting of a Light Railway Order on 1 August 1989, the company was able to offer a steam-hauled service on a mile-long section of the line between Bodmin General and Bodmin Parkway. After further upgrading of the line and platform at Bodmin Parkway, since 1990 regular services have been run, which are seasonally adjusted. In its first season, over twelve thousand passengers were carried and the line, operating both steam and diesel locomotives, is now a major tourist attraction. It is hoped to provide a regular commuter service from Bodmin General to the main line station, Bodmin Parkway. Although now ceased, a freight service was operated for three years with BR wagons from Bodmin Parkway to a siding at Walker Lines Industrial Estate for Fitzgerald Lighting.

Ambitious plans concerning the former sections of the B&WR owned and operated by the LSWR and their successors include the restoration of the line to the ECC driers at Wenford Bridge for the transportation of clay traffic, which currently goes by road. To that end, negotiations have taken place between the company, British Rail and the County Council; planning consent has been granted and the Light Railway Order applied for. Once obtained, the final stage would be to raise the necessary finance for this environmentally acceptable project. The extension of passengers workings to Boscarne would also be facilitated.

168
Dunmere Junction
200 SX 045674

An elevated view looking west and taken from a redundant signal post, shows the extent of the area once occupied by the exchange sidings and towards the site of the former Boscarne Junction signal box and crossing in the background, where a crossing gate lies cast aside in the undergrowth. A solitary oil tank wagon has been shunted to the far end of the remaining sidings, which mark the current limit of the Bodmin & Wenford Railway. The 'Camel Trail' occupies the area which was previously the clay reception road. *Date: 2 May 1993.*

A few chains round the bend from Boscarne Junction, the line crossed the River Camel and divided once again at Dunmere Junction: the Wenford Bridge branch dipped slightly to head north-east to follow the River Camel in its valley for a further six miles or so, whilst the branch to Bodmin North continued east for a short distance to the terminus on the north side of the town. Beattie 2–4–0WT No 30585 waits behind the gate at Dunmere with a train from Wenford Bridge. The points were operated from a cabin containing a ground frame behind the photographer. On the right is the branch to Bodmin North and a few yards round the bend is Dunmere Halt. *Photo: H. C. Casserley. Date: 19 August 1954.*

A minor tragedy is captured on camera: a small child has just fallen off its bicycle and lies in a crumpled heap wailing loudly as a would-be rescuer dashes to give assistance, while others just look on. With a few kisses and kind words of comfort, balance was soon restored and the family went on its way along the trail towards Wadebridge!

The gate and hut remain exactly the same, but the cottage beyond has been given a facelift. The 'Camel Trail' divides at this point, one branch ending at Bodmin at a dismantled bridge on the north side of the town and not far from the old gaol, while the Wenford Bridge section continues to the ECC clay driers works. It passes through Pencarrow Woods, once the site of a water tank and column used for the replenishment of locomotives, but no trace of it remains today. *Date: 2 May 1993.*

169
Dunmere Halt
200 SX 046675

The halt, the only intermediate one on the Bodmin branch from Dunmere Junction, was built on a curve and located just to the west side of the bridge that now carries the A389 road. Despite the fact that the shelter was built of corrugated iron to the pattern provided at all other halts, with its exaggerated roof lines it still had an elegant and charming look about it. Although it was on an LSWR branch, it is curious to relate that it appears to be of the same style as the one at Nanstallon, which may stem from the modernisation of the line

and improvement of the service when the GWR joined with it in 1888. The lamp posts exuded quality and seemed somewhat incongruous when compared with the rather spartan nature of the platform itself. The halt closed on 30 January 1967, along with the others on the line. *Photo: Andrew Muckley/Ian Allan library. Date: 7 September 1964.*

Although vegetation and grass have been allowed to encroach on its surface slightly, the platform remains in good condition. Note how the tree on the far side of the bridge has grown over the last 29 years. *Date: 2 May 1993.*

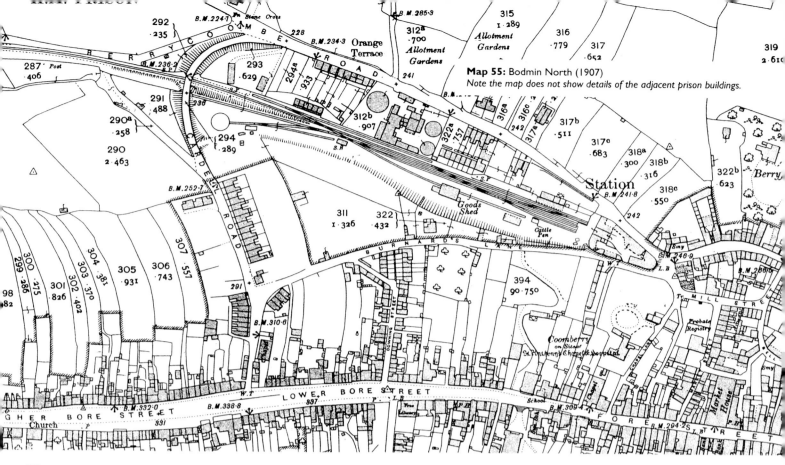

Map 55: Bodmin North (1907)
Note the map does not show details of the adjacent prison buildings.

170
Bodmin North station
200 SX 064673

On leaving Dunmere Junction, the line soon passed the grim building of Bodmin Gaol before entering the terminus, one of two built in the former Cornish county town. The station had one platform, protected by an extensive canopy along the front of its main building. Several sidings and a goods shed were provided for the handling of freight, but these operations ceased when facilities were withdrawn on 29 November 1965. The original B&WR station was superseded on 1 November 1895 by Bodmin North and contiguous to it, following reconstruction work carried out by the LSWR.

By the time this photograph was taken, Bodmin North was very much in decline: a diesel railbus waits at the terminus after arrival with the 13.15 service from Boscarne Junction. The little four-wheeled vehicle was introduced to the branch the previous June to operate the shuttle service between here and the junction, just a mile or so to the west. Of note are the centrally mounted steps on the railbus, which facilitated access from track level. Just visible on the left of the picture is Bodmin Gaol. *Photo: Andrew Muckley/ Ian Allan library. Date: 7 September 1964.*

The old terminus has disappeared entirely: the site has been given over to a retail park (including a large supermarket) and fire station, to which the road in the foreground provides access. The old gaol can still be seen, but there are no longer any inmates and it is a tourist attraction open to visitors. This comparison was taken by standing hard up against the wall of the Bodmin Health Centre now built here. *Date: 2 May 1993.*

171
Wenford Bridge clay dries
200 SX 084746

The clay works and dries soon became the mainstay of the railway and remained so until September 1983, when rail services were discontinued. Apart from its winding course through the spectacularly beautiful wooded Camel valley, the charm of the branch was the fact that three surviving ex-LSWR Beattie 2–4–0WTs worked the line until August 1962, which proved an irresistible magnet to railway photographers. Henry Casserley was no exception, and here he captures the now-preserved No 30585 indulging in some shunting at the clay works. The line ran on beyond the buildings for about thirty chains to the freight-only terminus at Wenford Bridge, where there was a connection with a cable-worked incline to the De Lank quarry. *Photo: H. C. Casserley. Date: 19 August 1954.*

English China Clays now send all clay by road and there are some twenty lorry movements a day. The road infrastructure is poor and they have to negotiate narrow lanes, much to the consternation of some local inhabitants, who would be glad if the Bodmin & Wenford Railway's plan to re-establish a rail link here succeeds, which ECC supports in principle. Although the main running line has been removed in the works, the sidings alongside the buildings survive. This part of the works, however, is now disused. Currently, the workforce employed here numbers 24.

A car park has been built on the west side of the work's access road and provides a link with the 'Camel Trail'. The only portion of the line to remain *in situ* is where it crosses the A389 at Dunmere and still lies embedded in the road surface. *Date: 2 May 1993.*

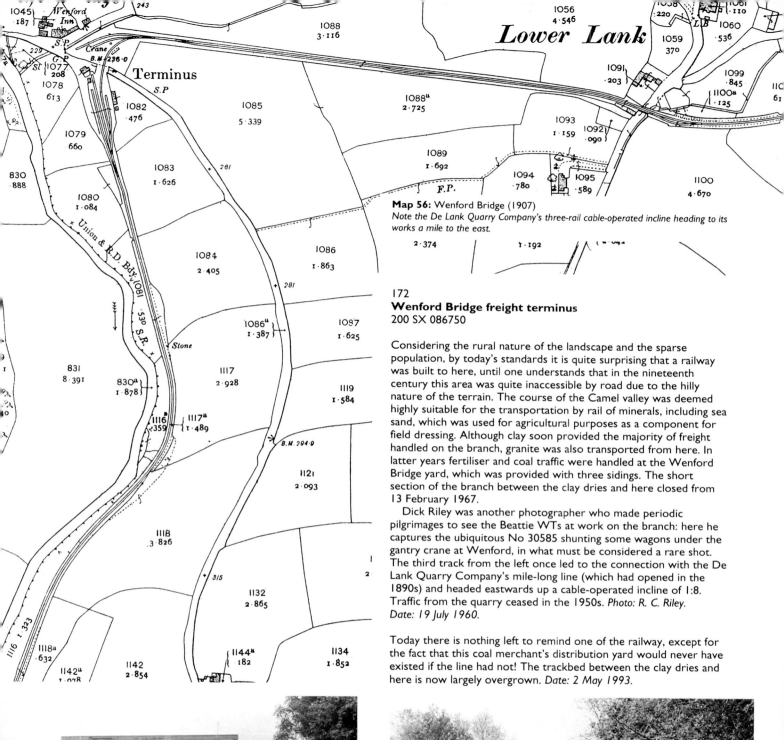

Map 56: Wenford Bridge (1907)
Note the De Lank Quarry Company's three-rail cable-operated incline heading to its works a mile to the east.

172

Wenford Bridge freight terminus
200 SX 086750

Considering the rural nature of the landscape and the sparse population, by today's standards it is quite surprising that a railway was built to here, until one understands that in the nineteenth century this area was quite inaccessible by road due to the hilly nature of the terrain. The course of the Camel valley was deemed highly suitable for the transportation by rail of minerals, including sea sand, which was used for agricultural purposes as a component for field dressing. Although clay soon provided the majority of freight handled on the branch, granite was also transported from here. In latter years fertiliser and coal traffic were handled at the Wenford Bridge yard, which was provided with three sidings. The short section of the branch between the clay dries and here closed from 13 February 1967.

Dick Riley was another photographer who made periodic pilgrimages to see the Beattie WTs at work on the branch: here he captures the ubiquitous No 30585 shunting some wagons under the gantry crane at Wenford, in what must be considered a rare shot. The third track from the left once led to the connection with the De Lank Quarry Company's mile-long line (which had opened in the 1890s) and headed eastwards up a cable-operated incline of 1:8. Traffic from the quarry ceased in the 1950s. *Photo: R. C. Riley. Date: 19 July 1960.*

Today there is nothing left to remind one of the railway, except for the fact that this coal merchant's distribution yard would never have existed if the line had not! The trackbed between the clay dries and here is now largely overgrown. *Date: 2 May 1993.*

Callington branch

East Cornwall Mineral Railway

Mineral mining and quarrying around the Callington and Gunnislake areas reached its peak of prosperity in the mid-nineteenth century, and the need for better transportation soon became evident in an area which was poorly served. The East Cornwall Mineral Railway's 7¾-mile 3ft 6in gauge line opened on 7 May 1872 to Kelly Bray, 1¼ miles from Callington and 640ft above sea level. It incorporated a cable-operated incline, worked on the counterbalance principle, assisted by a stationary engine, which rose for 35 chains from Calstock Quay at 1:6 to a point 350ft higher up the valley to the tramway. The incline had been built by a mercantile company in 1859, and three years later the Tamar, Kit Hill & Callington Railway was formed in order to extend the track to Kelly Bray, but lack of funds had prevented completion. In 1869, after several years lying derelict, the Calstock & Callington Railway took over and completed the line, by which time the company had become the ECMR. A proposal was made in 1876 to convert the line to standard gauge and extend across the Tamar to link with the Devon Great Consol Mine to Morwellham Quay, but the depressed state of the mining industry put paid to the idea.

In 1891 the existing company was taken over by the Plymouth, Devonport & South Western Junction Railway, which had been incorporated in 1883 to build 22 miles of line from Lidford (sic) to Devonport and opened in June 1890. The PDSWJR (in which the LSWR had an increasing shareholding) fully absorbed the ECMR in 1894; then under Light Railway Orders of 1900 and 1905, the gauge was converted to standard, linking with Bere Alston via a graceful 12-arch viaduct of 60ft spans built over the Tamar at Calstock. The line opened on 2 March 1908 and the old incline at Calstock Quay was replaced by an impressively high wagon lift built adjacent to the viaduct, which was to be used until 1934.

Apart from Bere Alston, intermediate stations were provided at Calstock, Gunnislake, Chilsworthy, Latchley and Luckett; the terminus at Kelly Bray was renamed Callington (apart from Calstock and Chilsworthy, these had been little more than concentration points for rail-bound minerals).

For a time after Grouping in 1923, when the Southern took over from the PDSWJR, which had been fully absorbed by the LSWR the previous year, the celebrated entrepreneur of light railway fame, Colonel H. F. Stephens, became associate engineer. In 1907 the PDSWJR had purchased three Hawthorn Leslie locomotives, becoming LSWR/SR No 756 (ex-No 3) *A. S. Harris*, an 0–6–0T, whilst No 757 (ex-No 4) *Earl of Mount Edgecumbe* and No 758 (ex-No 5) *Lord St Levan* were 0–6–2Ts. They operated on the branch for many years and were replaced in 1929 by O2 class 0–4–4Ts (later to be usurped by Ivatt 2–6–2Ts) on passenger workings, but two continued to be employed on various duties in the Plymouth area until the 1950s (No 756 had previously left the district).

Between 1950–8, the 9 mile 50 chain branch from Bere Alston to Callington came under the control of the Western Region for commercial reasons, reverting to the SR until 1963. It was then dieselised, with DMUs working most passenger services, whilst Class 22 diesel-hydraulic locomotives hauled the occasional freight. The section beyond Gunnislake closed on 7 November 1966; but the remaining portion forms part of the 11¾-mile Tamar Valley line from St Budeaux, with reversals necessary at Bere Alston. Its future is reasonably secure, because the difficult geography it passes through (the reason for its original promotion and later the ease of access to Plymouth across the Tamar) will ensure its survival – at least in part.

173
Calstock Viaduct
201 SX 432685

Of the Callington branch, only 1½ miles were in Devon before the line crossed into Cornwall over the magnificent viaduct spanning the Tamar, marking the county boundary. Calstock Viaduct was a triumph in aesthetics: its elegance was unsurpassed, and the slender stone structure of 12 arches stood 129ft above the river. The attachment of the 20-ton capacity wagon lift detracted only slightly from its uncomplicated design; however, the latter had been sold and removed by the time this study was taken, showing Adams O2 class 0–4–4T No 30192 crossing with the 14.26 train from Gunnislake to Bere Alston, comprising two vans and three coaches, including one of the ex-LSWR railmotor gated trailer units. Calstock station can be seen on the far side of the viaduct. *Photo: R. E. Vincent/Ian Allan library. Date: 25 September 1954.*

A Class 118 DMU, one of the last to remain in service, crosses the viaduct with the 17.20 Gunnislake–Plymouth train. Although the viaduct is unchanged, it is self-evident how the lineside embankments have been allowed to become overgrown, obscuring two of the arches from view when standing in the same position. There has been limited development which has taken place over the years, and it is interesting to spot the subtle changes to the village of Calstock in Cornwall sitting snugly on the west bank of the River Tamar. *Date: 8 September 1992.*

174
Calstock station
201 SX 434688

The station was built rather awkwardly on a sharp curve situated near the viaduct. The building on the platform, of wooden construction and clad in corrugated iron, had a ramshackle appearance; apart from similar ones at Gunnislake and Luckett, the other two intermediate stations were even less well equipped and some only had small shelters. By 1900 the mineral traffic on the line was in decline, but new businesses flourished, helped by the ECMR linking with the PDSWJR's system. Receipts for passengers carried and freight transported were respectable, allowing a dividend to be paid to shareholders. Over the years the small yard at Calstock handled a variety of goods, mainly market garden produce, particularly flowers and fruit; however, general freight facilities were withdrawn on 28 February 1966.

Despite this photograph being fairly recent, it does show the relationship of the station to the viaduct and the buildings on the platform, but by this date the sidings in the foreground had been lifted, as the remaining sleepers testify. A Birmingham RC&W suburban DMU, without its centre car, forms the 16.36 Plymouth–Gunnislake service and arrives at Calstock. Note the 10mph restriction imposed on this side of the viaduct because of the sharp curve into the station (the maximum speed limit for the line was 25mph, but in places was as low as 5mph). *Photo: Les Bertram/Ian Allan library. Date: c1977.*

Sprinter No 150241 is captured in exactly the same position, but is heading in the opposite direction and leaves with the 17.20 Gunnislake–Plymouth service at 17.31 on a bright spring evening. A small platform shelter has been provided in place of the buildings, although it cannot be seen in this view. In the up direction the speed limit across the viaduct is 15mph, as indicated by the sign on the parapet. *Date: 21 April 1993.*

Map 57: Calstock (1906)
Note the line under construction and the piers for the viaduct drawn on the map, printed two years before the opening of the PDSWJR's Callington branch.

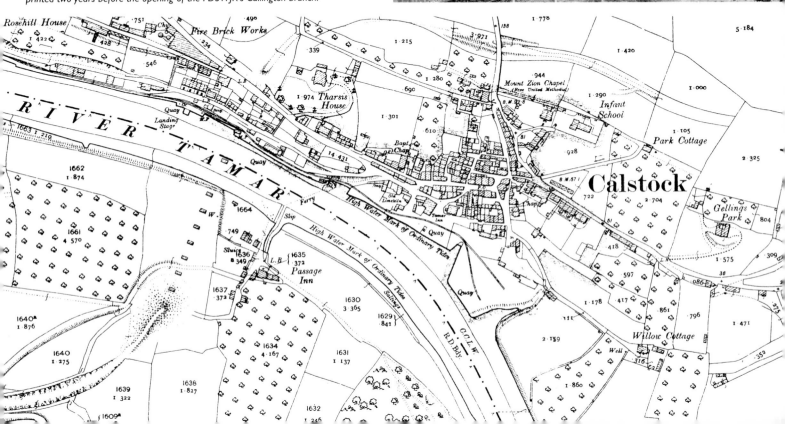

175
Gunnislake station
201 SX 427710

From Calstock, the line ran along the hillside of the Tamar valley in an east south-easterly direction climbing mostly at 1:40, before turning through 180° to follow closely a minor road to head north, passing the point where the formation of the tramway leading to the original incline built from the quay emerged, to enter Gunnislake station, a little over a half-mile beyond. In freight-only days, before the station was built, it had been Drakewalls Depot.

The station, like Calstock, was basic in its design, but had reasonably extensive sidings on the west side of the island platform, upon which the building had a double-sided canopy. Here Class O2 No 30236 stands at Gunnislake with the 13.00 train from Callington to Bere Alston. *Photo: R. E. Vincent/ Ian Allan library. Date: 7 April 1953.*

The platform has been shorn of its building and a small barrel-type shelter provides the only passenger comfort. Class 150 Sprinter No 150241 waits at what is now the branch terminus with the 16.25 from Plymouth; it is about to depart with the 17.20 return service. There are provisional plans to resite the station on the south side of the A390, to allow a low bridge to be demolished, which will lift the restrictions on heavy goods vehicles. *Date: 21 April 1993.*

A panorama of Gunnislake, showing the station layout to full advantage. Having recently replaced the PDSWJR 0–6–2Ts on this work, Ivatt 2–6–2T No 41315 shunts wagons in the yard. *Photo: R. C. Riley. Date: 30 August 1954.*

COMMENT: *Due to the growth of trees now surrounding the site and the west side of the station platform, it was impractical to obtain a direct comparison to this and several other photographs taken of here, but I decided to include it anyway, as it gives a better idea of the layout of Gunnislake than the one I was able to replicate.*

176
Chilsworthy station
200 SX 418720

Having followed the contours of the land closely from Gunnislake, the tiny station of Chilsworthy was built high on the side of a hill overlooking the Tamar valley, giving distant views to the north. Opened on 1 June 1909, the station itself was basic in the extreme: the platform face was built of stone, but the surface was compacted chippings and only a tiny corrugated iron shelter was provided for passengers. This early view shows the platform, upon which is a primitive wooden lower quadrant signal with two arms: presumably one for each direction of running. The smartly attired young man adopts a suitably relaxed pose for the camera and leans against the post and rail fencing backing the platform. *Photo: Lens of Sutton. Date: c1910.*

Sections of the platform survive, but it is totally overwhelmed with gorse and scrub. Only very careful study will reveal one or two hedgerows seen in the distance as being identified with the original photograph. *Date: 21 April 1993.*

COMMENT: *Quite apart from a terrible stench emanating from something horribly dead somewhere in the undergrowth, this shot was acquired with difficulty, as the gorse bushes had to be held down with three spare limbs, whilst the other operated the camera!*

The bridge seen in the first view is still in use. A few of the platform's concrete and wooden posts remain *in situ.*
Date: 21 April 1993.

177
Latchley station
200 SX 402719

Before it was built, the site was known as Cox's Park Depot and served as a mineral concentration point for a nearby quarry. Stark simplicity: that is how Dick Riley captioned this view taken of Latchley, named after the village 1½ miles to the north on the lower slopes of the Tamar valley. Facilities could not have been more rudimentary here; the platform shelter was ridiculously small and could not have provided protection for more than three or four people. Freight ceased to be handled here in 1949 and the station closed to passengers on 7 November 1966, along with the others between Gunnislake and Callington. The road crossing was ungated and extreme caution was necessary by locomotive crews and road users alike.

Opening in June 1910 to serve the Phoenix Pleasure Ground, Seven Stones Halt was situated between Latchley and Luckett. Although the excursion traffic was heavy, the halt and ground closed in 1914 on the outbreak of war. *Photo: R. C. Riley. Date: 12 July 1955.*

The former railway cottage has been renovated to make a fine home and is in much better condition now than it has been for years – probably in all its life! The platform is still extant and sits alongside a garage built on the trackbed. Much of the line formation either side of the station is still defined, although some is overgrown and unwalkable. *Date: 21 April 1993.*

178 (Opposite)
Luckett station
200 SX 385718

Originally another mineral traffic concentration point, it was known as Monk's Corner Depot before the station was constructed here in 1908; it then became known as Stoke Climsland until 1 November 1909, when it was renamed. Luckett not only had a passing loop, but also a few short sidings and a small loading dock; goods ceased to be handled here from 10 September 1962. The station building was typically built of wood clad with corrugated iron, but nevertheless looked proportionally sound, with a small saw-toothed canopy on its front.

After the demise of steam, Class 22 diesels were employed on freight duties, but sometimes worked the occasional passenger train as here, on the first day of operation on the line. North British Type 2 Bo-Bo diesel-hydraulic No D6323 calls at Luckett with the 17.24 from Bere Alston on a dull and wet Monday afternoon. The sidings had been lifted by this date. *Photo: Andrew Muckley/Ian Allan library. Date: 7 September 1964.*

Spring blossom adorns the tree that now blocks the view of the station site from the minor road bridge. The former railway cottage, a portion of which can just be seen in both photographs, has been renovated and the loading dock made into a feature of the garden. Although it cannot be seen clearly, much of the platform remains in very good condition, despite the grass that has been allowed to grow on its surface. The building has not survived, but the recess in which it sat is clearly defined. *Date: 21 April 1993.*

179
Callington station (1)
200 SX 362714

When the ECMR opened on 7 May 1872 to serve the mining industry in the area, particularly around Kit Hill, the north side of which the line circumnavigated, the terminus was simply known as Kelly Bray, the village in which it was situated and just over a mile north of Callington. When the line was converted to standard gauge by the PDSWJR, the station built here became Callington Road, until renamed on 1 November 1909.

Kit Hill, with the chimney of a defunct mine on its summit, provides a dramatic backdrop to a perfect rural scene: Adams O2 class 0-4-4-T No 30236, the last of the class built, arrives at Callington with the 15.13 from Bere Alston. The train is comprised of ex-LSWR steam railmotor No 4 (renumbered as coach No 565575) and two vans. The driver, an ex-LMS man at Worcester, found work on the PDSWJR a little different from what he had previously been used to! The locomotive would have had quite a climb to Callington on a number of steep grades ranging between 1:40 and 1:50, with a short stretch of 1:33 on the approach to the station. Callington's small two-road engine shed is seen over the train. *Photo: R. C. Riley. Date: 30 August 1954.*

With the evening sun shining, Kit Hill and the chimney provide the instant clue, being immediately identifiable, as is the gable end of a cottage behind the factory unit on the left. The area of the station and goods yard has been turned into an industrial estate. In front of the building on the right are crates full of aircraft components bought by a company operating from the site. *Date: 21 April 1993.*

180
Callington station (2)
200 SX 361714

What better scene with which to end this book than a shot of the Callington terminus? The station was well placed in the centre of Kelly Bray and adjacent to the main crossroads in the village (now the A388 and B3257). As befitting a terminus, a large part of the station had a covered roof, making the wooden main building which it protected seem a little gloomy; however, its neat appearance speaks volumes for the staff. Here O2 class No 30183 stands at the station with a typical mixed train. The sturdy wooden starter signal was of PDSWJR origin. The goods yard was small, but a variety of freight was handled here during its active life; however, it and the station closed on 28 February 1966, when the line was truncated at Gunnislake. *Photo: G. M. Kitchenside/Ian Allan library.*
Date: 17 June 1959.

All has gone; not a trace left of the station, which is now a plot of waste ground used for parking cars on the industrial estate which covers the site. The cottages on the right provide some continuity with the past.

As we move on through a different age – that of the car and heavy goods vehicle – it is difficult to comprehend just how much of the nation's heritage has been lost with the demise of Britain's rural railways. If by magic they suddenly reappeared, many would still be hopelessly uneconomic and, as sure as night follows day, there would be yet another Dr Beeching to come along and wield the axe.
Date: 21 April 1993.

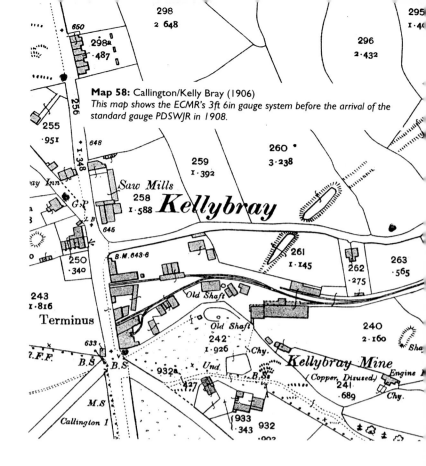

Map 58: Callington/Kelly Bray (1906)
This map shows the ECMR's 3ft 6in gauge system before the arrival of the standard gauge PDSWJR in 1908.

ACKNOWLEDGEMENTS

One of the privileges of being able to prepare such a volume as this is to experience the kindness and help of so many people, some of whom were previously strangers to me but, in many cases, have since become firm friends.

It is always difficult to single out individuals for special mention, but I feel that this is most appropriate in the case of Ron Lumber, who has given me generous and invaluable help, imparting his own extensive knowledge of the former LSWR lines in the West Country and also allowing me access to his photographic collection. In addition, he had the kindness to read through my manuscript chapter by chapter as it rolled off the word processor, which was of enormous help – at least any errors of fact can be put down to him!

I would particularly like to thank the following, some of whom are old friends, fellow authors and photographers, who have kindly helped with information and tolerated me pestering them on the telephone at various times, or allowed me to reproduce material from their photographic collections – often going to much trouble in printing them. They include: Dick Riley, Peter Gray, Mike Mensing, Phil Lynch, Philip Wells, George Heiron, Brian Morrison, Sid Nash, John Scrace, Bernard Mills, Les Elsey, David Cross, Ron Toop, Terry Nicholls, Colin Caddy, Mike Esau, Stanley Creer, Edwin Wilmshurst, Dennis Cullum, Richard Casserley, Roy Hobbs, H. B. Priestley, Gordon Buck, Andrew Muckley, Colour-Rail, National Railway Museum, Lens of Sutton, Stratton Creber Estate Agents and especially Peter Waller of Ian Allan Ltd.

A special mention must go to George Reed and Steve Drabwell of British Rail, Exeter, who kindly organised trips to Meldon Quarry and to Salisbury in cabs of locomotives,
enabling me to gain much valuable experience of some of the routes about which I was to write. My thanks go to Richard Lucas of Meldon Quarry, who gave me a guided tour of the works and has supplied much of the technical and historical information about it. I have received enormous help in innumerable ways from other members of staff working for the various divisions of British Rail; they include David Mather, Garth Ponsenby, Richard Burningham, Ian Hitchcock, Ian Dinmore and the drivers who tolerated me in the cab of their locomotives.

I am also indebted to those companies and individuals encountered during my travels, who allowed me to photograph from their properties, many of which were former stations; also to the management of the Bodmin & Wenford Railway and the Launceston Steam Railway for their help in supplying historical information on their operations and future plans. Valuable assistance was also given by the map library staff at the universities of both Exeter and Plymouth.

It would be remiss of me not to give special thanks to Michael Head, who designed this volume and two of my previous titles. His flexibility in adapting to my way of thinking so readily is remarkable! He has done a superb job to follow the exacting parameters set before him, as has Derek Mercer with the printing of my negetives. I am indebted to him for both his patience and skill, which have equally been tested to their limits.

Finally, I am grateful to my wife Jenny, whose support is my strength – as ever: she has acted as my much-treasured and patient chief critic, photograph selector, proofreader and sometime safari companion.

INDEX